Profiles
Volume I:

Historic & Influential People
from Buffalo & WNY
the 1800s

*Residents of Western New York that
contributed to local, regional and national
history, commerce and culture.*

Rick Falkowski

10/29/19

Published by
Rick Falkowski
P.O. Box 96
Williamsville, NY 14231
buffalomusichistory.com
info@buffalomusichistory.com
Facebook: Historic & Influential People from Buffalo & WNY

Profiles Volume I: Historic & Influential People from Buffalo & WNY – the 1800s
ISBN number: 13-978-0578569239

1. Buffalo, NY
2. Local History
3. Historic People, Nonfiction

Edited by: Angela Keppel, Carol Jean Fremy Swist, Marsha Falkowski
Layout and Design: Nancy Wise
Research Assistant: McKinley Falkowski
Photo enhancement and optimization: Steve Loncto
Foreword by: Angela Keppel, Discovering Buffalo, One Street at a Time

Front Cover Photo: Buffalo Harbor with a view up Main Street 1855.
    Collection of The Buffalo History Museum
    With photos of Joseph Ellicott, Peter Porter, Red Jacket and Samuel Wilkeson

First Edition: October 2019
First Printing: October 2019
Printed in the U.S.A.

Dedicated to my wife Marsha
for all her assistance and support.

TABLE OF CONTENTS

FOREWORD

I first met Rick through the Buffalo History Museum's Annual Local Author Day. We bonded over a shared interest in the people who make up Buffalo's history.

I write a blog called Discovering Buffalo, One Street at a Time (buffalostreets.com). For those who follow my blog, some of the information in this book will seem familiar. For the past eight years, I have been writing about the origins of the street names of Buffalo, and the people the streets were named after. As an urban planner and historian, I find our region's history to be particularly exciting. I think it is important to know about our history and where we have been as a region, in order to better see where we are going as we move forward. Many of the people included in this book are also people whose names are found on street signs. Because of the natural overlap, Rick asked me to write this foreword.

Even if you are not familiar with my blog, some of the names will be very familiar to you – Grover Cleveland and Millard Fillmore, our illustrious Buffalo presidents. Some of the names will bring back nostalgic times of downtown shopping – William Hengerer of Hengerer's Department Store and the Adams of AM&A's and JN Adam. Some names, you may not know, but upon reading, you will realize that you know about things they accomplished, institutions they created, etc. Others in the book may be entirely new to you, nevertheless important to the progression of our city and region. You will learn about 100 people here who lived and worked here in Buffalo. The learning of history can be captivating. Buffalo's influence can be seen in many places. As you read the book, you will learn about the creation of the greenback dollar bill, the invention of the fire hydrant, the donation of land to create Letchworth State Park, and so much more! After you read the book, I hope that you are filled with a sense of wonder at all the different ways that Buffalonians have made an impact. If you are picking up this book and not from Buffalo, I hope you'll learn that we are so much more than snow and chicken wings.

One thing of note is that Rick included several important women in his book. This is important because many early books chronicling the important people of Buffalo were titled things like *The City of Buffalo: Its Men and Institutions*, and women were often an afterthought. I think you will enjoy reading about Anna Katherine Green, Maria Love and the other women included here.

Rick has spent a lot of time preparing this book. His diligent research is evident throughout the text, and you can see the long list of sources at the end. The book will serve as a valuable reference for those wanting to learn more about the City and region. You will also be fully stocked with tidbits that you can use to impress your friends or win at local trivia night.

I hope you enjoy the book, and I hope that you, like me, look forward to seeing whose lives Rick chronicles next!

Angela M. Keppel, AICP
Discovering Buffalo, One Street at a Time

ACKNOWLEDGEMENTS

When the Erie County Public Library bookmobile came to Woodrow Wilson Elementary School in the Cheektowaga Sloan School System, I probably checked out every book on the early explorers and early American history. In fact, I still remember the distinctive smell of the bus and the excitement when an attendant informed me that new books were added that may be of interest to me.

In grammar school, I looked forward to the history lesson section of the day and recall the influence of my Junior High School and Senior High School teachers, Mrs. Coyne, Mr. Ward and Mr. Mahoney, at John F. Kennedy High School. Upon entering college at SUNY Fredonia, I aspired to become a history teacher but was told that in 1969 there was an overage of teachers, so I should consider a different career path. After proudly serving in the United States Air Force and graduating from the University of Buffalo, I began working in sales and business management. My love of history turned to local history and I became involved in the Buffalo Music scene, writing hundreds of profiles on bands and musicians in the self-published grassroots music magazine *Buffalo Backstage* and the in *Annual Buffalo Music Awards Programs*.

After retiring from the cable company (TCI, Adelphia and Time Warner), I focused on my interest in local history by publishing *History of Buffalo Music & Entertainment* in 2017. I began giving talks at area senior centers through the Erie County Senior Services University Express Program, coordinated by Pat Dowling. In addition, I gave presentations at libraries, senior housing communities, private clubs and organizations. Enjoying these talks I wanted to give a wider variety of presentations, so I decided to create a historical book about people from Buffalo.

Over a year ago, I visited the Buffalo History Museum to begin research on a book about the individuals who shaped WNY and to showcase the accomplishments of people from our area that current area residents may not be aware. Cynthia Van Ness, the Director of the Research Library and Archives at the Buffalo History Museum, researched the subject and found no recent books were written covering historical profiles. Eventually, I discovered the last similar book of this type was published in the early 1900s. I began accumulating quite a library of old Buffalo History books. Since the books were in the public domain, many were digitized, with some available as reprinted books or only in digital format. I was also pleased to find several local history internet sites and blogs. These books and internet sites are referenced in the source notes and bibliography.

Since this book covers a time that was over one hundred years ago, most of the data was found in books and online. However, to augment the printed material, I traveled to various historical sites, societies and museums.

Some of the locations visited were: Artpark State Park, Black Rock Historical Society, Buffalo & Erie County Public Library, Buffalo History Museum, Buffalo Niagara Heritage Village, Buffalo Science Museum, Canalside, Delaware Park, Devils Hole State Park, Forest Lawn Cemetery, Fort Erie, Fort Niagara, Grand Island

History Museum, Holland Land Office Museum, Larkin Gallery Museum, Niagara County Historical Society, Niagara Falls State Park, North Tonawanda History Museum, Old Stone Chimney, Reinstein Woods Nature Preserve, Schoellkopf Power Station, Seneca Indian Park, Seneca-Iroquois National Museum, St. John the Baptist R.C. Church, St. Paul's Episcopal Cathedral, St. Stanislaus R.C. Cemetery, Tifft Nature Preserve, Tonawanda History Museum and the Twentieth Century Club.

I would like to thank the following for their suggestions and information: Rich Andres, Jare Cardinal, Steve Cichon, Mary Cooke, Doreen DeBoth, Ryan Duffy, John Edens, McKinley Falkowski, Gerry Halligan, Rick Heenan, Jennifer Jimerson, Angela Keppel, Francis Lestingi, Toni Louden, Amy Miller, Wayne Mori, Sharon Osgood, Lois Ringle, David Rumsey, Shane E. Stephenson, Erin Sullivan, Cynthia Van Ness, and Sami Wnek. My sincere apologies if I overlooked any contributors.

Thank you to the following who assisted in the production of this book. Editing was done by Angela Keppel and Carol Jean Fremy Swist. Photos were enhanced and optimized by Steve Loncto. Nancy Wise created the layout and design of the book. Final proofing was completed by Mike Reid, Carol Jean Fremy Swist and Nancy Wise. Marsha Falkowski assisted with ideas, research, photos, editing and proofing.

A special thanks to the many people who purchased my first book and came to my presentations on Buffalo Music and Buffalo History. Numerous comments and suggestions were received, but the most recurrent were people wished the photos were larger and that there were more pictures. Therefore, in this book there are more and larger photos. I cannot wait until this book is completed and sent to the printer, so I can get to work on Profiles Volume II: Historic & Influential People from Buffalo & WNY – the 1900s. That book has already been started and it will be published in October 2020, in time for the Erie County Bicentennial in 2021.

INTRODUCTION

Over one and a half million people now live in the Western New York (WNY) area, with almost one million in Erie County and over 250,000 in Buffalo. However, it is possible to identify the first settlers and properties that existed in this area.

A community begins with the first people that settled that area and following are the first settlers of Buffalo and WNY. Many of these individuals are referenced throughout this book and later residents built upon the foundations set by these pioneers.

Cornelius Winney (or Winne) arrived in Buffalo as early as 1783 and in 1789 he erected the first building on the site of what would become the city of Buffalo. It was a small log house near the corner of Washington and Quay Streets, in the rear section of the area where the Mansion House was later built. At this location he opened a post for trading with the Indians, Haudenosaunee. Winney was the first white settler on Buffalo Creek.

William Johnston first visited Buffalo as the British Indian Agent in 1780. When the British vacated Fort Niagara in 1794, he decided to remain in WNY. He married a Seneca woman and built a home next to Winney's store, with this home being located north of Exchange Street and east of Washington Street. His half-brother Captain (later Colonel) Powell accompanied Johnston to Buffalo as a British Indian Agent and also decided to remain in the area. He purchased an interest in Winney's store but moved to Canada where he died not far from Fort Erie.

In 1794, Johnston gave consent to Martin Middaugh to build a log house next to his block house. Middaugh had come from Canada with his son-in-law Ezekiel Lane, who was a cooper and the first mechanic in Buffalo. They built a double house, and the homes of Winney, Johnston and Middaugh were the first three homes built in Buffalo.

When surveyor Augustus Porter came to Buffalo in the spring of 1795, he recollected only four people lived in the area near Buffalo Creek: Captain William Johnston, Martin Middaugh, Ezekiel Lane and Cornelius Winney. Joseph Landon, who passed through Buffalo in June 1796 on his way to survey Ohio, identified these pioneers as well as Mr. Skinner who had a log tavern on a nearby hill, and Joseph Hodge, an African American trader and scout, who had a whisky shop near Little Buffalo Creek.

John Palmer operated a tavern in a building owned and built by Johnston in 1795 on Exchange Street about 100 feet west of Main Street. Palmer was the first innkeeper in Buffalo and remained in the city until 1802. He was married to the daughter of Lewis Maybee, who lived in Canada across the Niagara River from Black Rock.

Prior to 1796, runaway slave Joe "Black Joe" Hodge lived in a cabin just west of the Winney home. Hodge was married to a Seneca Indian and was fluent in the Seneca languages. He was often hired as a guide and interpreter. Hodge died at an advanced age on the Cattaraugus Reservation.

In 1797, Sylvanus Maybee established himself as an Indian trader and lived in a log building on the west side of Main Street approximately 300 feet north of Exchange Street. He had moved to Buffalo from Canada but was originally from the Mohawk valley.

Asa Ransom arrived in Buffalo in 1797, with his wife and daughter, and built a log cabin near Main and Terrace. He was a silversmith and he sold trinkets to the Indians. Their second daughter Sophia was the first white child born in Buffalo.

William Robbins was a blacksmith who arrived in Buffalo in 1798, providing the forging services required by every early community.

These people were the entire population of Buffalo in 1798 and can be considered the original, non-Indian, residents of the city of Buffalo.

Joseph Ellicott and The Holland Land Company began selling land in Buffalo in 1804, with the first deed being issued to William Johnston. When Dr. Cyrenius Chapin purchased a lot in Buffalo in 1805 there were a total of 15 real estate holders in the village of Buffalo Creek, all others were squatters or tenants. In addition to Dr. Chapin, the legal landowners were William Robbins, Henry Chapin, Sylvanus Maybee, Asa Ransom, Thomas Stewart, Samuel Pratt, William Johnston, John Crow, Joseph Langdon, Erastus Granger, Jonas Williams, Robert Kain, Vincent Grant and Louis LeCouteulx.

There were 16 dwellings in the village in 1806. Three were on the Terrace, three on Seneca Street, two on Cayuga and eight on Main Street. There were two stores: one owned by Vincent Grant on Main and Seneca and one by Samuel Pratt on Main and Crow (now Exchange) Streets. Pratt's store was next to Crows Tavern on Crow Street, at the later site of the Mansion House. Judge Barker also had a tavern on Main and Terrace and LeCouteulx had a drug store on Crow Street.

William Hodge Jr. compiled a list in 1856, given to him by his uncle Lorin Hodge who was in Buffalo in 1806, before moving to Ohio. Hodge recalled 18 heads of households in 1806, with his list verifying and expanding upon the listing in the above paragraphs. 1 – Zenus Barker was an innkeeper on the Terrace about 100 feet west of Main. 2 – John Crow was on innkeeper on Crow Street (Exchange) between Main and Washington. 3 – Erastus Granger's office as Collector of the Port was in Crow's Tavern. 4 – Joshua Gillet was a merchant with his store east of Baker's Tavern on Terrace near Main. 5 – Vincent Grant was a merchant on the west side of Main near Seneca. 6 – Louis Stephen LeCouteulx had a drug store across from Crow's Tavern on the north side of Crow Street. 7 & 8 Sylvanus Maybe and William Johnston were merchants that traded Indians goods at a store adjoining the east side of LeCouteulx's store. 9 - Captain Samuel Pratt was a merchant with his store and home west of Crow's Tavern on Crow and Main Streets. 10 – William Hull was a silversmith with his store on the east side of Main between Crow and Seneca. 11 – David Reese was the blacksmith for the Indians with his shop at the northeast corner of Washington and Seneca, with his house across the street on the southeast corner. 12 – William Robbins had a blacksmith shop, with a home behind it, on the west side of Main next to Grant's store near Seneca. 13 – Dr. Cyrenius Chapin lived on Main Street near the Square or Swan Street. 14 & 15 – Michael Middaugh and his son in law Ezekiel Lane lived on Main near Little Buffalo Creek on the south end of Samuel Pratt's lot. 16 – Black Joe lived near Little Buffalo Creek on the east side of Main. 17 – John Despar had a bakery on Washington between Crow and Seneca. 18 – He recalled that Mr. Mann also lived in Buffalo but could not remember the location of his home, only that he was married to the daughter of Ezekiel Lane.

In 1802, the first immigrants began arriving in WNY and settled in Clarence and Newstead. Asa Ransom established his tavern in Clarence in 1799 and in 1802 Peter Vanderventer built a tavern in Newstead. Western New York was still very much a wilderness because at what is considered the first town meeting on March 1, 1803, held at Vanderventer's tavern, elections were held and an ordinance was passed offering a bounty of five dollars for wolf scalps, two-fifty for whelps and fifty cents for foxes and wildcats.

The first settlers in 1805 of outlying towns and villages included Jonas Williams, who purchased the abandoned Benjamin Ellicott and John Thompson home and mill in Williamsville, and William Warren, who built a home in East Aurora. The southeast corner of Tonawanda was first settled by John Hershey, John King and Alexander Logan in 1805, with Oliver Standard settling along the Niagara River in 1806. In 1806, Joel Henry opened a tavern in Evans at the foot of 18 Mile Creek, John Cummings built a mill upstream in the southwestern part of the county, William Allen built the first home in Wales and the Quakers organized a "Friends meeting" place at Potter's Corners in Hamburg, which in 1807 was the first church building in the county. The Quakers also built a school on the property. In 1807, Christopher and John Stone built a home on streams which emptied into the Cattaraugus in Springville, Phineas Stephens built the first grist mill in the southeastern part of Erie County and William Warren converted his log cabin in East Aurora into a tavern, while his original cabin became a school. In 1807, Archibald S. Clark opened the first store outside of Buffalo at his farm in Newstead and Arthur Humphrey made the first settlement in Holland. In 1808, the first settler in the village of Tonawanda was Henry Anguish (who later opened a tavern in 1811), Jacob Taylor built a sawmill at Taylor's Hollow in Collins (followed by a grist mill the following year), and George Richmond opened a tavern three miles east of Springville.

The town of Buffalo was formed in February 1810, containing all land west of the transit (now Transit Road), between Tonawanda Creek to the north and Buffalo Creek to the south. In 1813, the Villages of Buffalo and Black Rock were formed. The boundaries of Buffalo were basically Franklin, Exchange, Washington and Chippewa Streets, and Black Rock was from the current location of School Street on the south to Austin Street on the north. Scajaquada Creek separated Lower Black Rock to the north and Upper Black Rock to the south. The town of Amherst, which included Cheektowaga, was removed from the town of Buffalo in 1818. The County of Erie was established when it was separated from Niagara County in 1821. When the city of Buffalo was incorporated in 1832 the boundaries were North Street and Porter Avenue to the north and Jefferson Street to the east, the Niagara River to the west and Buffalo Creek to the south.

In 1836, the town of Tonawanda, which included Grand Island was removed from the town of Buffalo. In 1837, the village of Black Rock was incorporated and in 1839, the town of Black Rock was incorporated from the remainder of the town of Buffalo outside of the city limits. Finally, the City of Buffalo established its current day city limits when it annexed all the town of Black Rock in 1853.

Building off of this foundation, this book will profile one hundred people that helped shape the WNY community during the 1800s. It includes individuals from various backgrounds and occupations, who contributed in different ways. Some lived in Buffalo for their entire lives, while others were here for a short time, but left their mark. Most contributions were local in nature, but some affected the region, state, country or world. However, all assisted in establishing the significance of Buffalo and WNY.

ROBERT BORTHWICK ADAM & J.N. ADAM

AM&A's and J.N. Adam Department Stores

Robert Borthwick Adam was born in 1833 and his brother James Noble Adam in 1843 at Peebles on the River Tweed in Scotland. Their father Thomas Adam was a Presbyterian pastor and mother was Isabella Borthwick. Edinburgh was about twenty miles from Peebles and both brothers apprenticed at dry goods stores in that city when they were young.

In 1857, Robert emigrated to the U.S., with his wife Grace Harriet Michie, whom he married in Scotland. They settled in Boston where he worked in the importing business for ten years before moving to Buffalo in 1867, along with two associates from Boston. In Buffalo they opened Adam, Meldrum and Whiting at 308 – 310 Main Street. The company then became Adam, Meldrum and Anderson (AM&A's) in 1876 when Whiting left and was replaced as a partner by William Anderson. In 1886, AM&A's was one of the pioneer stores in the use of electricity when they purchased a Westinghouse generator to light the store.

The original store was on the site of the current Main Place Mall, where they continually expanded their operations, purchasing the Hudson's store at 410 Main Street. In 1960, the department store was moved across the street to 385 Main Street, the former J.N. Adam & Company building, where at both locations they were known for their elaborately decorated Victorian Christmas window displays. AM&A's became the first downtown store to expand to suburban branch locations when they opened a store at The University Plaza in 1948 followed by stores in major plazas and malls throughout WNY. The store remained family owned and in 1942, Robert B. Adam III, the grandson of the founder, became president. He served as CEO until his death in 1993, with the department store chain being sold to The Bon-Ton in 1994.

Robert Borthwick Adam purchased a three-story Victorian mansion at 448 Delaware Avenue in 1876. He became a director of the YMCA in 1879 and served as president of the organization. Adam was also president of the Merchants Exchange and when the legislature established the Grade Crossing Commission, he became chairman of this commission and worked to make the crossings safer for

Figure 1 Adam Meldrum & Company in 1870s, before William Anderson became a partner in the company

the public. Upon his death in 1904, his son Robert B. Adam II moved into the Delaware mansion. The Robert B. Adam house is currently utilized as office space.

James Noble Adam opened his own dry goods store in Scotland when he was 21. In 1872, he married Margaret Paterson in Edinburgh and emigrated to the U.S. They settled in New Haven, Connecticut, where he opened a dry goods store with William H. Hotchkiss. When visiting his brother in Buffalo, he was told that space for a dry goods store was going to be available in the White Building and his brother preferred him, rather than some stranger, as his competition. J.N. Adam and William Hotchkiss relocated and opened their store in the White Building at 298 Main Street on October 20, 1881. They continued expanding their operations and moved to larger facilities down Main Street, at the corner of Main and Eagle, where they acquired several properties from 383 to 393 Main Street. In 1946, the store was remodeled with a 12-story addition with the current building being a combination of five historic buildings.

J.N. Adam and his wife lived in a large home at 60 Oakland Place and did not have any children. Every summer they vacationed in Scotland and his wife died in Edinburgh while visiting there in 1895. Upon returning to Buffalo, J.N. turned his attention to politics and to enhancing the community. He was elected to the City Council in 1895 and served as Mayor of Buffalo from 1906 to 1909.

At the Pan-American Exposition, the Emmons Howard Company of Westfield, Massachusetts built and installed one of the largest organs in the U.S. at the Temple of Music. The cost of the organ was $18,000 dollars, over half a million current dollars. J.N. Adam purchased the organ and since it did not fit in St. Louis Church at Main and Edward, it was installed in the Elmwood Music Hall at Elmwood and Virginia. This organ remained at the music hall for 36 years, after the debut concert in October 1902.

Figure 2 AM&A's original store before they moved across the street to the J.N. Adam location

Near the end of J.N. Adam's term as mayor, the city of Buffalo was authorized by NYS to build and operate a hospital for tuberculosis patients. Adam purchased a 293-acre site in Perrysburg for $20,000 in 1909 and donated it to the city. The hospital was named the J.N. Adam Memorial Hospital in his honor. It opened in late 1912 but J.N. Adam died at the age 69 earlier that year.

JOHN JOSEPH ALBRIGHT

Coal, steel, banking and the Albright Art Gallery

John Albright was born on January 18, 1848 in Buchanan, Virginia. He was descended from Andrew Albright, a gunsmith who supplied guns to the Continental Army during the American Revolution. His father Joseph J. Albright was an iron manufacturer, bank president and coal agent for the DL&W (Lackawanna) Railroad. Joseph moved his family to Scranton and after John Albright graduated from Rensselaer Polytechnic Institute in Troy, New York, with a degree in Mining Engineering, he moved back to Scranton, Pennsylvania.

Coal was in demand in the Western U.S., and in 1868 Albright began shipping railroad cars filled with coal to the West. These cars previously returned empty, but he had them filled with grain to be shipped back to the East. This business idea made him a profit of $100,000 in his first year. His partner in this business was Andrew Langdon, whose sister Harriet Langdon married Albright in 1872. The next year Albright and Andrew Langdon started working for the Philadelphia & Reading Coal & Iron Company in Washington, DC. While in Washington, Albright started an asphalt paving business with his brother-in-law, Amzi L. Barber, who was married to his wife's sister. They obtained contracts to pave the streets of Washington, DC, Scranton, PA and Buffalo, NY. After Albright left that company, it obtained a monopoly concession to Trinidad asphalt and paved the streets of over 70 American cities.

In 1883, the Philadelphia and Reading Railroad began shipping coal direct to Buffalo. Albright moved to Buffalo, where he formed the company Albright & Smith, with fellow RPI graduate Thomas Guilford Smith. In Buffalo they handled all coal sold by railroads in WNY and Canada, along with forwarding all shipments west from Buffalo. His concept of shipping the railroad cars west with coal and returning east with grain, was now earning Albright the current equivalent of almost two million dollars a year.

Figure 3 Albright home on West Ferry near Elmwood Avenue

In 1887, Albright started the Ontario Power Company located in Niagara Falls, Canada, but with a headquarters in Buffalo. The company provided power to Buffalo and many of Albright's companies. It became Hydro-Electric Power Commission of Ontario, later called Ontario-Hydro, a province-owned enterprise. In 1905, with George Westinghouse's brother Henry Herman Westinghouse, Albright purchased the Niagara Lockport and Ontario Power Company, the company that distributed Ontario Power Company generated electricity in the U.S. After several mergers and reorganizations, that company evolved into Niagara Mohawk and National Grid.

Albright and Edmund B. Hayes purchased Buffalo Bolt in 1897, which later moved from Buffalo to North Tonawanda and employed 1,500 people. Hayes also worked with Albright in helping move Lackawanna Steel to Buffalo.

In 1899, Albright began working with William Walker Scranton to move Lackawanna Iron & Steel Company to Buffalo. He purchased the land for the factory often accompanied by John Milburn, who was president of the Pan-American Exposition committee, of which Albright was a member. To purchase the land, they worked with realtor Charles Gurney (of current day Gurney, Becker & Bourne – established in 1864). People thought they were purchasing land for the Pan-Am, not a steel company, and it only took one month and one million dollars to complete the land purchase. In 1922, Lackawanna Steel was acquired by Bethlehem Steel, becoming one of the largest employers in WNY. Lackawanna Steel, along with the Buffalo & Susquehanna Iron Company, (a company Albright formed with the Goodyear brothers), helped build the Union Ship Canal. Due to the success of these companies, the city of Lackawanna was split from the town of West Seneca, becoming a city looked after by the steel plants and populated by their employees.

Albright purchased the Wadsworth house at 730 West Ferry in 1887 and in 1890 hired Frederick Law Olmsted's company to landscape the grounds. He lived in this house with his wife Harriet Langdon, who was a first cousin of Olivia Langdon Clemens, the wife of Samuel Clemens (Mark Twain). When his wife died in 1896, Albright hired Susan Fuller to tutor his and Harriet's three children. Two years later Albright married Susan Fuller and they had five children. Their son Fuller Albright was a renowned endocrinologist, who made numerous contributions to this field of medicine. The Wadsworth mansion burned down in 1901, and Albright hired E.B. Green to design a grand mansion. Green's association with Albright began when he designed the Albright Memorial Library, in honor of Albright's parents in Scranton in 1890. Landscaping of the twelve-acre estate was handled by Olmsted's company, with the address being 690-770 West Ferry and the property extending to Cleveland Drive. This majestic mansion and grounds were adjacent to the equally grand Rand Mansion on Delaware Avenue, which is now part of Canisius High School. For a second residence, in 1914 he purchased Joseph Pulitzer's cottage on the exclusive Jekyll Island in Georgia.

Albright was a director of the Pan-American Exposition, and in 1900 he donated $350,000 to build a permanent home for the Buffalo Fine Arts Academy, founded in 1862, and had a board consisting of the most prominent families in Buffalo. The

Figure 4 Grand opening of Albright Art Gallery on May 31, 1905

building was designed by E.B. Green and was to be the Fine Arts Pavilion of the Pan-Am. Construction of the building was delayed, and it opened on May 31, 1905 as the Albright Art Gallery. Beginning in 1939, Seymour H Knox Jr. and the Knox Family provided funds to establish the Room of Contemporary Art to exhibit modern art. Gifts of artwork from A. Conger Goodyear, Seymour Knox Jr. and other donors necessitated additional exhibit space. In 1962, donations from Knox and hundreds of other donors provided for a new addition and the renaming of the building as the Albright Knox Art Gallery.

In addition to the Albright Art Gallery and Scranton Memorial Building, Albright's philanthropy extended to numerous other projects. He donated the land for Unitarian Universalist Church on Elmwood and donated a building for Nichols School. The Botanical Gardens were established with plants that he donated. Albright also supported the Elmwood School, which became Elmwood Franklin School, the oldest K-8 school in WNY.

In 1908, Albright founded Fidelity Trust & Guaranty Company with George Forman. The Fidelity Trust Building at 284 Main Street, now known as Swan Tower, was designed by E.B. Green and built in 1909. In 1925, the bank merged with Manufacturers & Traders Bank to become Manufacturers & Traders Trust Company. In 1908, he served on the board of Marine Bank and was later president of Marine National Bank of Buffalo and a director of Marine Trust Company which eventually became Marine Midland Bank.

Albright lost much of his fortune in the Great Depression and died in 1931 at age 83. His home on West Ferry was demolished in 1935 and subdivided into multiple parcels. All that remains of the estate is the Queen Anne's Gate and part of the wall which are still standing on West Ferry Street.

LEWIS ALLEN

The father of Allentown

L ewis Allen was born in Westfield, Massachusetts in 1800. He worked for an uncle in Sandusky, Ohio at 18 years of age and returned to New England three years later to work with family. In 1827, he moved to Buffalo as secretary and financial manager of Western Ensurance Company. When that charter expired in 1830, he formed Buffalo Fire & Marine Insurance Company. At that time insurance companies could make loans and all the loans Allen made were paid in full.

When Allen moved to Buffalo, he arrived with his wife Margaret Cleveland, who he married in 1825. Margaret was born in Salem, Massachusetts and was the daughter of William Cleveland, who was a resident of Norwich, Connecticut at the time of the marriage. Her younger brother, Reverend Richard F. Cleveland was the father of Grover Cleveland, the future U.S. president. Lewis Allen and Margaret had six children, two of whom lived to adulthood. Their daughter Margaret married Dr. Daniel A. Bailey and their son William Cleveland Allen married May Barclay.

In 1829, Allen purchased 29 acres on Main Street extending to the mile reserve, at a cost of $2,500. On his land he started planting orchards and raising shorthorn cattle. Every day he would walk the cattle down a path from the back of his home to pastureland, owned by Thomas Day, about of a quarter mile away. The path upon which he took the cattle became Allen Street and the pasture is now in the area of Days Park.

Figure 5 Portrait of Lewis Allen in 1857

When Buffalo was incorporated as a city in 1832, North Street became the northern boundary. Allen's land was ideally situated to increase in value, so he began selling off parcels. He also purchased other parcels of land at auctions and sold them at significant increases. He often replaced old wooden homes with new brick buildings before reselling them. It appears that Allen was involved in flipping homes before it became fashionable almost two centuries later.

In 1833, Allen worked with the East Boston Lumber Company of Massachusetts to purchase 16,000 acres of Grand Island at $6.00 per acre. This was almost the complete island. They purchased the land to cut down the white oak and other trees that

Figure 6 Lewis Allen home, River Lea, in the early 1900s prior to the front porch being removed
Photo: Courtesy Grand Island Historical Society

grew on Grand Island. Most of the white oak was transported to the company's shipyards on Noodle Island in Boston Harbor, for the construction of clipper ships. The company built a factory settlement on Grand Island called Whitehaven, which included a sawmill, store, school and church. Stephen White directed the lumber enterprise from his home across the Niagara River on Tonawanda Island, which later became an important center for the lumber trade, with Tonawanda and North Tonawanda becoming the largest lumber supply center in the U.S. Orator and statesman Daniel Webster was one of the owners of the East Boston Lumber Company. He was a frequent visitor at the White mansion; Webster's son married White's daughter and Webster Street in North Tonawanda was named after Daniel Webster.

When the company moved out of Grand Island, Allen purchased 600 acres for his farm called Allenton. At this farm he conducted experiments in improving milk production with cows and the meat production of swine. He also had orchards of apple, pear and cherry trees. The home, River Lea, built by Allen as a gift to his son, and often vistied by his nephew Grover Cleveland, is now the Grand Island Historical Society Building and is located inside of Beaver Island Park. In addition, Allen was one of the founders of the Falconwood Private Club on Grand Island.

In 1841, Allen re-started the Erie County Fair which was held behind the Court House on Lafayette Square. The Erie County Agricultural Society was originally begun in 1820 and held county fairs in 1820 and 1821 on the Buffalo waterfront near Terrace and Main Streets. Dr. Cyrenius Chapin was the initial president of the organization, but fairs were not held from 1822 until 1840. After being held behind the Court House, the fair was moved to various locations before settling in Hamburg in 1868. The society finally purchased the former Hamburg Driving Park in 1881 from Maria Clark, Naomi Clark and George N. Pierce.

In 1837, Allen purchased Peter Porter's home in Black Rock on Niagara Street and lived there for over 50 years. Stephen Grover Cleveland was his nephew and he stayed at the Niagara Street home while on his way to Ohio. Allen told Cleveland that if he wanted to study law, he could have a successful career in Buffalo. Allen sent him to the firm of Bowen & Rogers who handled his legal business. The 18-year old Cleveland presented himself at the office but did not bother to mention his relationship with Allen. Unimpressed with his credentials, he was told there were no job openings.

The next morning Allen stormed into the office of Bowen & Rogers and told them if they did not want the services of his nephew, they also did not need his legal business. The firm reconsidered and gave Cleveland a job as a clerk. This convinced Cleveland to remain in Buffalo and he read law at Bowen & Rogers. Cleveland passed the bar in 1857 and remained with the firm until 1863. Allen was a former Whig and was the first chairman of the Republican Party in Erie County, serving in the NYS assembly for over 10 years. Cleveland was a Democrat. They parted ways over their political views, with Allen never voting for Cleveland in any elections.

Figure 7 Falconwood was built by Lewis Allen in 1858 and became the most popular private club on Grand Island Photo: Courtesy Grand Island Historical Society

BENJAMIN BARTON

Freight forwarding business along the Niagara River with both Peter Porter and Samuel Wilkeson

Benjamin Barton was born in Sussex County in New York and in 1787, at age seventeen, he accompanied his father in delivering cattle and sheep to Fort Niagara. After completing this delivery, they returned to their farm near Geneva, New York, but the trip got Barton interested in WNY.

In 1805, Barton attended the sale by New York State of lands in the Mile Strip along the Niagara River. At this sale the lease was offered for the docks and warehouses, including Steadman farm, at Lewiston and Schlosser. Barton attended the sale with his relative Joseph Annin, who surveyed the Mile Strip. Also attending were Peter Buell Porter and Augustus Porter. These four men decided to form a partnership and bid together on the lands and lease.

Figure 8 Benjamin Barton Portrait

Porter, Barton and Company was successful in obtaining the Lewiston/Schlosser lease for thirteen years and purchased the land around Niagara Falls, including many other farms and village lots. In 1805, Benjamin assisted in building a gristmill at the falls and moved his family to Lewiston in 1807. Their company was successful in establishing the first regular and connected line of transportation between Lake Ontario and Lake Erie on the American side of the Niagara River.

The company's holdings at both Lewiston and Schlosser were destroyed by the British during the War of 1812. Barton joined his business partner General Peter Buell Porter as quartermaster of the militia and was granted a regular army commission by President Madison. After the war he moved back to Lewiston and in 1815 rebuilt his home Barton House, on the hill at Center and Third Streets. Barton served as Lewiston supervisor from 1819 to 1827, retiring to his estate where he died at age 72 in 1842.

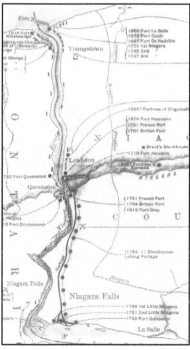

Figure 9 Map showing Porter, Barton & Company portage around Niagara Falls

When he was twelve years old in 1807, James L. Barton started working with his father. After the Porter Barton & Company warehouse was rebuilt, he began working in Black Rock in 1815. Living in Black Rock and being the Postmaster at Black Rock from 1817 to 1827, James Barton was aligned with Porter in arguing for Black Rock to be the western terminus of the Erie Canal. When the Buffalo harbor was granted the award of being the western terminus, Barton moved to Buffalo and formed a partnership with his former adversary Samuel Wilkeson. Their forwarding partnership, one of the first in Buffalo, lasted for an amicable two years, when Wilkeson decided to retire from the business. He rented the docks and warehouse to Barton for only $250 a year, an annual rent that remained the same until the business closed in 1835. Barton also owned a line of boats on the canal and ships on the lake.

In 1835, James L. Barton built a home at 2 Delaware Avenue at Church Street, which was the first house on the Avenue. Barton retired from active business in 1848 and died on October 6, 1869 at age 74. He had the distinction of working with both Porter and Wilkeson, the two antagonists of the Black Rock – Buffalo argument regarding which town would be the western terminus of the Erie Canal.

Figure 10 The Barton House was rebuilt in 1815 on the hill on Center Street at 3rd Street in Lewiston

PHILIP BECKER

Wholesale grocer, president of the German Insurance Company and the first German born Mayor of Buffalo

Philip Becker was born in Oberotterbach, Bavaria, Germany on April 25, 1830. When he was 13 years old, he started attending college in France and graduated from a German college at age 16. In 1847, he and his brother convinced their parents to allow them to move to America, where they had relatives living in Buffalo.

Upon arriving in Buffalo, Becker obtained a job in the retail and wholesale grocery business, working for Jacob Dorst at a salary of $4.00 per month. In 1854, after working for Dorst for seven years, he saved $400 and borrowed $2,000 to open his own delicatessen business at 390 Main Street near Court Street. A year later he moved to larger facilities at 384 Main and admitted George Goetz as a partner. Business continued to increase and by 1862 he was located at 468 and 470 Main Street, with his brother-in-law Michael Hawsauer admitted as a partner in Philip Becker & Company. After 39 years in the business, Becker retired from Philip Becker & Company in 1893, with the business being continued by his partners.

In 1867, Becker was one of the founders of the German Insurance Company and served as its president from 1869 until his death in 1898. There were three businesses in what was called the Roos Block in 1868. The lots encompassed 89' x 99' on Main Street between the Tifft House and Broadway or Lafayette Square. The German Insurance Company purchased the lots in 1873 and 1874, hiring architect Richard Waite to design a six-story cast iron building. The ornate building was fireproof, cost $200,000 to build and opened in 1876.

Next to the German Insurance Building on Lafayette Square was the Lafayette Presbyterian Church. When the church was moved to Elmwood Avenue, that building was sold in 1901 and remodeled into a burlesque house known as the Lafayette Theater. It became the Olympic Theater, a vaudeville and movie theater in 1913. Next to the Olympic was a private home that after it was demolished, the Park Hof Restaurant was built on the corner of Broadway and Washington. When the theater and restaurant were torn down, in their place, the Rand Building opened in 1929, which at 405 feet was the tallest building in Buffalo. The Buffalo German Insurance Company moved to 220 Delaware Avenue and it was replaced by the Tishman Building in 1957, the first large post war downtown Buffalo construction, ushering in the construction of other skyscrapers in the city. It is now the Hilton Garden Inn, with apartments and the Hamister Group on the upper floors.

Due to the anti-Germany movement after the U.S. entered WWI, the German Insurance Company became the Buffalo Insurance Company in 1918. The German American Bank, founded in 1882, was diagonally across the street at the corner of Main and Court Streets. The anti-German sentiment also resulted in the bank changing its name in 1918 to Liberty Bank.

Figure 11 German Insurance Company at Main and Lafayette Square. To the left on Main Street is the Tifft House and to the right on Broadway is the Lafayette Presbyterian Church, later the Olympic Theatre Photo: Buffalo History Museum

In the early 1870s, Becker was a member of the commission to build a new City and County Hall. The site selected was the former Franklin Square Cemetery on the southern portion of the lot which was already owned by the city. Philip Becker was elected mayor in 1875 and on February 7, 1876 he set the tower clock in motion by initiating the swing of the giant pendulum, the building lights were illuminated by gas on March 10 and on March 13 the new City and County Hall opened for business.

Since Becker took his oath of office as Mayor of Buffalo on January 3, 1876, he was called the Centennial Mayor and received an annual salary of $2,500. In 1878, third party candidate Edward Bennett obtained sufficient Republican votes, resulting in Becker's defeat and the election of Democrat Solomon Scheu. Becker remained active with the Republican Party but did not seek office again until 1886, when he was elected for two more terms, becoming the first three term mayor of Buffalo. In 1890, he decided not to seek re-election for a fourth term.

Becker married Sarah Goetz, the sister of his business partner George Goetz in 1852. They lived in a home on Pearl Street near Court and then moved to a brick mansion on Franklin and Mohawk. In 1890, Becker built a mansion at 534 Delaware Avenue, near Allen, where his neighbor across the street was Jacob Schoellkopf. In 1883, Becker and Schoellkopf were responsible for bringing the second Saengerfest to Buffalo. For this German singing festival, they built the Saengerhalle, or First Music Hall at the southwest corner of Main and Edward, across from St. Louis RC Church. That building burned down in 1885 and a Second Music Hall was built in 1887, and was remodeled into the Teck Theater in 1900. Becker was active with various societies and served as president of the Saengerbund, as well as other German societies and area cultural organizations.

When he died in 1898, his estate was valued over $750,000. Philip and Sarah Becker did not have any children and in his will, he provided for his wife, along with establishing trusts for various charities including: Buffalo General Hospital, the German Deaconess Home, Sisters Hospital and St. Vincent's Female Orphan Home. In 1899, Sarah had a polished black granite truncated obelisk monument created for Philip's gravesite. The 48-ton monument, the heaviest ever manufactured in its day, was transported to Forest Lawn Cemetery by a team of 30 horses. Their home at 534 Delaware is now the Plaza Suites Executive Office Building.

Figure 12 These buildings in Franklin Square were the City and County Buildings until the present County Hall was opened in 1876

LEWIS J. BENNETT

The founder of the Buffalo Cement Company and creator of the
Central Park area of Buffalo

The family of Lewis J. Bennett can be traced back to John Bennett, who was sheriff of Wiltshire, England in 1266. Six of his ancestors immigrated from Scotland in 1770 and participated as patriots in the Revolutionary War. His parents William and Elma Strong Bennett were living in the town of Duanesburg, Schenectady County, NY when Lewis was born on July 7, 1833.

When Lewis was four years of age, the family moved to Glen, NY, where his father established a large farm. Lewis was not of the physical constitution for farm work and even though he was the oldest son of a prominent farmer, he entered the retail sales business. In 1849, he began working as a clerk in Fultonville, then attended high school in Fort Plain, before returning to Fultonville to work with Mr. Chapman at his grocery store. Eventually that store became Bennett & Company, where Bennett worked until he sold his interests and moved to Buffalo in 1866.

While in Fultonville, Bennett became involved in schools, the Erie Canal, iron bridges and government. He was a Fultonville school trustee in 1860, where he changed the rate bill system to a free public-school system supported by taxes. It was one of the earliest school systems to adopt this now universal system. Starting in 1861, he served two terms as state canal board collector of tolls at Fultonville, becoming familiar with canal operations. He was elected a Fultonville supervisor in 1865, when during his term he replaced a wooden bridge with an iron one. His administration also sold the country poor farm, devising a new system of caring for the poor.

Upon relocating to Buffalo, he assumed contracts for repairs on the Erie Canal. He formed a company with Andrew Spaulding and John Hand, contracting harbor work and the building of iron bridges, specializing in iron bridges for country towns. In 1874, he became treasurer of the Buffalo Hydraulic Cement Company and in 1877 he formed Buffalo Cement Company. This company was located at Main and Amherst Streets, including the quarry on Amherst Street. Buffalo Cement became a leading company in the manufacture of hydraulic cement and Bennett was president for 35 years, until the company transitioned into a real estate investment and development company in 1911.

Beginning in 1889, Lewis Bennett began planning the 200-acre Central Park neighborhood, purchasing lots from various property owners. The boundaries were Main, Woodbridge, Parkside, Linden, Starin and Amherst Streets, with nineteen stone markers originally identifying the boundaries of the neighborhood. Preparation of the neighborhood took four years and $300,000 to lay out the streets, blast out the underlying bedrock and plant 1200 elm trees. Strict deed restrictions required the houses to be at least two stories, barns built behind the house and minimum home

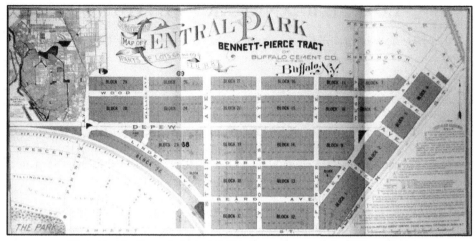

Figure 13 Advertisement by Bennett's Buffalo Cement Company for lots in Central Park

construction costs of $4,000 on Depew Avenue, $3,500 on Main Street and $2,500 on Starin Avenue. Bennett built the first house in the development at 354 Depew Avenue, a magnificent 24 room mansion. When that house was razed in 1935 it was replaced by twelve building lots.

The Central Park neighborhood was developed by Bennett due to its proximity to Delaware Park and it was made possible by the completion of the Belt Line Railroad in 1883. The Starin and Amherst Station of the Belt Line was owned by the Buffalo Cement Company and leased to New York Central Railroad. That station is the only one that remains from the Belt Line. The neighborhood included the Otowega Club at Starin and Linden, which consisted of a bowling alley, billiard hall, card room, dance hall and dining room for the people of Central Park.

Bennett made generous contributions back to the community. In Central Park he donated land for three churches and deeded Burkes Green Park to the city. The area of the Buffalo Cement Quarry on Amherst Street is now McCarthy Park, with a small portion of the quarry still existing next to it. Due to his early involvement with schools, he donated the land for All High Stadium and Bennett High School to the city of Buffalo, with the school on Main Street being named after him.

LOUISE BLANCHARD BETHUNE

The first woman to practice as a professional architect in the United States

Louise Blanchard Bethune was born in Seneca Falls, NY in 1856 and attended high school in Buffalo. Upon graduation in 1874, she started preparing to enter the newly opened architecture program at Cornell University. In 1876, she accepted an apprenticeship at the office of Richard Waite, a prominent Buffalo architect, and worked part time at the office of F.W. Caulkins. Rather than attending Cornell her five-year apprenticeship and study allowed her to start her own firm in 1881. Later that year she married Robert Bethune, who joined her in forming the architectural company Bethune & Bethune.

In 1885, she applied for membership in the Western Association of Architects and was unanimously accepted. She was the Vice President of the WAA in 1888 and when it merged with the American Institute of Architects in 1889, she became its first female member.

Figure 14 Louise Bethune memorial plaque in Forest Lawn Cemetery

Bethune designed 150 buildings of all styles in Buffalo and New England but concentrated on public buildings, especially schools. She designed 18 schools including Hamburg High School, Lockport High School and several Buffalo Public Schools. Two of her major projects were the 74th Armory, which became the Elmwood Music Hall, and the Hotel Lafayette. Her firm also designed the Denton, Cottier & Daniels store at Court and Pearl Streets, one of the first buildings designed in Buffalo utilizing poured concrete slabs and steel frame construction. She also designed the former Jehle's Grocery Store at Bryant and Ashland, which became Just Past and is now Trattoria Aroma.

Bethune was active in women's rights and championed equal opportunities and pay for women. She refused to enter the architectural design competition for the Women's

Figure 15 Hotel Lafayette designed by America's first female architect, Louise Bethune
Photo: Buffalo History Museum

Building at the 1893 Chicago World's Fair because the prize offered to men was $10,000 but only $1,000 to women. She did not believe in competitions and felt women should be paid the same as men.

To honor Bethune, in 1971 the University of Buffalo purchased the former Buffalo Meter Company Building and renamed it the Louise Blanchard Bethune Hall. It housed the Architecture Department, Art Department and portions of the university's Division of Continuing Education. The building is located at 2917 Main Street, next to Bennett High School and a block from the LaSalle light rail station. The University of Buffalo vacated the building in 1994 and it was subsequently purchased by Ciminelli Real Estate Corporation, who refurbished the property into 87 loft apartments, known as Bethune Lofts.

In addition to Buffalo, only three other cities in the U.S. have an Olmsted park and buildings designed by Henry Hobson Richardson, Louis Sullivan and Frank Lloyd Wright, who are considered the trinity of American architecture. Those three cities are New York City, Chicago and St. Louis. The fact that the first female architect was from Buffalo, only further solidifies Buffalo's reputation as a historically significant architectural city.

WILLIAM A. BIRD

*Central figure in establishing Black Rock and president of
Erie County Savings Bank*

William A. Bird was born on March 23, 1796 at the home of his maternal grandfather, Colonel Joshua Porter, in Salisbury, Connecticut. William's mother, Eunice Porter, married John Bird, a Yale graduate who studied law with Judge Tappan Reeve in Litchfield, Connecticut. His parents relocated to Troy, New York, where John served in the NYS Legislature from 1796 to 1799 and was a member of the U.S. Congress in 1801 and 1802.

William studied at Yale in 1813 for one year but returned to Troy, where he studied mathematics and prepared for a career as an engineer. He obtained a position with the Boundary Commission in 1817, to survey the border between the U.S. and Canada in the western Great Lakes. His uncle Peter Buell Porter was the commissioner of the Boundary Commission and William moved to Black Rock after he completed his work at Lake Superior with the commission. He built a home at 1118 Niagara Street in 1820 and lived in that house on the west side of Niagara Street for the next 58 years, until he died in August 1878 at age 81.

During the construction of his home, while excavating the foundation a large brass kettle was found. Inside this kettle were 12 skeletons and each one had a hatchet in its head. It was believed that these were the remains of French explorers, who went missing while traveling to Detroit in 1763.

A fifth generation American, Bird married Joanna W. Davis of Troy in December 1820. They had four children, but Mrs. Bird died in 1837 and William remained a

Figure 16 William A. Bird house at 1118 Niagara Street, built in 1820

widower the rest of his life. He was involved in the promotion of Black Rock, its harbor, pier, public works, canal commerce and other enterprises. William A. Bird, Peter B. Porter and Robert McPherson built the first flouring mill at Lower Black Rock and this mill ground the first cargo of wheat, that came down the Niagara River from the Western States.

Figure 17 William A. Bird was president of Erie County Savings Bank from 1854 to 1878

He assisted in the building of Black Rock Harbor and piers, but the Bird Island Pier was not named after William Bird. It was named after Bird Island which previously existed at the southern end of the pier that connected Squaw (Unity) Island to Bird Island. Bird also served as a government inspector of the Marine Navigation of the Great Lakes and established a code of rules for boats that is still valid today.

In 1824, Jasper Parrish sold Bird 172 acres on the northern edge of the square mile tract that he was given by the Seneca Nation, for his services as an interpreter at major treaties. The land that Bird purchased became known as Bird Farm and extended from the Niagara River to Military Road. This remained undeveloped farmland and the road on the southern edge of the property is now Hertel Avenue. He was also responsible for laying out and developing several streets in the Black Rock area, with Bird Avenue being named after him.

In 1834, William A. Bird and his uncle Peter B. Porter started the Buffalo & Black Rock Railroad. It was a horse drawn track down Niagara Street from Main Street to School Street in Black Rock. In 1836, it was converted to steam engines and construction supervised by Bird replaced the low-quality horse drawn tracks. The line was extended to Tonawanda in 1827 and to Niagara Falls around 1840, becoming the Buffalo & Niagara Falls Railroad which later consolidated into the New York Central Railroad in 1853. These companies were the first horse drawn and locomotive railroads in Buffalo.

Bird was one of the founders of Erie County Savings Bank in 1854. He served as president of the bank for 24 years, until his death in 1878. He was active in local politics, being elected as supervisor for the town of Black Rock and serving two terms in the NYS Assembly. Bird and his family are buried in the family plot at Forest Lawn Cemetery.

GEORGE BIRGE

President of the M.H. Birge & Sons wallpaper company and
Pierce-Arrow Motor Car Company

Richard Birge came to America from England on the 1630 voyage of the ship Mary and John, settling in Dorchester, Massachusetts. Richard's grandson Joseph Birge was one of the first settlers of Litchfield, Connecticut. Joseph's grandson David Birge fought in the American Revolution and married Abigail Howland, a descendant of John Howland who arrived on The Mayflower. Their son Elijah Birge was a Captain during the War of 1812. He married Mary Olds, and their son Martin Howland Birge was born in Underhill, Vermont on July 30, 1806.

After attending school and running a dry goods and general store in Middlebury Vermont, Martin moved to Buffalo in 1834. He opened a store selling dry goods and paper hangings on Main Street near Seneca. He sold that business in 1846 and opened the largest paper hanging business trade in the Western section of New York and the first store offering French and Italian wallpaper in Buffalo. Martin formed M.H. Birge & Sons in 1878, the first paper hanging factory west of NYC.

M.H. Birge & Sons Company became world-renowned as a manufacturer of wallpapers. Their first factory was in the former Tifft Furniture Manufacturing on Perry Street near Washington, later moving to a plant at 390 Niagara Street, between Maryland and Hudson. The company was known for its 12-color process of wallpaper production, offering top-price quality on handmade paper and expensive designs. In 1921, Charles Burchfield was hired as a designer and worked at the company for a decade before leaving to concentrate on his paintings, becoming one of Americas most innovative artists of the 20th Century. The Niagara Street factory closed in 1976 and the company went out of business in 1982 when wallpaper fashions changed.

Figure 18 M.H. Birge & Sons Company factory complex Photo: Buffalo History Museum

George K. Birge was born in Buffalo on December 19, 1849. After attending Buffalo Public Schools, Buffalo Academy and Cornell University, he began working with his father at M.H. Birge & Sons, soon becoming a partner. The business continued until 1890, when the family sold it to National Wallpaper Company. In 1900, the Birge family bought the business back, retaining the headquarters in Buffalo and maintaining branch offices in Chicago, New York, San Francisco, St. Louis, Boston and London, England. Their products were sold throughout the U.S., Europe, South America, South Africa and Australia. The M.H. Birge & Sons Company redesigned the wallpaper business, raising the status of the product from trade work to artistic decoration.

In 1896, George Birge invested in the George N. Pierce Company, which was manufacturing bicycles while its owner George Pierce was experimenting with making steam engine automobiles. Birge and the other investors convinced Pierce to switch to gasoline engines, which most early car makers were making. The first Pierce Arrow was premiered on opening day of the Pan-American Exposition in 1901. After winning the Glidden Tour – American Automobile Association car race, the Pierce Arrow was one of the best-known cars in the U.S. By 1905 they were selling the biggest and most expensive automobiles in the U.S. When Pierce left the company, Birge became president from 1908 to 1916. Under his leadership the company built the Pierce Arrow complex on Elmwood and Great Arrow, which had over one million square feet of floor space and the capability to employ over 10,000 workers.

During the Pan-American Exposition, George Birge was elected a director and Executive Committee member. He was also a member of the Building Committee with J.N. Scatcherd, Colonel Thomas W. Symons, Carlton Sprague and Harry Hamlin. The M.H. Birge & Sons Company and George N. Pierce both participated as exhibitors at the Pan-Am and his future son-in-law, George Cary, designed the New York State Building, the only permanent building at the exposition and now the Buffalo History Museum. The new Pierce Arrow manufacturing plant was built on the land that was the Pan-Am Midway.

In 1878, George Birge married Carrie Humphrey, daughter of former Congressman James. M. Humphrey and Adeline Bowen Humphrey. They had three children: Humphrey, Marion and Allithea. Humphrey became president of M.H. Birge & Sons and was one of the original residents of the 800 West Ferry Street Apartments. Marion married Thomas B. Lockwood who donated the Lockwood Memorial Library and his book collection from their home at 844 Delaware to The University of Buffalo. The library was donated in memory of Thomas Lockwood's father Daniel N. Lockwood and his wife's father George K. Birge. Allithea married George Cary, architect and member of the Cary family of Buffalo.

George built a home at 477 Delaware in the Midway in 1895, and his brother Henry lived at the house. The Birge mansion at 33 Symphony Circle was built in 1896 and 1897, modeled after a villa he saw while visiting the Riviera. George Birge lived in this home until his death in 1918. After George's death, his wife Carrie moved to

Figure 19 Birge Memorial at Forest Lawn Cemetery

Palm Springs, California, and later to France, where she had an apartment in Paris and a home on the Riviera in Monte Carlo.

George and Carrie Birge were local patrons of music, with George writing the theme song "Cornell" for the Cornell University Glee Club. Thomas B. Lockwood established the George K. Birge and Allithea Birge Cary Chair of Music at the University of Buffalo in memory of his wife's father and sister. It is appropriate that across from the Birge Mansion on Symphony Circle, Kleinhans Music Hall was built, which is the home of the Buffalo Philharmonic.

JOHN BLOCHER

Shoes, real estate, Blocher Homes and the Blocher Mausoleum

John Blocher moved to Clarence when he was one year old and was the youngest of three children. His father died when Blocher was ten, so he had to go to work at an early age and did not receive much formal education. After working on a neighboring farm for four dollars a month, at twelve years old he was apprenticed to a tailor and started his own tailoring shop in Williamsville when he was eighteen. That shop became a ready-made clothing store, expanding to a general country store. At age twenty, he married Elizabeth Neff of Williamsville in 1846.

When the Civil War broke out Blocher was in his middle thirties and a successful merchant, yet Blocher was one of the first to enlist. He was a Second Lieutenant in the 74th New York Regiment when his health became impaired and he was honorably discharged after only one year of service. He returned and purchased a farm in Amherst, also working in the lumber business. Blocher then moved to Buffalo and opened a boot and shoe factory on Wells Street (which no longer exists), where one of their contracts was manufacturing boots for the U.S. Army. The company had 200 employees, and John Blocher ran it with his son Warren. Upon his son's death in 1884, John retired from the business and concentrated on real estate, along with furthering his interest in electric transportation by serving as the president of the Buffalo and Williamsville Railroad.

In 1878, he purchased the 168 Delaware Avenue home of forwarding merchant Ozias Nims, who had facilities on the Central Wharf. Nims built the home in 1869 next to Public School #10 on a lot that was previously utilized by traveling circuses. The Blocher family lived in this home until Elizabeth died in 1904 and John died of old age in 1911. This spacious home was elegantly furnished with some of the belongings later moved to Blocher Homes.

Upon the death of Warren Blocher, his parents decided to build an elaborate memorial for him at Forest Lawn Cemetery. The mausoleum depicts John and Elizabeth Blocher looking down at their son Warren, who is laying on a marble slab. Hovering above is an angel that resembles Katherine Margaret Sullivan, who was a maid at the Blocher home. It was said Warren loved Katherine, but his parents did not approve of a marriage between their upper-class son and domestic help. They sent her away when Warren was in Europe on family business. Warren was heartbroken, unsuccessfully searched for his lost love and died after a prolonged illness. The tomb included a cap stone sculptured from a 90-ton slab of granite into a 29-ton bell. The monument cost $100,000, equivalent to over two million current dollars.

Elizabeth, driven by a maternal blend of love and guilt, insisted that the memorial be erected for her son. John could not find a monument designer, so he crafted it himself. After the monument was completed, Blocher told his wife that he now

Figure 20 Interior of Blocher Monument at Forest Lawn Cemetery

wanted to pursue his goal of ensuring that aging men and women would have a true home when they could no longer live on their own. He sent inspectors across the state to visit homes for the aged and find the best features to incorporate in a home he would build. This culminated in the building of a fifty-five room limestone mansion called Blocher Homes at 135 Evans Street in Williamsville, which was opened in 1906. He had hoped to build two more homes for the aged, but he passed away in 1911, leaving the bulk of his estate to Blocher Homes.

Blocher's Williamsville land had extensive orchards, where he allowed area residents to help themselves to the harvest. At the turn of the 20th Century, Old Home Days were celebrated on his land at Blocher Park Pavilion, located at the current site of Ed Young's Hardware. Forty acres were donated for Blocher Homes, and Mrs. Blocher donated several acres to the Holy Family Home on Mill Street in Williamsville. When the original building was considered not safe for occupancy, the Board of Directors built a new Blocher Homes which opened for 55 residents on February 1, 1970. Blocher's philanthropy lives on at Blocher Homes, he set a new standard for homes for the aging and the monument to his son remains a feature at Forest Lawn.

WILLIAM WELLS BROWN

Abolitionist, speaker and author, who was active in the
Underground Railroad in the Buffalo area

William Wells Brown was born a slave in Alabama in 1814. He grew up near St. Louis, Missouri, where he was hired out to a steamboat captain and learned about the steamship service industry. William was then put to work at the printing office of abolitionist Elijah P. Lovejoy, where he learned about the anti-slavery movement. Just before his 20th birthday, while William was working on a steamboat, he escaped slavery in January 1834 and took the name of a Quaker, Wells Brown, who assisted him when he was a runaway.

He settled in Cleveland, Ohio and obtained employment on lake steamers, where he would conceal fugitive slaves on the vessels headed to Buffalo. Upon arriving in Buffalo, the fugitives would be led to abolitionists who would transport them across the Niagara River to freedom in Canada. In 1836, Brown and his wife Elizabeth Spooner (a free black woman), moved to Buffalo because there was a larger black population and work could be obtained during the winter months when the lake steamers could not operate due to ice on the Great Lakes.

While living in Buffalo, he became actively involved with the Western New York Anti-Slavery Society, speaking out against slavery and using his connections to secure passage for runaway slaves across Lake Erie to Canada. In addition, Brown and other members of the Anti-Slavery Society would lure slaves, who were visiting Niagara Falls with their Southern masters, to inform them that according to NYS law that their journey in this free state made them free men. They encouraged the slaves to remain in New York, freeing themselves from slavery. This legality was reversed by the Dred Scott ruling in 1854.

During the summer of 1843, Buffalo hosted a national antislavery convention, organized by the National Convention of Colored Citizens. At this convention Brown sat on committees and became friends with black abolitionists, including Fredrick Douglass and Charles Lenox Remond. Buffalo became a center for the anti-slavery movement as in August 1843 it also hosted conventions for the National Convention of Colored People and the National Convention of the Liberty Party.

William W. Brown also gravitated to the Michigan Street Baptist Church, which in addition to being known as a legendary station on the Underground Railroad, was a meeting place for abolitionists and reformers. Due to his service to the anti-slavery movement and his increased sophistication as a speaker, he was invited to speak at the 1844 annual meeting of the American Anti-Slavery Society in NYC. Inspired by the success of Douglass' *Narrative of the Life of Frederick Douglass, an American Slave,*

Figure 21 The Underground Railroad Freedom Crossing Monument in Lewiston

Brown published *Narrative of William W. Brown, a Fugitive Slave*. It was initially published in Europe and became widely read in the U.S.

Now a best-selling author and public speaker, Brown received an invitation to speak at the 1849 International Peace Conference in Paris and at locations across England. He remained in England until 1854, because with the passing of the Fugitive Slave act, since he was an escaped slave and due to his celebrity, he could have been apprehended and returned to his previous owners. After abolitionists in England bought his freedom from the slave owner he had escaped from 20 years earlier, Brown was free to return to America.

Upon returning to the U.S., Brown continued his speaking engagements and publishing. He released a book about his travels in Europe and the novel *Clotel*, about the fictional slave daughters of Thomas Jefferson, one of the first novels published by an African American author. He was also a playwright and it was reported that when his anti-slavery play was produced at Buffalo's Eagle Theatre, it was so emotionally charged that it provoked a small riot.

It was claimed that during a lecture in Rochester on October 4, 1854, Brown discussed the rescue of a man who had been accused of being a fugitive slave. Brown and other abolitionists retained lawyer Millard Fillmore as counsel. Fillmore, whom as President signed the Fugitive Slave Act of 1850, represented the alleged fugitive without accepting a fee, explaining that he considered it "his duty to help the poor fugitive."

After becoming a doctor in 1860, Brown continued writing, publishing books about histories of black Civil War soldiers, Haiti's 18th century slave rebellion, plays and compilations of antislavery songs. Until his death at age 70 in 1884, he continued campaigning for temperance, women's suffrage, and prison reform.

TRUMBULL CARY

Purchased Chautauqua County from the Holland Land Company and became a pillar of WNY Society

Trumbull Cary was born in Mansfield, Connecticut on August 11, 1787, the son of Ebenezer and Sarah Trumbull Cary. He moved to Batavia in 1805 with his parents, his father being one of two merchants in the city. Trumbull was elected to the NYS Assembly and Senate, agent for the Holland Land Company and founder of the Bank of Genesee, serving as its president until his death in 1869. In 1817, he married Margaret Brisbane, daughter of James Brisbane, one of the surveyors of the Holland Land Company. Her brother was utopian socialist Albert Brisbane.

In 1835, Trumbull Cary and George Lay purchased all the Holland Land Company holdings in Chautauqua County for $919,175. There was a question about the Holland Land Company title to the lands, and the farmers who had land purchases revolted against the property owners. William Henry Seward was the attorney that successfully represented Trumbull Cary in this dispute and he remained a lifelong friend of the family.

Dr. Walter Cary was born in Batavia in 1818, the only child of Trumbull Cary and Margaret Brisbane. Walter received his medical degree from the University of Pennsylvania but due to his wealth, he spent his life as a world traveling member of society, not as a doctor. In 1848, he married Julia Love, the daughter of Thomas Love who was taken prisoner at Fort Erie during the War of 1812. Thomas Love returned to Batavia after the War and later moved to Buffalo where he was a judge and member

Figure 22 The Genesee House at Main and West Genesee Streets

of Congress. He gave his daughter three houses on Franklin Street as a wedding present and Trumbull gave Walter the Genesee House on Main and West Genesee Street.

Walter and Julia had six sons and one daughter. They traveled extensively, with some of their trips lasting several months or up to a year. During several of their trips the children were educated at schools in Europe. In 1852, they began building the house at 184 Delaware Avenue, at the corner of West Huron and originally extending to West Chippewa. The mansion was called Cary Castle because of its castellated exterior and three-story octagonal entrance tower. The 1870 census listed 23 people living at 184 Delaware, eight members of the Cary family, the two Love sisters, five domestics in the main house and the coachman and his family above the stables. In 1870, the mansion was raised an additional story and a French roof was added. Cary Castle was the social center of Buffalo with at least three presidents, many dignitaries and members of the social elite dining or staying at the house.

The Cary children were: Trumbull, Thomas, Charles, Walter, George, Seward and their sister Jennie. Trumbull was educated at universities in Europe and studied at Harvard. He was president of the Bank of Geneseo and an expert horseman. Thomas managed the family estate, especially the Genesee Hotel, and was appointed to the Taft Commission by President McKinley to establish civil government in the Philippines. Walter was educated in Europe, graduated from Harvard and received a master's degree from Cambridge. Majoring in English, unlike his brothers he did not pursue a business career, choosing to devote himself to literary pursuits. Seward graduated from Harvard and married Emily Scatcherd, daughter of wealthy lumberman James Scatcherd. They lived in the Scatcherd mansion at 615 Delaware and in a home at Hempstead Long Island. Dr Walter Cary died in Marseilles in 1881 and specified that upon his death he be cremated. Upon returning to Buffalo, his family funded the Buffalo Crematory on West Delavan, where most of the Cary family was later cremated.

Their son Charles Cary was also a medical doctor, and unlike his father, he actively practiced the medical profession. He married Evelyn Rumsey, daughter of Bronson C Rumsey. Charles was a respected physician and sportsmen. He had a polo team that included himself, his brother Thomas, Lawrence Rumsey, Bronson Rumsey and John M Scatcherd. They lost a match in Newport, Rhode Island against the team that was considered the top polo team in America. Charles' team later defeated that team in a rematch that took place at the Driving Park on East Ferry in Buffalo. Charles also promoted golf in America and was an organizer of the Aeronautical Club of America, the second oldest aviation club in the world. Evelyn was a suffragist, artist and patron of the arts. She painted The Spirit of Niagara, which became the official emblem of the Pan-American Exposition.

Their son George Cary received his bachelor's degree from Harvard and master's in Philosophy from Columbia. After graduation he accepted an apprenticeship with the architectural firm of McKim, Mead and White, before further studying in Paris. Two of the many buildings he designed were the Buffalo History Museum and Pierce-

Arrow Car Company. The History Museum is the only remaining building from the Pan-American Exposition and the Pierce Arrow Building set the standard for automobile manufacturing plant design. On December 13, 1908, George married Allithea Birge, daughter of George Birge, president of Birge Wallpaper Company and the Pierce Arrow Motor Car Company.

Their daughter Jennie married Laurence D. Rumsey, so two Cary children married Rumsey children. Lawrence graduated from Harvard and worked for the family tanning business until it was sold to United States Leather in 1893. He spent the rest of his life managing his father Bronson Rumsey's estate. They had five children. Their son, Charles Cary Rumsey was a sculptor and world class polo player. He married Mary Harriman, daughter of railroad industrialist Edward Henry Harriman and sister of William Averell Harriman, the 48th Governor of New York.

The last member of the family to live at Cary Castle was Maria Love. She was born on a farm in Clarence and was an actress and benefactor of the Red Cross and Fitch Creche. After her death in 1931, the house became a rooming house and later the Normandy, a steak house. It was sold to the federal government in 1964 and the GSA Building was built on Delaware between Huron and Cary Streets.

Figure 23 Cary Castle became the popular Normandy Restaurant, it was later demolished and the site of the mansion became a government office building
Photo: Buffalo History Museum

CYRENIUS CHAPIN

One of the earliest settlers and the first physician to practice medicine in Buffalo

C yrenius Chapin was born on February 7, 1769, in Bernardston, Massachusetts, where he studied medicine with his brother Caleb Chapin. Cyrenius practiced medicine in Winhall, Vermont for several years before moving to Sangerfield in Oneida County, New York.

In 1801, Dr. Cyrenius Chapin visited Buffalo and was impressed with the location of the settlement. He returned to Oneida county and wrote to Joseph Ellicott advising that he had a group of 40 individuals who were interested in purchasing the township at the mouth of the Buffalo River. Since the area had not yet been surveyed, Ellicott turned him down.

Chapin returned to Buffalo in 1803, but since land was still not available, he moved across the Niagara River to Fort Erie, where he practiced medicine for two years. In 1805, he purchased lot 40 on Swan Street (between Pearl and Main), where he built his home. His practice extended from north of Fort Erie in Canada and south to Erie, PA, all serviced on horseback. He also started the first drug store in Buffalo. His service to his patients was appreciated, and he was also respected by the Indians who called him "The Great Medicine Man."

When the War of 1812 began, Chapin raised a group of volunteers and offered his services as an officer and a surgeon. He fought in battles in Canada and rose to the rank of Lieutenant-Colonel. After the American capture of Fort George in 1813, the British set up an embargo and Chapin's mounted volunteers scavenged the Canadian countryside for food and supplies. His group earned the nickname of "The Forty Thieves" because contrary to Chapin's claims, it was said they stole from private as well as public property. Chapin and his men were captured at the Battle of Beaver Dams but later overpowered the guards that were transporting them to Kingston when the guards stopped to drink grog. The boat they were being transported on was redirected to Fort George, with the British guards now Chapin's prisoners.

The British attacked the American side of the Niagara River on December 30, 1813, in retaliation for the American burning of Newark (now Niagara on the Lake), and Chapin organized a force that tried to protect Black Rock. Due to the soldiers being killed, wounded or dispersed, that force reduced to five men retreated to Buffalo. He then set up a force of thirty men at Main and Niagara Streets in attempt to defend against the British attack coming down Main St. and Black Rock Road. Their cannon broke after firing a few volleys, and they surrendered to the British. General Riall did not accept Chapin's terms because he was not the commanding officer and therefore not authorized to offer the surrender. His negotiations with the British did not save the city from being burned, but it gave the people of Buffalo time to escape the city. He admitted he failed to save the town but secured the retreat of many of its inhabitants. After he surrendered, Chapin was taken as a prisoner to

Montreal for nine months. He was released in a prisoner exchange and returned to become a surgeon at an American military hospital.

At the time that Buffalo was burned, the boundaries of the city were Chippewa, Exchange, Franklin and Washington. The only buildings left standing were the home of Mrs. Margaret St. John, the blacksmith shop and jail. There was also a barn on the property of Captain Samuel Pratt at Ellicott near Seneca recently built of fresh timber, so it did not burn down. The British did not proceed down Main (Batavia Road) Street toward Cold Springs and Hodge Tavern until January 1. The destruction did not reach as far as the farms of Erastus Granger and Daniel Chapin, which were near or past Scajaquada Creek.

Cyrenius Chapin and Captain Samuel Pratt obtained verbal permission from Joseph Ellicott to use Franklin Square, the city block bounded by Church, Delaware, Eagle and Franklin Streets, as a cemetery. People previously buried their dead on their property or at a burial plot set up on the property of Captain Johnston on Seneca and Washington Streets. The first person buried at Franklin Square was John Cochrane, a traveler from Connecticut who died while staying at Barker's Tavern on the northwest corner of Main and Terrace. The soldiers and civilians killed during the burning of the City of Buffalo were buried there and Seneca warrior Farmer's Brother was buried with full military honors. Franklin Square became the main burial grounds in Buffalo, but formal title was not received from the Holland Land Company until 1821. During the cholera epidemic of 1832, Dr Chapin and others, banned additional burials at Franklin Square, unless by special permit. The cemetery was closed, and in 1852 the 1158 graves were moved to Forest Lawn, where a monument was built in 1862 to mark the reinternments. In 1852, the initial Buffalo city hall was built on that land, and in 1876 the new city and county hall was constructed on the site. County hall still stands on the former grounds of Franklin Square Cemetery.

After the War of 1812, Chapin reopened his medical practice, with his office being on the second floor of the building he rebuilt on Swan near Pearl Street. Orlando Allen had come to Buffalo to study medicine with Dr. Chapin. Due to the number of Seneca patients treated at the practice; Chapin insisted that Allen learn the native Seneca language so he could prescribe for their minor ailments. There was a drug store operated by William Keese below the medical office, and Chapin offered to purchase the store if Orlando Allen and Hiram Pratt agreed to run it. They agreed, and later both Allen and Pratt became successful businessmen and future mayors of Buffalo, with Allen marrying Pratt's sister.

In 1820, the first agriculture fair was held in Buffalo when it was still part of Niagara County. (Not to be confused with the Erie County Fair which started in 1841.) Chapin was president of the Niagara County Agricultural Society and the fair was held near Main and Terrace. Chapin owned several farms in WNY from Clarence to Hamburg and his animals were presented at this fair.

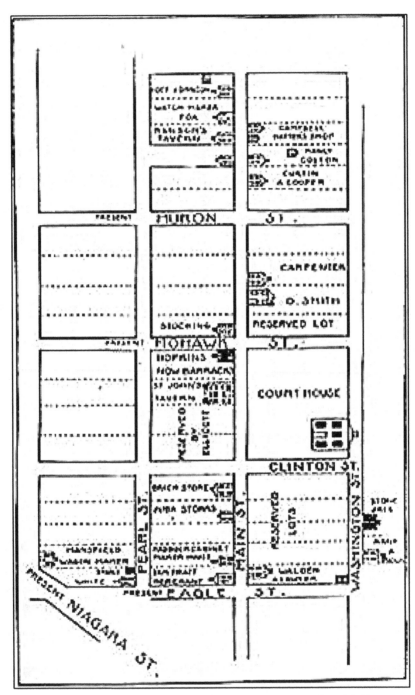

Figure 24 Map showing the size and buildings of Buffalo before it was burned during the War of 1812

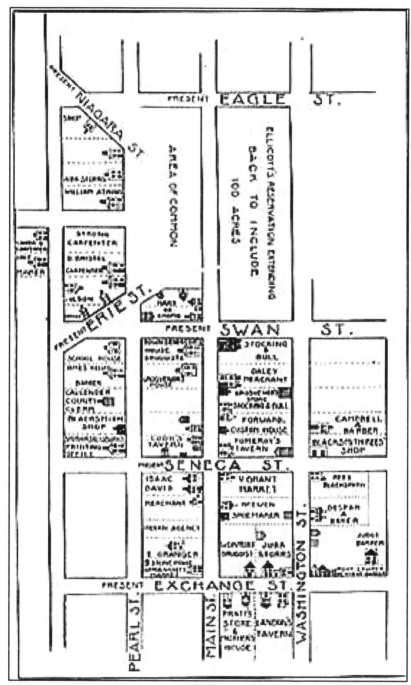

Figure 25 Southern section of map drawn by Juba Storrs of early Buffalo

When the Erie County Medical Society was formed in 1821, Chapin was named its first president. In 1836, the city of Buffalo honored him with a dinner where he was presented a silver plate for his contributions to the city as a citizen and a soldier.

When Chapin died in 1838, he was buried with full military honors at the Franklin Square Cemetery, later being reinterned at Forest Lawn Cemetery.

Other members of the Chapin group that proposed purchasing Buffalo moved to the city and with other early 1800s settlers, helped establish the community.

John Palmer built a log home on the Terrace about 100 feet west of Main Street. Palmer later added a frame building to the log structure and opened a tavern. In 1801, his younger brother Joseph Palmer, requested a lot to build a schoolhouse. He was interested in establishing a school because prior to moving to Buffalo, Joseph Palmer taught school to children at the garrison in Fort Erie. Joseph Ellicott gave the village the land on Pearl Street with the stipulation that the citizens finance the building of the school. The school was not completed until 1809 and was burned during the burning of Buffalo in 1813.

John Crow was a member of Chapin's original group, and he moved to Buffalo in 1802. He purchased inner lot #1 near Washington and Crow (now Exchange) Streets, where he built a tavern called Crow's Tavern. In 1809, it was sold to Joseph Landon, who called it Landon's Tavern until it was expanded to the Mansion House. This became first tavern in the County, which gained fame as a place of good cheer. The Mansion House was burned during the War of 1812 and rebuilt closer to the corner of Exchange and Main Streets, eventually extending to three stories with balconies on Main Street. Over the years it was continually expanded, until by 1883, it was six stories high and extended to Washington Street.

Zerah Phelps was also a member of the original Chapin group and he moved to Buffalo around the time Crow arrived. He remained in Buffalo until 1804, when he moved to the Batavia area.

In 1803, David Reese moved to Buffalo, financed by the government as the first blacksmith in the city. He purchased outer lot 176 and built a shop at the corner of Washington and Seneca and a house across the street on what was once William Johnston's lot. His blacksmith shop was one of buildings not burned by the British in 1813, and he operated from that building until 1823.

Louis LeCouteulx was a French nobleman who left the violence of the French Revolution and moved to America. He arrived in Buffalo in 1804 and was the first pharmacist in Buffalo but identified himself as a gentleman. LeCouteulx donated the land for St. Louis Church at the corner of Main and Edward Streets.

DR. DANIEL CHAPIN

Early Buffalo physician and owner of property that became Delaware Park

Dr. Daniel Chapin came to Buffalo from Connecticut in 1807 and settled on a 175-acre farm on the Buffalo Plains, just east of Erastus Granger's property. It extended from Main Street, through the present locations of Delaware Park and the Buffalo State College campus.

From this then rural location, Dr. Daniel Chapin treated patients from Buffalo and Niagara Falls, traveling on foot to their homes. He built a rustic log cabin on the grounds and insisted on retaining the indigenous trees and plants, to keep the farm in a natural state. Dr. Cyrenius Chapin and Dr. Daniel Chapin were not related but when Erie County was created from a portion of Niagara County, Cyrenius organized an Erie County medical society. The first meeting was on January 9, 1821, with Cyrenius being elected president and Daniel vice-president. Later in 1821, Dr. Daniel Chapin died from exposure after walking to treat a patient at their home.

His son, Colonel William W. Chapin, was a commander of the Erie County militia during the War of 1812. He led them into engagements during some campaigns of the war. In 1820, William built a larger cabin, closer to the corner of Main and Jewett. Over the years he made the home larger and more aesthetically pleasing, resulting in it being called Willow Lawn. The home became one of Buffalo premier mansions, with the name derived from the many willows that were planted by Dr. Chapin.

The Army of Niagara Frontier was comprised of regular army commanded by Brigadier General Alexander Smyth and militia commanded by Major General Steven Van Rensselaer. After the Battle of Queenston Heights in October 1812, the army set up winter quarters on the eastern end of Flint Hill, in what is now Forest Lawn Cemetery. The army was attired in the summer linen jackets and knee-high breeches. The government did not send food, there were no blankets and the summertime tents

Figure 26 Flint Hill Encampment memorial plaque
Photo credit: Angela Keppel

Figure 27 Stone in Delaware Park memorializing the burial of 300 soldiers that died at Flint Hill during the winter of 1812
Photo credit: Angela Keppel

were not designed for the snow and cold. Many of the men were from the South and not accustomed to the very unpredictable weather of WNY.

Conditions were so bad at the encampment that the soldiers stacked their arms and threatened to leave the camp and go back home. Many of the soldiers deserted and when General Smyth and the other commanding officers executed five soldiers, four for desertion and one for mutiny, there was nearly a rebellion by the troops. The executions took place under a large oak tree on either the current corner of Main and Dewey or Florence and Crescent. The soldiers knelt in a row to be shot and their bodies were later hung to discourage others considering desertion.

Buffalo's harsh winter conditions resulted in the death of 300 soldiers from exposure, frostbite, pneumonia and other diseases. Bodies of the dead soldiers were stacked in tents because the ground was too frozen to dig graves. In spring, they tried to bury the dead, but they could not dig deep into the ground. Since there were so many bodies, the hard dirt placed upon the pile of men only provided a shallow covering and bodies were protruding from the improper grave.

Dr. Daniel Chapin was appalled by the dishonorable sight of the botched burial. Since the Forest Lawn area had hard graveled ground, he relocated the bodies to the sandy soil of the Meadow where he dug a trench allowing for a proper burial. Chapin purchased 300 coffins, which were built by William Hodge, proprietor of Brick Tavern on the Hill, at Main and Utica.

The bodies were buried on the property line of the Daniel Chapin and Captain Rowland Cotton farms. Caskets were stacked side by side, two-or-three-deep, to fit between the Willow trees Chapin planted at each end of the hallow ground. The burial ground is now near the center of the Delaware Park Golf Course, between the third hole green and fourth hole tee box. A large rock was placed on July 4, 1896 by the Buffalo Historical Society, to mark this travesty, where 300 American soldiers froze to death.

NED CHRISTY

*Leader of Christy's Minstrels and helped make minstrel shows the most
popular form of mid-1800s entertainment*

E dwin Pearce (Ned) Christy was born in Philadelphia in 1815 and at an early age
 sang with Purdy & Welch's Circus in New Orleans. While performing in the
south, Christy studied the rhythms of speech and music in the African American
culture. After leaving the south he gained a reputation as a traveling blackface
performer, musician and comic singer.

Christy arrived in Buffalo where he met and in 1835 married Harriet Harrington,
a widow who owned Harrington's Dance Hall on Canal Street, the notorious Red-
Light District, referred to as the Barbary Coast of the U.S. In the late 1800s it was
reported that 60% of the buildings on Canal Street between Erie and Commercial
Streets were houses of prostitution, 30% were saloons and 10% were grocery stores
of other types of businesses.

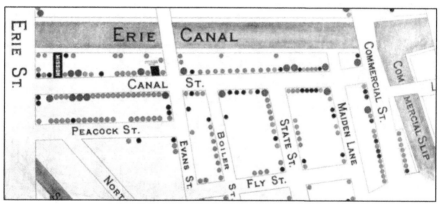

Figure 28 Map showing location of taverns and brothels in Canal Street district

Soon after he arrived in town Christy began performing at his wife's dance hall.
Ned's stepson George Harrington (later called George Christy) and his friend Dick
Sliter performed song, dance and comedy routines in front of the dance hall, to draw
people inside for the shows. These shows featured Ned as the ballad singer and
violinist, Sliter as the jig dancer and George playing bones (a percussion instrument
made from animal bones), along with tambourine players, banjo players and an
additional violinist. Performing as the Darkey Minstrel Show, they packed the people
into Harrington's Dance Hall.

Regarding Christy's place in the history of the minstrel show, Thomas D. Rice was
the first famous blackface performer and he appeared in Buffalo at the Eagle Street
Theater in 1835. Dan Emmett and the Virginia Minstrels made the minstrel show
synonymous with blackface, while the Ethiopian Serenaders removed what was

considered low comedy. However, it was Christy that established the three-set template and brought respectability to the minstrel shows.

After performing under other names, the quartet known as Christy's Minstrels gave their first performance at Harrington's Dance Hall in the summer of 1842. They

Figure 29 Poster for Christy's Minstrels, who were formed at a Canal Street Dancehall in 1842

continually packed the dance hall and began performing concerts at downtown Buffalo concert halls. Christy's Minstrels gave a "Grand Concert" at the American Hotel in September 1845 and were heading towards national acclaim. On April 27, 1846, they opened at Palmo's Opera House and a year later moved to Mechanic's Hall on Broadway in NYC. Their run of 25 cent nightly performances did not end until July 13, 1854, interrupted only by a few concert tours. When visiting NYC during the later 1840s and early 1850s there were two mandatory stops for entertainment: P.T. Barnum's Museum and a Christy's Minstrels concert.

It was Ned Christy's association with Stephen Foster that brought national attention to his minstrel show. Foster was influenced by Thomas D. Rice to write minstrel style material and titled his songs as Ethiopian Melodies. Christy's Minstrels were performing in Cincinnati, Ohio and they performed a benefit concert for Foster, which included a rendition of his song "Oh! Susanna." Foster gave Christy the rights to perform his songs prior to them being published and even sold Christy the song "Old Folks at Home (Swanee River)" for ten dollars. It was originally published as written by E.P. Christy, but Foster later requested the songwriter's credit be returned to him. The other Foster songs that Christy's Minstrels introduced and helped popularize included: "Camptown Races," "My Old Kentucky Home," "Nelly Was a Lady," and "Jeanie with the Light Brown Hair." Not to be outdone, in 1844 Christy wrote, "Buffalo Gals Won't You Come Out Tonight," as a tribute to the women of Canal Street.

Ned Christy was the leader and manager of Christy's Minstrels, but the main attraction was his stepson George Harrington Christy, who was considered the greatest blackface comic of the minstrel era. Nine months after George left his father's group to form Christy and Wood's Minstrels, with George Wood, Ned retired Christy's Minstrels, managed some minstrel shows and invested in P.T. Barnum's Circus. Other groups performed under the Christy Minstrels name, some of which included former members from the original group. Several former members moved to England, where Christy's Minstrels was the name given to any blackface minstrel show. In the minstrel show as developed by Christy, the second part or act was known as the olio or variety section. This part included singers, dancers, comedians, other novelty acts and parodies of legitimate theater, which was a precursor to vaudeville.

Ned Christy was depressed and afraid that the Civil War would damage his remaining entertainment business and on May 9, 1862 he committed suicide by jumping out of the window of his NYC home, dying several days later. During his career Ned Christy made the equivalent of five million dollars from performing his minstrel show. Unfortunately, Steven Foster, who wrote the songs he performed and was acclaimed as America's first songwriter, died with only 38 cents in his pocket. Foster's plight was one of the driving factors behind the formation of the American Society of Composers, Authors and Publishers (ASCAP), an organization formed to protect the musical copyrights and guarantee songwriters are paid for the public performance of their compositions.

GROVER CLEVELAND

The only president to serve two non-consecutive terms — being the 22nd and 24th President of the U.S.

Grover Cleveland was born in Caldwell, New Jersey on March 18, 1837. His father was a minister and Grover was the fifth of nine children. When he was young his father moved to Fayetteville, NY and later to Clinton, NY in Oneida County.

In 1855, he decided to move west and considered moving to Ohio where a distant relative General Moses Cleveland was the person for whom Cleveland, Ohio was named. He stopped in Buffalo and his uncle Lewis Allen secured him a clerical job at the law firm of Rogers, Bowen and Rogers, who offered him a clerkship to read law.

After being admitted to the bar in 1859, he worked for Rogers, Bowen and Rogers for three years and in 1862 he started his own practice. In 1862, he was drafted but paid Polish immigrant George Benninsky, a Lake Erie sailor, $150 to serve in his place as a substitute. George was injured before serving in any campaigns and survived the Civil War.

Figure 30 A Young Grover Cleveland

He was not acquainted with former president Millard Fillmore, who was still living in Buffalo at this time. However, he was a friend of Millard's son Millard Powers Fillmore, who lived in the same apartment building, in the back of the Weed block. Since he lived in bachelor apartments or rooming houses, he took his meals at area taverns, eating rich foods and drinking tankards of German beer. After he put on a few pounds he became known as Big Steve (his actual first name) to his friends and Uncle Jumbo to his nephews.

Cleveland was elected Erie County Sheriff in 1870. This was a very lucrative position because as part of his pay, the sheriff received a portion of the funds he collected. During his two-year term, Cleveland made $40,000, which in today's money is over $800,000. As the sheriff he became aware of the bribes and illegal profits from contracts in the department. While sheriff, Cleveland was also responsible for the execution of two murderers and he personally pulled the lever for the hangings. He was the only U.S. president to serve as an executioner.

After his term expired, he formed a law firm with friends Lyman K. Bass and Wilson S. Bissell. They became a successful law firm and Bissell was the Postmaster General during Cleveland's second term. His other law partners included Laning, Folsom, Sicard and Goodyear.

In 1874, Maria Crofts Halpin gave birth to a son named Oscar Folsom Cleveland. Grover Cleveland acknowledged the child and paid child support. Halpin accused Cleveland of rape and abduction of the child, but he accused her of being an alcoholic and consorting with various men. Some contended that since Cleveland was the only unmarried member of a group of men that knew Halpin, he said he was the father to protect his friends, especially since the middle name was Folsom, his best friend. After the child was born Cleveland had Halpin committed to Providence Asylum, which did not detain her because they determined that she had been drinking but was not insane. It is believed that the director of the asylum, Dr. William G. King, adopted the child and changed his name to James E. King Jr., who became a Buffalo gynecologist that died in 1947. King did not have any children, so the DNA cannot be checked to verify paternity. During the Presidential election of 1884 the Republicans adopted a chant of "Ma, Ma, where's my Pa?" When Cleveland won the election, the Democratic Party responded to the chant with, "Gone to the White House, ha, ha!" Halpin later claimed that when she confronted Cleveland with the assault and abduction charges, he paid her $500 to surrender her son and make no further demands upon the father of the child.

In 1882, Cleveland was elected mayor of Buffalo, running a campaign to clear up corruption in government. During the 1870s municipal government in Buffalo had become corrupt, with the leaders of the Democratic and Republican Party sharing the spoils. The Republicans nominated a corrupt slate and the Democrats approached Fillmore who agreed to run if all corrupt Democratic candidates were removed from the slate. Upon taking office he vetoed a contract where the highest, rather than the lowest bid, was accepted for a city street cleaning contract. The winning bid had political connections and Cleveland accused the city council of squandering the public's funds. The council reversed their vote and properly gave the contract to the lowest bidder. Other actions to safeguard the public's funds gained Cleveland the reputation of a leader willing to purge government of corruption. People outside of Erie County took notice.

Later in 1882 when the New York State Republican Party was split, the Democrats nominated Cleveland for governor, even though he had only served less than a year as mayor of Buffalo. He won by the largest margin of a contested election up to that time. Cleveland did not disappoint in his opposition to political corruption by vetoing eight bills in his first two months in office. He also opposed the influential Tammany Hall of New York City. In Albany he got the reputation for working every day until after midnight, often in an office he had installed in the governor's mansion. In 1883, he returned to give a speech in Buffalo and attended a picnic at the Pine Ridge estate of George Urban Jr., who was a republican but was a friend of Cleveland. Brewer

Gerhard Lang raised a glass and toasted "Here's to Grover Cleveland, our next president." The only person that seemed surprised by the toast was Cleveland.

In the presidential election of 1884, the Republicans nominated James G. Blaine of Maine, who had the reputation of being ambitious, immoral and was involved in several questionable corrupt deals. His nomination alienated the Mugwumps, reform minded Republicans who were opposed to corruption in government and were more concerned with morality instead of party lines. If the Democrats could come up with the proper anti-corruption candidate, they could win the White House. Cleveland fit the profile of that candidate. During the campaign the Republicans, brought up the Halpin scandal, aided by sermons by a reverend from Buffalo, George H. Ball. Cleveland responded to the scandal by instructing his supporters to "Above all, tell the truth." He took responsibility and admitted paying child support to the woman that accused him. This acknowledgment gained him the trust of the people.

After just two months as governor of New York, he was elected President. As president he continued with his reform agenda. As with his predecessor Chester Arthur, he continued to base political appointments on merit, not party affiliation. Cleveland worked to reduce government spending and he vetoed twice as many congressional bills as all 21 presidents who preceded him. During his first term he vetoed 414 bills. He fought to lower tariffs, which resulted in him losing support in the industrial Northeast and losing his re-election bid in 1889.

One of Cleveland's closest friends was attorney Oscar Folsom. Cleveland, Folsom and about 20 other friends formed the Beaver Club on Grand Island, located in what is now Beaver Island State Park and familiar to Cleveland from his uncle Lewis Allen

Figure 31 Grover Cleveland often stayed at his uncle Lewis Allen's home on Grand Island
Photo: Courtesy Grand Island Historical Society

owning land on Grand Island. Folsom often brought his daughter Frances to the club and Cleveland knew her shortly after she was born, purchasing her first baby carriage as a gift. After Folsom died in a carriage accident in 1875 Cleveland assumed legal guardianship of Frances, took care of the finances for Folsom's widow and was executor of Oscar Folsom's estate. When Frances was young, she called Cleveland - Uncle Cleve.

When Cleveland took office, he was a bachelor, so his sister Rose Cleveland took the responsibilities of acting First Lady from March 4, 1885 to June 1886. Rose Cleveland was an intellectual, educator and lecturer. She did not fit the high society mold of a first lady, but admirably served in the capacity of first lady until her brother married. After Millard married, Rose returned to education, working as a school principal and magazine editor. In 1890, she began a relationship with a wealthy widow, Evangeline Marrs Simpson. Their relationship cooled when Mrs. Simpson married Episcopal Bishop Henry Whipple. However, after Whipple died in 1901, Rose and Evangeline moved to Bagni di Lucca, Italy in 1910, where they lived together until her death in 1918.

Cleveland married Frances Folsom on June 2, 1886 in the Blue Room of the White House. She was born in 1864, was 27 years younger than the president and at 21 years of age was the youngest First Lady. Cleveland became the second president to be married while in office and the only to be married in the White House. They had five children and British philosopher Phillippa Foot was their granddaughter.

Cleveland won the popular vote in the election of 1888 but did not win the electoral college. He was re-elected in 1892 after a re-match against Benjamin Harrison. During his second presidential term, in 1893 he had cancer surgery on a yacht off Long Island, keeping the operation secret so as to not cause a panic and worsen the existing financial depression. The cover story for the operation, falsely reported he had two teeth removed.

After the presidency he moved to Princeton, New Jersey. He never forgave the people of Buffalo for bringing up the Halpin affair and only returned once to Buffalo, in 1903 for the burial of his friend Wilson Bissell. Cleveland died in 1907 and was buried in New Jersey.

GEORGE WILLIAM CLINTON

*Member of New York's politically influential Clinton family,
a lawyer, a judge and Mayor of Buffalo*

George William Clinton was born on April 21, 1807 in New Town, NY, which is now part of Brooklyn. At the time of his birth his father DeWitt Clinton was Mayor of New York City, later becoming a four term Governor of New York and known as the Father of the Erie Canal. Dewitt Clinton was a presidential candidate in 1812, with James Madison receiving 128 electoral votes to Clinton's 89 electoral votes.

The family is descended from Geoffrey de Clinton, Lord High Chamberlain and Treasurer to King Henry I of England from 1100 to 1135. Revolutionary War General James Clinton was George William Clinton's grandfather. The Fourth Vice President of the U.S. and former NYS Governor George Clinton was his great-uncle. Former members of the House of Representative, George Clinton Jr. and James G. Clinton were his uncles.

George began attending Hamilton College at age 14, graduating in 1825. That year he accompanied his father DeWitt Clinton on the ceremonial voyage of the Seneca Chief from Buffalo to New York City, to commemorate the opening of the Erie Canal. Due to his interest in science and botany, he studied medicine at Fairfield Medical School during 1826 and 1827. However, upon the death of his father in 1828, he switched his field of study to law.

He attended Tapping Reeve's law school in Litchfield, Connecticut, the first law school established in the U.S. There he studied under Judge James Gould at the school which graduated two U.S. Vice Presidents, six Cabinet Members, three justices of the U.S. Supreme Court, 28 U.S. Senators, 101 members of the House of Representatives, 14 State Governors and 13 state supreme court justices. George completed his legal training by reading law with Judge Ambrose Spencer.

Upon being admitted to the bar in 1831, he moved to Canandaigua, NY, where he formed a law partnership with John Canfield Spencer, the son of his legal mentor. Spencer later became Secretary of War and Secretary of the Treasury under President John Tyler. George married Spencer's daughter Laura Catherine Spencer on May 15, 1832.

Moving to Buffalo in 1836, he and his wife settled on East Mohawk between Washington and Ellicott Streets. In 1836, with 20 other area residents, George Clinton formed the local Democratic Party. In 1838, he was appointed Collector of Customs at Buffalo by President Martin Van Buren. He was elected president of the Young Men's Temperance Society of Buffalo in 1841, which included over 150 prominent citizens advocating total abstinence from all forms of alcohol and intoxicants.

When he was 35 years old, Clinton was elected Mayor of Buffalo in 1842. He defeated the sitting mayor Isaac Harrington by over 500 votes. During his term he advocated increased pay for public servants, especially teachers, to prevent discontent among city employees. Due to his position regarding alcohol, Clinton wanted to eliminate the unlicensed sale of ardent spirits because he felt they led to increased crime. As mayor, he was given a $100 bonus by the Common Council at the end of his term for rewriting the city charter.

After his term as mayor, Clinton was appointed U.S. Attorney for the Northern District of New York by President James K. Polk, serving in this position from 1847 to 1850. When the Superior Court of Buffalo was created in 1854, he and Judge Isaac Verplanck were chosen as judges. Upon Verplanck's death in 1870 Clinton became chief judge, a position he held until he was forced to retire at age 70, in 1877. He was offered a cabinet position by President James Buchanan but turned it down to remain in Buffalo.

In addition to political endeavors, Clinton was active in numerous community organizations. In 1846, the State Legislature granted a charter to establish a medical school in Buffalo. George W. Clinton and former President Millard Fillmore were two primary members of the group of influential Buffalo citizens that brought the medical school to fruition. Buffalo General Hospital was incorporated that year and Clinton was elected secretary. In 1856, Clinton was secretary of the Children's Aid and Reform Society and secretary of the Buffalo Juvenile Asylum. He became a Regent of the University of the State of New York in 1856, becoming Vice-Chancellor in 1871.

His primary community contribution was his association with the Buffalo Science Museum. The Young Men's Association, founded in 1836, had accumulated a collection of numerous specimens, minerals, fossils, shells, insects, pressed plants, sea weeds and various painting and articles of historic value. They required a separate science museum to exhibit their collection. At the first meeting of the museum in 1861, George W. Clinton was elected the first president of the Buffalo Society of Natural Sciences. He served as president for 20 years and gave frequent lectures on botany and geology. When Clinton moved to Albany, where he died in 1885, the Society dedicated its plant collection in his honor.

Figure 32 George W. Clinton was the first president of the Buffalo Society of Natural Sciences and assisted the Young Men's Association in building the Science Museum

Figure 33 Spencer Clinton was president of Buffalo Savings Bank when they built their iconic Gold Dome building

Clinton and his wife, Laura Catherine Spencer, had seven children, with two of his sons following him into the legal profession. Spencer Clinton was born in Buffalo on June 29, 1839 and was educated at schools in Buffalo, Albany and Brockport. He studied law under Solomon G. Haven and William Dorsheimer, being admitted to the bar in 1860 at age 21. After practicing law in New York City, he was appointed Assistant U.S. District Attorney, serving under his former instructor William Dorsheimer. In 1866, he became involved with Buffalo Savings Bank, becoming a director in 1892 and president in 1898. Leaving the legal profession to work for the bank, it was Spencer Clinton who was responsible for building the new Buffalo Saving Bank in 1901, with its signature gold leaf dome, still standing at 1 Fountain Plaza.

His son George Clinton followed in his grandfather's and father's footsteps. Born on September 7, 1846 in Buffalo, he graduated from Buffalo Central High School in 1865 and received his law degree from Columbia University. After being elected to the NYS Assembly, he was chairman of the Assembly Canal Committee and president of the Union for the Improvement of the Canal. In 1898, NYS Governor Black appointed him chairman of the commission to improve state canals, including the Erie Canal that his grandfather was instrumental in building. President Roosevelt appointed him a member of the American section of the International Waterways Commission, for the purpose of establishing water boundaries and water levels on the Great Lakes. Continuing the work of his father, he was selected to prepare the new Buffalo City Charter (that his father rewrote when he was Mayor), helped establish the Buffalo Law School at the University of Buffalo (that his father assisted in creating) and was involved with the Buffalo Society of Natural Sciences (of which his father was president). George Clinton also continued the family tradition of practicing law with his children, when his son George Clinton Jr. joined him in the law firm of Clinton & Clinton.

BELA D. COE

Operated stagecoach lines across the state of New York and
owner of Mansion House

B ela, Canfield and Chauncey Coe were born and raised in Trenton, New York, north of Utica. In 1814, Bela built a tavern in Canandaigua that he sold for a profit two years later. He joined his brother Canfield and purchased William Boswick's tavern in Auburn. After three years, Bela sold his share of the Auburn business to his brother Chauncey and reacquired the Canandaigua tavern and stage agency.

The Coe family acquired the Old Line (stagecoach business) from the Marvin family and Chauncey Coe moved to Buffalo. Coe did business with Benjamin Rathbun of the Eagle Tavern and brought Edward L. Stevenson to Buffalo as his agent. Rathbun decided he wanted both the hotel and stage business for himself, so he solicited potential investors in a competing stage company. Chauncey returned to Buffalo from Auburn to confront Rathbun, negotiating an agreement to make the

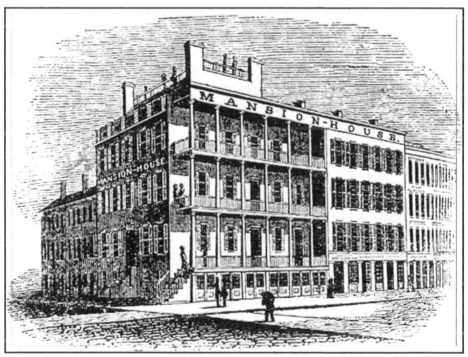

Figure 34 Stagecoach line owner Bela A. Coe purchased and expanded the Mansion House at Main and Exchange 1842 engraving by J.W. Orr

Eagle Tavern the headquarters of the stage operations in Buffalo and accepted Rathbun as a partner in the stage franchise. Rathbun agreed to finance improvements to the stage lot, but this construction only further benefited the Eagle Tavern. Chauncey discussed the situation with his older brother Bela, and they decided to exchange agencies, with Chauncey moving to Canandaigua and Bela coming to Buffalo.

When he came to Buffalo in 1825, Bela purchased a home from Ebenezer Walden at the corner of Main and Eagle Streets, diagonally across the street from Rathbun's Eagle Tavern. To counter Rathbun's influx of business at the Eagle Tavern, Coe invested in the Mansion House in 1827. He remodeled the building, that was previously owned by John Crow and Joseph Landon and even hired Rathbun to do some of the work. Coe only considered the Mansion House as an investment, hiring people to manage it and leasing it out for others to run. In 1831, Coe purchased 1676 acres across Buffalo Creek which later became Tifft Farms; and in 1832, he was one of the drafters of the Charter of the City of Buffalo.

Coe was so respected and influential in the stage coach business that when Thomas Abell started a stagecoach line between Erie, PA and Buffalo in the late 1820s, his partners were R.S. Reed in Erie and Bela D. Coe in Buffalo. In 1828, the Old-Line Stagecoach Company changed their name to the Buffalo and Albany Coach Lines. They survived competition from the new Pioneer Line, who built competing routes but only remained in business for two years. Coe was a shrewd businessman and realized that the Erie Canal and railroads would result in the end of the stage business. After his brother Chauncey died, he sold out his interests in Old Line Mail company to Rathbun in 1835, but he retained his position as official mail contractor. To protect his interests in the sale, in addition to a mortgage Coe insisted that Rathbun additionally provide a bond and insurance policy to secure the transaction. This resulted in Coe not experiencing any losses when Rathbun's empire collapsed in 1836. Coe also avoided the real estate speculation that ruined many other investors in the Panic of 1837.

In the early 1840s Coe purchased the Prospect Hill estate at Niagara and Prospect from the family of Hiram Pratt. Coe and his wife Elizabeth were active in forming the high society of the city of Buffalo, giving lavish garden parties, entertaining and creating a salon where young authors and poets would gather. These events were initially held at their mansion on Main and Eagle and expanded when they moved to the Prospect Hill mansion. The new home was surrounded by gardens, labyrinths of hedges and Elizabeth's roses, including rare hybrids she imported from France.

Upon Bela Coe's death in 1852 at age 62, his widow married former state senator and U.S. congressman William B. Mosely. Bela and Elizabeth Coe did not have any children, so upon her death in 1855, Prospect Hill was sold to Porter Thompson, who further embellished the mansion.

GEORGE COIT

One of the founders of the City of Buffalo and Buffalo Harbor

The Coit family arrived in America in the 1630s, and George was born in Norwich, Connecticut on June 10, 1790. He was trained in the druggist trade and worked at a Norwich store with Charles Townsend. In 1811, Coit and Townsend moved to Buffalo and purchased property at Swan and Pearl Streets, from Samuel Pratt Jr. for $2,000, plus an additional $20 to buy a silk dress for Mrs. Pratt. There was a frame building on the lot, where they opened a drug store on the first floor, while living in rooms on the second floor. Coit and Townsend worked together for the next forty years and Coit married Townsend's sister Hannah.

On December 29, 1813, the day before the British attacked and burned the Village of Buffalo, Coit and Townsend took a wagon full of their merchandise to Williamsville. After the city was burned, they returned to Buffalo and purchased a building on Erie Street, where they did business until selling the store to Dr. James. E Marshall in 1817. Their entrance to the shipping industry began in 1818 when they built the Old Red Warehouse at Little Buffalo Creek. However, they started in shipping in 1816 when they owned the Hannah, the first ship registered at Buffalo Creek. Eventually they owned many ships and steamboats that navigated the Great Lakes.

From 1818 to 1821, Coit and others worked on creating a navigable Buffalo harbor. Coit, Townsend, Oliver Forward and Samuel Wilkeson even obtained a bond and mortgage for $12,000 to secure a State bond for the construction of the Buffalo Harbor. They were successful in making the channel deep enough for ships to utilize the Buffalo harbor, and these four men lobbied to ensure that Buffalo, not Black Rock, became the western terminus of the Erie Canal.

There were numerous private slips on the Buffalo waterfront during the Erie Canal era. The Coit slip was parallel to Erie Street, with Coit and Townsend owning the slip and the land on either side. In the 1940s, it was filled in, along with the Erie Canal, but a portion remains behind Templeton Landing restaurant, formerly Crawdaddy's. Coit and Townsend also had a warehouse at the southern end of Commercial Street, along the western edge of the Commercial Slip. The Coit Block or Coit Building, also

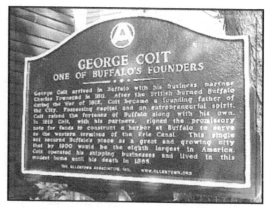

Figure 35 Coit memorial plaque in front of the new location of the Coit House

referred to as the McCutcheon Building, stood at that location from 1840 to 1947. Portions of the building foundations were found during the archaeological investigations of the Erie Canal Harbor project, which created the uncovered Commercial Slip at Canalside. The new Buffalo & Erie County Naval & Military Park & Museum building is now located at the site of their warehouse.

Freight forwarding businesses were formed in Albany and Troy on the Hudson River to benefit from the Erie Canal shipping business. Coit and Townsend formed a freight forwarding company in Buffalo, while Sheldon Thompson operated a freight forwarding company in Black Rock. These two Buffalo companies joined forces with Griffith & Company from Troy to form the "Troy and Erie Line" of Erie Canal boats. They were the first company, and for many years the largest, to operate on the entire canal from Buffalo to the Hudson River. The freight forwarding companies of Coit & Townsend and Thompson & Company merged in 1836 to form Coit, Kimberly & Company. In the 1840s, both Coit and Townsend retired from active management of their companies.

In 1815, Coit built a house on the lot that he and Townsend purchased when they initially moved to Buffalo at 53 Pearl Street on the southeast corner of Swan. Coit had the wealth to move to a mansion in less commercialized areas of Buffalo but lived at that home for 50 years, until his death in 1865. In this home he and his wife Hannah Townsend Coit raised their eight children.

After Coit's death, Charles T. Coit lived in the house until selling it in 1867 to Anson U. Becker. Since the Pearl and Swan area had become commercialized, the home was moved to 412 Virginia Street near Elmwood. Ironically, the property to which it was moved was previously owned by Coit's business partner Charles

Townsend, who sold the land, along with the home at 418 Virginia to Anson U. Becker. The home was subsequently sold to Lewis Baker, who sold it to Nancy Jones and then purchased by Betsey E. Tregilgus and Jennie E.B. Westcott. Jennie's husband Byron H. Wescott owned it from 1878 to 1923.

Figure 36 Built in 1815, the Coit House is the oldest home in Buffalo

By the 1880s the Coit House became an apartment building, with eleven people from five different families residing in the home.

The Elmwood Music Hall was next to the current location of the Coit House on Virginia Street. There were plans to build a new music hall, with Ansley Wilcox and others forming the Virginia Park Corporation to purchase the land near the Elmwood Music Hall, including the Coit House,

Figure 37 Buffalo History Museum frieze of Coit, Clinton, Townsend and Wilkeson opening the Erie Canal

to build the larger music hall. When the Elmwood Music Hall was demolished in 1938, instead of becoming an expanded new hall, Kleinhans Music Hall was built on Symphony Circle. So, the Coit House was first saved by being moved in 1867 and a second time when the music hall was not expanded. If it were not for these two events, the Coit House would not have survived.

In 1962, a group was formed by concerned citizens who wanted to save neglected buildings. These volunteers worked with the Buffalo Chamber of Commerce and City of Buffalo Division of Conservation to repair the Coit House. It was slated for demolition in 1969 when the Landmark Society of the Niagara Frontier was formed, which saved the home by completing the necessary repairs. They sold the building, with deed restrictions that prohibited modification of the historic restoration of the house. It was purchased by Henry and Linda Priebe, who lived there for 30 years, when it was purchased by the Allentown Association. The association completed further major renovations and sold it to Gerhart Yakow, who sold it to the present owners Tim Boylan and Sue-Jolie Rioux Boylan. Due to all these efforts, the Coit house was saved and is now the oldest existing house in Buffalo.

Coit and Townsend were awarded the final contract to dig the Erie Canal in Buffalo. Coit was responsible for the excavation of the Little Buffalo Creek and its connection with the Erie Canal, and it was Coit who dug the Commercial Slip. The Seneca Chief barge, upon which Governor Clinton traveled from Buffalo to New York City, was owned by George Coit. The frieze called Wedding of the Waters at the Buffalo and Erie County Historical Society Building depicts Governor DeWitt Clinton with George Coit, Charles Townsend and Samuel Wilkeson to memorialize their contributions to the building of the Erie Canal.

S. DOUGLAS CORNELL

Cornell Lead Works and amateur theater impresario

S. Douglas Cornell was a member of the eighth generation of the Cornell family in America. Thomas Cornell of Essex County, England, born in 1595, was the first U.S. Cornell arriving in the 1630s and settling in Portsmouth, Rhode Island. The father of S. Douglas was Samuel G. Cornell, who was born in Glenville, Connecticut, where he founded the Union White Lead Company, manufacturers of lead pipe, with his brothers Peter and Isaac. His son S. Douglas was born in Connecticut in 1839.

In 1852, Samuel moved the company to Buffalo as the Cornell White Lead Company. The lead company was at the northeast corner of Delaware Avenue and Virginia Street from 1854 to 1889, being the last of the factories along Delaware Avenue to be razed. The location of the two-acre factory is now the site of the Midway, a block of row houses. Row houses were popular in eastern cities, but this was most representative grouping of attached grand townhouses in Buffalo. It was called the Midway because it was halfway between Niagara Square and Forest Lawn Cemetery on Delaware Avenue.

After graduating from Hobart College, S. Douglas went to work with his father at Cornell Lead Works. During 1862-1864 he took a hiatus from the company and pursued the prospects of gold mining in Colorado. He was very successful in that endeavor but returned to manage the family company and continued to operate it until 1888, when the company closed.

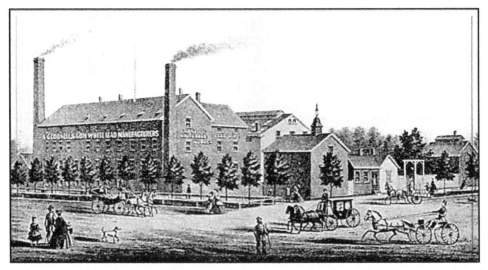

Figure 38 Cornell Lead Works factories at Delaware Avenue and Virginia Street

Across the street from the Cornell Lead Works, S. Douglas Cornell razed two cottages and in 1894 built a mansion, designed by Edward Kent, at 484 Delaware. S. Douglas Cornell excelled in dramatics at Hobart College and he built a theater, complete with a stage, lighting and seating, on the fourth floor of his house. He had been stage manager of the Buffalo Amateurs since the drama group was formed in 1872. They presented four plays a year on the fourth floor of 484 Delaware during the 1890s and early 20th century. The group included members of Buffalo gentry, including Maria Love, Peter Norton, Charles Clifton, Townsend Davis, Lars and Eva Sellstedt, Walter, Thomas Charles and Jennie Cary, Carlton Sprague, S. Douglas Cornell and his children Peter, Douglas and Lydia.

His son Peter Cortelyou Cornell was born on January 18, 1865 in Buffalo. He married Alice Gardner Plimpton and was pursuing graduate medical studies in Berlin, Germany when his daughter Katherine was born on February 16, 1893. Peter returned to Buffalo and lived at 174 Mariner Street, practicing medicine and being active in plays at his father's home theater. In 1901, Peter's love of theater prevailed, and he left medicine to become the manager and part owner of the Star Theater, on the corner of Pearl, Mohawk and Genesee Streets. Peter was later associated with fellow theater manager John Oishei, from the Teck Theater. In 1916, Cornell became a partner of Oishei and investor in his company which made hand operated windshield wipers. That company was later incorporated as Trico.

Peter's daughter Katherine attended the early plays at her grandfather's house but was too young to participate in them. The Cornell family also had a summer home in Cobourg, Ontario, Canada, where the family presented outdoor plays, in which Katherine participated. After Katherine attended Maude Adams' *Peter Pan* at her father's Star Theater, she decided to devote her life to the theater. Katherine Cornell became one of the greatest stage actresses of her day.

The home that S. Douglas Cornell built to foster his love of theater and subsequently influenced the lives of his son and granddaughter is still standing today. In 1994, it was restored by attorney Thomas J. Eoannou into offices. Eoannou is also known for his restoration of Buffalo's North Park Theater on Hertel Avenue.

JOSEPH DART

Created the steam powered grain elevator that transformed the grain industry in Buffalo

Joseph Dart is credited with inventing the grain elevator, but it was actually invented by Joseph Dart and Robert Dunbar, with Dunbar being the person that obtained a patent # US226047A for a grain elevator improvement invention.

Joseph Dart was born in Middle Haddam, Connecticut in 1799. He moved to Buffalo in 1821 and became a partner of Joseph Stocking in a hat, cap and fur business located on the southeast corner of Main and Swan Streets. He learned the Seneca language so he could trade with Indians at his store.

When the Erie Canal opened in 1825, Western farmers began shipping their grain to Buffalo to be forwarded to the east coast. The grain was unloaded in barrels or in sacks carried on the shoulders of dock workers. It was a slow process, and it could take up to a week to unload a boat filled with grain.

Dart recalled that American inventor Oliver Evans devised a system in flour mills where buckets were attached to a conveyor belt to move wheat to the top of the mill for processing. This bucket elevator was not an original concept as it went back to antiquity when the Romans attached buckets to chains to raise water.

In 1842, Dart approached engineer Robert Dunbar, who he had met when Dunbar designed a water-powered flour mill in Black Rock that utilized a new mechanized system for handling grain and flour. They built the large wooden 50 x 100-foot grain mill near the mouth of the Buffalo River at the junction of the Evans Ship Canal (near the present Vietnam Veterans Memorial on the Buffalo Harbor). By using a steam powered vertical conveyor belt made of leather or canvas and equipped with buckets, the marine leg could be inserted into the ship's hull. The workers that previously carried barrels on their back, now shoveled grain into the buckets. These workers came to be called scoopers and were dominated by Irish laborers. With this method, they unloaded their first ship in a matter of hours. The original system was able to raise 600 bushels an hour, ten times more than workers could previously carry. Improvements increased the capacity to 2,000 bushels an hour, and grain elevator storage was increased from 55,000 bushels to 110,000 bushels. Previously 2,000 bushels was the maximum manual labor removed per day from lake vessels and now that was accomplished in an hour.

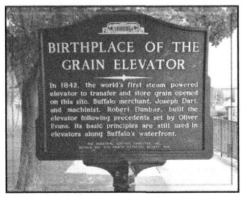

Figure 39 Memorial plaque of Dart's grain elevator in Canalside

The grain that was scooped up was carried up the grain elevator structure by the steam powered loose leg to a scale where it was weighed. The grain was then transferred to storage bins. To remove the grain from the building, by gravity, grain from the bottom of the storage bins was loaded into Erie Canal barges.

Grain elevators were the perfect structure for storing grain. They could protect the grain by keeping it dry, free from vermin and safe from pilferage. The elevators made it possible to weigh and sample the grain to determine the quality, quantity and grade, as a basis for payment. When damp grain was received from shipment on lake vessels, Dunbar's elevators had a drying facility (called a Marsh dryer) where the marine leg lifted the grain and deposited it on an 800 square foot metal surface perforated with small holes. The grain was raked across the surface and dried by blasts of hot air below the plate. The grain was cleaned by dropping the grain into a large cylinder. The chaff and other impurities, which were lighter than the grain, rose in the air and were dispersed by a steam-powered exhaust fan. Buffalo's George Clark later invented a combination drying and cleaning system.

By 1860, the success and utility of the Dart Elevator resulted in ten other grain elevators being built on the Buffalo waterfront. This increased the storage capacity in Buffalo to over one and a half million bushels. The addition of another 16 elevators by the end of the Civil War resulted in Buffalo becoming the World's Largest Grain Port, surpassing New Orleans, New York City, London, Odessa and Rotterdam.

Dart received the name recognition for the development of the grain elevator, but Dunbar designed most of the grain elevators in Buffalo and received orders to build elevators from around the world. He was called "the father of the great grain elevator system" and died a wealthy man in 1890.

Figure 40 Drawing of Dart's Elevator that changed the port of Buffalo
Photo: Buffalo History Museum

JOSEPH ELLICOTT

Surveyor and agent for the Holland Land Company

Joseph Ellicott was the chief surveyor of the Holland Purchase and for years the agent of the Holland Land Company. Some consider him the founder of the city; however, he was active in planning it but was not actively involved in its development.

His father Joseph Ellicott and uncles John and Andrew purchased land on the Patapsco River in Maryland, where they established a milling business. In 1772, they founded Ellicott's Mills, which became one of the largest milling and manufacturing towns in the East. The Ellicott brothers revolutionized farming in this section of Maryland by planting wheat, rather than tobacco. They also helped introduce fertilizer in order to revitalize the soil.

Ellicott was born in Bucks County, Pennsylvania on November 1, 1760. He worked with his father Joseph in farming and at his mill, but often assisted his older brother Andrew as a surveyor. Ellicott surveyed the disputed boundary between South Carolina and Georgia, worked on extending the Mason-Dixon Line and surveying the western and northern boundary of Pennsylvania, to determine the ownership of Erie, Pennsylvania. He also assisted in laying out the Major L'Enfant street plan of Washington, DC.

His first visit to WNY was in 1789, when he and his brother Andrew landed at the western end of Lake Ontario and traveled along the Canadian side of the Niagara River to Lake Erie. On this trip they stopped to view Niagara Falls. Ellicott made the first actual measurement of the Niagara River from Lake Erie to Lake Ontario. In 1797, he explored the boundaries of the Holland Land Purchase for Theophile Cazenove. The initial boundary of the Holland Land company was William Street – west to Lake Erie. He redrew the line so that the mouth of Buffalo Creek became part of the purchase not part of the Buffalo Creek Reservation. This resulted in the

Figure 41 Portrait of Joseph Ellicott

northern boundary of the Buffalo Creek Reservation following William Street through Cheektowaga and making a southern turn in East Buffalo, following Buffalo Creek to Child Street, just before the river turned north toward the mouth at Lake Erie. These negotiations were conducted with William Johnston, who was given this land by the Seneca and received other property from the Holland Land Company in consideration for the concessions. The one-mile strip along the Niagara River, including the harbor at Black Rock, was part of the New York Reservation and not considered part of the Holland Land Company.

In the Spring of 1798, Joseph Ellicott, with his brothers David and Benjamin, James W. Stevens, Ebenezer Cary and James Brisbane headed a party of 130 men for a survey that would last until October 1789 and cost the company $70,921.69. They established their headquarters at the corner of what is now Main and Exchange Streets in Buffalo. The crew had the best quality equipment and supplies, including scientific instruments required for surveying from Rittenhouse and Potts of Philadelphia, with the ax men, chainmen, horses, supplies and provisions being distributed across the territory from Genesee to Chautauqua. Those assigned to Buffalo included Seth Pease, George Eggleston and James Smedley. Other principal surveyors in the first season were John Thompson, Richard Stoddard, George Burgess, James Dewey, William Shepard, Aaron Oakford Jr. and Augustus Porter.

The General-Agent for the Holland Land Company was Paul Busti, headquartered in Philadelphia. In November 1800, Busti appointed Joseph Ellicott to the post of Resident-Agent in charge of land for the Holland Land Company, with a generous salary, a grant of six thousand acres of land and a five percent commission on his sales. Busti also appointed subagents in various areas. In the southern tier he

Figure 42 Drawing of Joseph Ellicott surveying the city of Buffalo, accompanied by William Johnston
Photo: Buffalo History Museum

appointed William Seward and N. Deveraux, in Buffalo agent L.A. Blossom, and in Niagara, Orleans and Genesee County area agent LeRoy Redfield.

In 1803, the Village of Buffalo was partially surveyed by William Peacock, who later married a niece of Joseph Ellicott and worked on surveys for the Erie Canal. Peacock spent the later days of his life in Mayville. At that time the name of the settlement was New Amsterdam, changed to Buffalo Creek and the Creek was later dropped. Ellicott participated in the survey and laid out the grid based upon L'Enfant's plan for Washington, DC.

Joseph Ellicott selected a manor size lot for himself in Buffalo. It was on Main Street from Eagle Street to Swan Street and extended to Jefferson, covering about 100 acres. The property included a semi-circular piece on Main Street, which faced the churches. Ellicott planned to donate that portion of the land back to the city upon his death to be used as a museum and park. He never built the house but purchased materials, which were used for the building of the first jail. The highway commissioners made a determination to straighten Main Street, which resulted in Ellicott deciding to make his home in Batavia, not Buffalo. The Ellicott Square Building was built and still stands on the Main Street frontage of the Ellicott lot. Prior to making his final move to Batavia, he worked out of Asa Ransom's Tavern in Clarence because of its location between Buffalo and Batavia.

The first building in Batavia, across from the site Ellicott selected as the office for the Holland Land Company, was a log house built by Abel Rowe called Rowe's Hotel. Ellicott suggested to Busti that the town be called Bustiville or Bustia, to which Busti countered that it should be called Ellicottsville. Ellicott suggested Tonawanta, but Busti officially named the town Batavia in August 1801. In the spring of 1802, the land office was moved from Ransom's tavern to a log building in Batavia. The current stone land office was added as an east wing to this building in 1803. All land west of the Genesee River was organized as Genesee County and Batavia became the county seat. Over time, the counties of Niagara, Erie, Chautauqua, Cattaraugus, Allegany, Orleans and Wyoming were carved out of Genesee County.

With Batavia being made the county seat, Ellicott built a courthouse and post office. James Brisbane opened the first store in Batavia and was named postmaster. David Evans moved to Batavia to serve as a clerk to his uncle Joseph Ellicott at the Holland Land Office. Joseph Ellicott's Batavia home was visited by dignitaries on their way to Buffalo and Niagara Falls. Ellicott was at the zenith of his success but some of the people who purchased land were not satisfied with his performance as land agent. In 1821, Paul Busti visited Batavia and it was agreed that Jacob S. Otto of Philadelphia would replace him as land agent and Ellicott would be given the option of forming a company to purchase all unsold property.

Negotiations between Ellicott and Busti for the purchase of 1,658,738 acres for $829,000 or about 50 cents per acre fell apart. Due to the near completion of the Erie Canal and increase in the sale of properties, Ellicott would have made over five million dollars from the transaction, but he was not satisfied with some terms and

Figure 43 The Holland Land Company office in 1890 Photo: Courtesy Holland Land Office Museum

conditions, so it never happened. His health deteriorated, Ellicott was hospitalized, and he died by committing suicide on August 19, 1826 at Bloomingdale Asylum in New York. Since he never married, in his will he bequeathed valuable property to his sisters, nephews and nieces, grand nephews and nieces. A total of sixty family members received some of the most valuable property in Western New York. The value of his estate was over $600,000 or thirteen million current dollars.

- *Much has changed since the days of Joseph Ellicott, especially the street names. He named the streets of his village of New Amsterdam, Buffaloe Creek, later to be called Buffalo after his superiors at the Holland Land Company and after Indian tribes.*
- *Main Street was called Willink Ave up to Church Street and Van Staphorst Avenue afterwards*
- *Niagara Street was Schimmelpennick Avenue*
- *Erie Street was Vallenhoven Avenue*
- *Court Street was Cazenove Avenue*
- *Church Street was Stadnitski Avenue*
- *Genesee Street was Busti Avenue*
- *Terrace was called Busti Terrace above Erie Street and Cazenove Terrace below Erie Street*
- *Ellicott Street was called Oneida Street*
- *Washington was Onondaga*
- *Pearl was Cayuga*
- *Franklin was Tuscarora*
- *Niagara Street was Missisauga*
- *Exchange Street was Crow – not after the Indian Tribe but after the innkeeper*
- *Delaware, Huron, Mohawk, Eagle, Swan and Seneca retain their original names*
- *The street names were changed in 1825 and 1826*

Benjamin Ellicott was the brother of Joseph Ellicott's and worked with Joseph and their older brother Andrew as surveyors. He worked for his brother during his employment as agent for the Holland Land Company, and purchased much land with Joseph, south of Buffalo and in Niagara County. Benjamin personally purchased land for himself in downtown Buffalo, bounded by Terrace, Franklin, Pearl and Seneca Streets. He also purchased outer lots #2, #3 and #5, which included twenty-four acres of land on the waterfront and the future area of the Peacock Slip and Evans Ship Canal. With John Thompson he purchased most of what became Williamsville, including the falls, where they built a mill and house. He was one of the first judges in Batavia and represented WNY in Congress. Benjamin never married and died on December 10, 1827, at the home of his nephew Lewis E. Evans in Williamsville. In his will he left one fourth to each of his sisters Ann Evans, Letitia Evans and Rachel Evans, making them, along with their children and grandchildren very wealthy. He also left one fourth to the nine children of his brother Andrew. After Benjamin died, he was buried in Williamsville but in 1849 his remains were moved to Batavia, where he was buried next to his brother beneath a thirty-two-foot monument.

Letitia Evans moved to Buffalo in 1835 to look after the property left to her by her brothers, especially the waterfront property from her brother Benjamin. Her son William Evans built two large homes on the west side of Washington Street and south of Eagle Street, where she enjoyed her children and grandchildren. It was their sister Rachel Evens, who was a twin of Benjamin, that built the monument in the Batavia cemetery. The Ellicott sisters were all members of the Society of Friends, living pious Quaker lifestyles.

Andrew A. Ellicott was the son of Joseph Ellicott's older brother Andrew. He accompanied his father during the 1796 survey to ascertain the northern boundary of Spanish Florida. Andrew later worked as one of the first clerks for his uncle at the Holland Land office and lived in a home in Williamsville, later owned by Lewis E. Evans. During the War of 1812, the volunteer militia of Batavia were asked to assist the U.S. Army detachment that held Fort Erie and was besieged by the British. The militia included all the clerks of the Batavia Holland Land Office, many of the citizens of Batavia, along with Andrew and his brother John. Under the Command of General Peter B, Porter, they attacked the British lines and helped break the siege. Andrew was married to Sarah Williams, who was the sister of Jonas Williams. The lands of Benjamin Ellicott and John Thompson in Williamsville were purchased by Jonas Williams, who he is considered the father of Williamsville.

WILLIAM CARYL ELY

*Pioneer in electric railways and first president of
International Railway Corporation*

William Caryl Ely came from a line of New York State politicians as his grandfather, father and himself were members of either the NYS Assembly or NYS Senate. He was born in Middlefield, NY on February 25, 1856, went to school in Cooperstown, attended Cornell University and was admitted to the bar in 1882.

Ely moved to Niagara Falls in 1885, working as a general counsel but later worked primarily in corporate law for manufacturing, railway and other business enterprises. He was one of the original incorporators and counsel of the Niagara Falls Power Company. Concerning electric railroads, he was the president of the Buffalo & Niagara Falls Electric Railway, president of the Buffalo & Lockport Railway and Lockport & Olcott Railway. Regarding bridges, Ely was counsel of the Niagara Falls & Clifton Suspension Bridge

Figure 44 Portrait of William Caryl Ely

Figure 45 Horse drawn streetcar of the Buffalo Street Railroad Company

Company and incorporator of the Lewiston & Queenstown Suspension Bridge Company.

Due to his involvement with the railways, it was Ely who conceptualized combining the electric railways in and between Buffalo, Niagara Falls, Tonawanda, Lockport and the adjoining towns uniting them with Niagara Falls, Ontario railways via the Niagara Falls and Lewiston-Queenstown bridges. This resulted in the formation of the IRC – International Railway Corporation in 1902. When this merger came into fruition, Ely became president of the IRC and stopped practicing law. The IRC owned and operated 352 miles of urban and interurban electric railways and two international bridges, evolving into the Niagara Frontier Transportation Authority (NFTA). He moved to 626 Delaware Avenue in Buffalo and from 1904 to 1906 was president of the American Street and Inter-Suburban Railway Association.

During his career he was actively involved with almost every large enterprise participating in expanding the cities of Buffalo and Niagara Falls, including the Niagara Falls Power Company and the Pan-American Exposition. He and his associates also created electric railway and utility companies in the Ohio Valley, Pittsburgh, Pennsylvania and Wheeling, West Virginia. In addition, they managed a large irrigation project in the State of Washington, constructing canals in the Yakima and Columbia River valleys.

In 1884, William Caryl Ely married Grace Keller who was a member of one of the oldest and most prominent families of Schoharie County in the Capital region of New York. Keller could trace six different routes of lineage back to families who arrived on the Mayflower and was a tenth-generation descendant of John and Priscilla Alden. Henry Wadsworth Longfellow, who was also a descendent of the Aldens, memorialized John and Priscilla in his poem *The Courtship of Miles Standish*.

Figure 46 International Railway Corporation High Speed Line train at Brighton Road in Tonawanda

WILLIAM EVANS & EVANS FAMILY

The Evans family inherited the estates of Joseph and Benjamin Ellicott

Each of the three sisters of Joseph and Benjamin Ellicott married brothers from the Evans Family. Since Joseph and Benjamin did not have any children, they left their estates to their sisters, along with their sister's children and grandchildren. The Evans Ship Canal and other locations associated with the Evans name in WNY are survivors of that left to the Evans sisters by Joseph and Benjamin Ellicott.

William Evans, the eldest son of John and Letitia Ellicott Evans, was born near Baltimore on December 3, 1778. His father died when he was fourteen years old and William was apprenticed to his mother's cousin Jonathan Ellicott to learn the milling trade. He was promoted to running one of Jonathan's mills and opened his own mill with William R. Gwinn, a portion of the capital to purchase it coming from his uncles Joseph and Benjamin Ellicott. William was successful in the milling business, being appointed one of three flour inspectors for Baltimore County.

In 1807, William married Margaret Randall, the youngest daughter of Christopher and Eleanor Carey Randall. Margaret's parents died before she was ten years old and she was raised by her uncle James Carey, one of Baltimore's most successful merchants. William received a salary of $2,500 as flour inspector, which allowed William and Margaret to raise their children in large homes and to attend the best schools. However, in 1832 William decided to move to Buffalo to look after the property that his mother inherited from her brothers, especially the waterfront property of Benjamin Ellicott.

Upon arriving in Buffalo, William's attention was directed to the completion of the Evans Ship Canal, in his mother's portion of outer lot #2. The canal was completed in 1833 and his mother provided him with eighty feet of land on Water Street, where he built a warehouse. He laid out lots on the Evans Ship Canal, creating Norton and Evans Streets. These improvements made William one of the pioneers of business on the waterfront. He died on March 9, 1840 only six days after he was elected

Figure 47 Letitia Evans home built by William Evans at Washington and Eagle Streets

alderman for the second ward of the city of Buffalo. His wife survived him by 32 years, living until age 90 in 1872.

The first Evans to move to WNY was David Ellicott Evans. David was the son of Lewis and Rachel Ellicott Evans and was born in Ellicott's Upper Mills on March 19, 1788. He started working for his uncle Joseph Ellicott in Batavia, serving as his clerk in 1803. He was well respected for his accounting work with the Holland Land Company. This resulted in him being a director of the Ontario Bank at Canandaigua, Bank of Genesee at Batavia, United Stated Bank Branch in Buffalo and Western Insurance Company of Canandaigua. He was elected to the State Senate and the U.S. Congress, but in 1827, resigned his seat in congress because he was appointed resident agent for the Holland Land Company. Evans replaced James S. Otto, who succeeded Joseph Ellicott, whose mansion David purchased. David successfully represented the company from 1827 to 1837, with the receipts being greater than all the receipts during the time of Ellicott and Otto combined. Due to the generous commissions and generous salary he received, in addition to the valuable real estate left to him by his uncle, he was one of the wealthiest people in WNY. David lost large sums of money during the Recession of 1837, with most of that money being lost to investments with Benjamin Rathbun. However, he served WNY and the Holland Land Company for approximately 50 years.

The sons of William and Margaret Evans were born in Ellicott's Upper Mills or Baltimore, Maryland area. They began their careers in the Baltimore area and moved to Buffalo and WNY to manage the properties left to them and their mother by her brothers Joseph and Benjamin Ellicott.

John Randell Evans was the eldest son of William and Margaret Evans, who was born in 1807. He visited WNY with his father in 1824 and 1827 and moved to Orleans County in 1832, where he purchased a farm near Medina in partnership with his brother James. That was followed by the produce business of Gelston & Evans and a partnership with his brother Lewis, located on the Evans Ship Canal, where they were agents of the New York Transportation Line of canal boats on the Erie Canal. John was elected alderman of the second ward of the city of Buffalo in 1852 and city treasurer in 1854 and 1855. In 1856, he formed the partnership of himself, Samuel F. Gelston, James C, Evans and William A. Evans, a steam planing mill called John R. Evans & Company

James Carey Evans, the second son of William and Margaret Evans, was born in Baltimore in 1809 and learned the mercantile business. In 1826, he became an assistant to David Ellicott Evans in the land department of Joseph Ellicott's estate in Batavia. He moved to Medina and worked keeping the books for the mercantile mill of David Ellicott Evans and his partner John B. Ellicott. In 1834, he moved to Buffalo and with Samuel F. Gelston formed Gelston & Evans, forwarding and commission merchants, operating on the Evans Ship Canal. They were agents for commercial canal boats and later became owners of lake steamboats. James invested all his transportation interests, propeller and canal boats, in American Transportation Company in 1855, becoming Secretary/Treasurer of the company, capitalized at

$900,000. That company went bankrupt during the financial Panic of 1857. His son Edwin T. Evans, with the assistance of several banks, purchased some of the canal and propeller boats of the company. They phased out the canal boats and concentrated on propeller boats. In 1862, they formed J.C. & E.T. Evans, building the Merchant which cost $85,000 and was the first iron propeller boat built for navigation on the lakes. The ship proved the be a great success and this business out of the Evans Line on the Evans Ship Canal thrived.

Charles Worthington Evans, the third son of William and Margaret Evans was born on March 13, 1812 in Baltimore. He worked in the family milling business but entered the insurance and banking business. Charles was the last member of the family to remain in Baltimore, he sold his father's Rural Mills property in 1833, visiting Buffalo in 1834, deciding to join the other members of his family and moved to Buffalo in 1835. Upon settling in Buffalo, he built a warehouse on the Evans Ship Canal and opened a produce and commission business with his brother William. Charles then entered into a partnership with Robert Dunbar (inventor of the grain elevator with Joseph Dart) as a storage and elevating business. In 1847, they converted the warehouses to a grain elevator for elevating the grain by steam. The business was so successful they purchased some adjoining lots on the Evans Ship Canal, giving them 165 feet of frontage on the Evans Ship Canal. Charles bought out Dunbar, added a brick addition to the elevator and expanded to the coal business. During this time period, he also settled the extensive estates of several of his relatives. On

Figure 48 The Evans House in Williamsville in 1860, built by John Thompson but owned by the Evans Family into the 20th Century Photo: Buffalo Niagara Heritage Village

September 10, 1857 he married Mary Peacock, niece of Judge William Peacock. By 1862 Buffalo was becoming the leading port for grain shipment. In September of 1862 the Evans grain elevator burned down, but by the terms of the Western Elevating Company, he continued to receive a share of the proceeds from other mills until the next shipping season. He then opened a new grain elevator the following season, in partnership with capitalist George W. Tifft. Charles spent 53 years of his life engaged in business at the family named Evans Ship Canal, which his father built in 1833. He died in 1889 in his home at 468 Delaware, at the corner of Virginia. Charles was the author of the history of the Fox, Ellicott and Evans Families, which he published in 1882.

William Alexander Evans was born near Baltimore in 1816 and moved with his parents to Buffalo when he was 16 years old in 1832. He worked with his brother Charles in a produce a produce company and became interested in his brother James' firm of Gelston & Evans. This interest resulted in him purchasing the steam planing mill of C.A. Van Slyke & Company. That company moved to Buffalo and evolved into John R. Evans & Company, consisting of John, James and William Evans, with Samuel F. Gelston. He was then involved in the lumber business and died in 1880 at his brother James farm near Lewiston.

Lewis was the youngest son of William and Margaret Evans and was born in 1818. When he was 14 years old the family moved to Buffalo, where William assisted his father in his warehouse on the Evans Ship Canal. After clerking for Gelston & Evans he entered into a partnership with his brother called John R. Evans and Brother, a transportation company that was an agent for New York Transportation Line. They partnered with S.G. Chase, who was the New York Transportation Line agent in Albany, forming Chase & Evans. Lewis later created his own company, transporting goods between Albany and Buffalo. In 1847, Lewis married Amelia La Grange, a descendant from one of the oldest families in Albany, residing in that city from when it was still called Fort Orange. They moved to Buffalo in 1852, where Lewis continued in the produce and transportation business, and purchased a house on Franklin Street, where they raised twelve children.

Lewis Ellicott Evans was the son of John and Letitia Evans, born on December 10, 1782 in the family mansion in Ellicott's Upper Mills, Maryland. He was trained in the milling business and married Miriam Hunt in 1807. After operating successful mills in the Baltimore area, Lewis and Miriam moved to Williamsville, residing on a 136-acre farm that was deeded to him by his uncle Joseph Ellicott. It was in this home that his uncle Benjamin Ellicott died in 1827. Their son Henry Brice Evans lived with Letitia on her Williamsville property after his father's death. He was the village Justice of the Peace and for a period of time owned a portion of the mill, next to the falls in Williamsville.

There are many things named after Joseph Ellicott in WNY. However, since he and his brother Benjamin never married, it is the Evans name that passed the Ellicott legacy into future generations.

WILLIAM FARGO

Founder of American Express and Wells Fargo

William Fargo was born on May 20, 1818 in Pompey, New York in Onondaga County. The eldest of 12 children, he left school at 13, after a very rudimentary education at a country school, to deliver the mail and help support his family. His father William C. Fargo was stationed at Fort Niagara during the War of 1812 and was wounded in the Battle of Queenston Heights, while his grandfather William Beebe Fargo fought in the American Revolution.

Fargo worked for grocers in Syracuse for four years before obtaining a clerkship with the forwarding house of Dunford & Company in Syracuse. In 1841, he became a freight agent and messenger for the Auburn & Syracuse Railroad in Auburn. He was the railroad resident agent in Buffalo in 1843 and left the railroad in 1844 to join Livingston, Wells & Company, as a messenger in Buffalo.

In 1845, he formed Western Express with Henry Wells and Daniel Dunning, to provide service from Buffalo to Cincinnati, St. Louis, Chicago and points between. The company operated as Wells & Company and since there were not any railroads west of Buffalo, transport was by steamboats in the summer and wagons, stages or sleighs in the winter. In 1846, Daniel Dunning withdrew from the company and Wells sold his interests to William A. Livingston, who became his partner in Livingston, Fargo & Company. In 1850, the companies of Wells, Fargo, Livingston and John Warren Butterfield consolidated to form American Express Company, with Wells as president and Fargo as secretary. The company was organized during an 1850 meeting at The Mansion House on Exchange Street in Buffalo. When Henry Wells resigned in 1866 and the company merged with Merchants Union Express Company, Fargo became president, a post he held until his death in 1881. At the time of the merger, American Express was one of the largest companies in the country, with capital of 18 million dollars,

Figure 49 The William Fargo Mansion covered two city blocks on the West Side

4,000 offices, over 10,000 employees and operating 30,000 miles of railways. Fargo was not a figurehead president as he was active in the everyday management and major decisions of the company.

In 1852, when the board of American Express objected to expanding services to California, Wells and Fargo formed Wells Fargo & Company. They offered banking services, including buying gold, selling paper bank drafts and express service from NYC to San Francisco, which included rapid delivery of gold and other valuables. They facilitated business between New York City and California by way of the Isthmus of Panama and overland stagecoaches into the west before railroads were built. The company opened for business in the gold rush city of San Francisco and had agents in other new cities and mining towns in the west, opening banks in many of these cities. In 1861, they purchased and reorganized the Overland Mail Company, which had the contract to carry mail via the Pony Express. They used the northern route from Salt Lake City to Sacramento and Oregon. That company was discontinued when the Transcontinental Railroad was completed in 1869.

When William Fargo died in 1881 his brother James C. Fargo succeeded him as president of American Express, a post he held until 1914. When J.C. was in Europe from 1888 to 1890, he found it difficult to obtain cash in smaller cities, even with a letter of credit. He approached Marcellus Flemming Berry, who invented the express money order in 1882, to create the American Express Traveler's Cheque which was launched in 1891. That became the main travel currency for the next 100 years.

In addition to these companies, Fargo was the Vice President of New York Central Railroad Company, as well as a director and shareholder in other railroads and several Buffalo manufacturing companies. He was president of The Buffalo Courier Company, which printed the Daily Courier, Evening Courier & Republic, Weekly Courier and books. It was considered one of the largest show-and-general printing houses in the country and stood in the location of HSBC or One Seneca Tower. Fargo was a proponent of businesses in Buffalo and was mayor of Buffalo during the Civil War, from 1862 to 1866. Fargo, North Dakota is named after him.

Fargo married Anna Hurd Williams in 1840 and they had eight children, with only three living until adulthood. Their first home was a brick Italianate at 47 Niagara Street at Franklin. In 1868, he started building The Fargo Mansion, which he completed in 1872. It covered two city blocks and cost $600,000 to build (about 12 million in current dollars) and $100,000 to furnish (about 2 million today). The house was the largest house in New York State outside of NYC at 22,170 square feet, five stories high, had an elevator, was rumored to have gold doorknobs and included wood from all states in the U.S. The lot was 5.5 acres. After he died in 1881 and his wife in 1890, his family could not upkeep it. It stood vacant for 10 years before being demolished and the area of Pennsylvania, West, Jersey and Fargo was subdivided and replaced by homes.

FARMER'S BROTHER – HONAYAWAS

A noted orator and Seneca warrior

Farmer's Brother was reportedly born in 1730 and fought for the British with General Braddock during the French & Indian War in 1755. During Pontiac's Rebellion, the Seneca chief, Cornplanter, was receptive to War Chief Pontiac's plan to drive the British colonists back east of the Allegheny Mountains. In 1763, Cornplanter appointed the young warrior Farmer's Brother to lead a force of 300 Seneca warriors. They attacked the British forts of Presque Isle (Erie), LeBeouf (Waterford) and Venango in Pennsylvania, killing the small garrisons and burning down the forts. Returning to their homes in WNY, Farmer's Brother's forces attacked the British at Devil's Hole Massacre on September 14, 1763.

At Devil's Hole, Farmer's Brother trapped John Stedman's wagon train between his forces and the Niagara Gorge. The teamsters, horses, mules and wagons were forced into the gorge, being smashed to death on the rock 80 feet below. The British at Fort Grey in Lewiston heard of the attack and rushed to rescue the wagon train. They were also ambushed. The British lost 81 soldiers and 21 teamsters, while the Seneca's had only 1 wounded. In retaliation for this attack, Superintendent of Indian Affairs, Sir William Johnson, made the Seneca cede a strip of land one mile wide on each side of the Niagara River and all islands upriver from Niagara Falls to the British. This was called the Mile Reserve.

Farmer's Brother was one of the Seneca representatives at the Treaty of Canandaigua in 1794 when the Six Nations signed away their land rights to the United States for most of New York State. The lands west of a line drawn from Buffalo to the PA border separated the New York and Seneca lands. The Seneca Chiefs that signed the agreement were: Cornplanter, Handsome Lake, Little Beard, Red Jacket and Farmer's Brother. The U.S. representative at the treaty was George Washington and the interpreters were Jasper Parrish and Horatio Jones.

During the War of 1812, Farmer's Brother was over 80 years old but led the Seneca forces with the vigor of a young man. An example of his leadership was during the war, an Iroquois warrior arrived at the Indian camp in Buffalo and proclaimed he was a deserter. When the Seneca were boasting about the English soldiers they killed in battle, he began talking about the Americans he had killed. During questioning by Farmer's Brother, the Iroquois acknowledged he was a spy. While the other members of the Seneca were still trying to decide what to do with this spy, Farmer's Brother took matters into his own hands and shot him, then demanded that the body of the traitor be removed from their camp.

Farmer's Brother's house was the first home on the Buffalo Creek Reservation, when entered from Buffalo. He never drank alcohol and commanded an influence over everyone he met, was a man of high character, unrivalled as a warrior and only equaled in eloquence by Red Jacket.

Figure 50 Medallion that George Washington presented to Seneca Chiefs

His name was coined when George Washington tried to show that agriculture was a very respectable work activity. During a conversation, Washington told Farmer's Brother that he too was a farmer and referred to him as his brother. He was proud to have met Washington and adopted this name. Washington also gave him a Silver Medallion, of which he was extremely proud.

He was a cousin or half-brother of Hiokatoo, who was Mary Jemison's second husband. Farmer's Brother remained friends with Mary Jamison, in a treaty with the U.S., he obtained lands for her on the Genesee River and she later moved to the Buffalo Creek reservation. When he died in 1815, he was initially buried, with full military honors, at the Franklin & Delaware Cemetery and was moved to Forest Lawn in 1851. His exact birth date is not known, it could have been 1716, 1718, 1730 or 1732, so he may have been almost 100 years old when he died.

MILLARD FILLMORE

*President of the United States and benefactor of numerous
Buffalo cultural organizations*

The 13th President of The United States was born into poverty in a log cabin on January 7, 1800 in Moravia, in the Finger Lakes region of New York. He was the second of eight children born to tenant farmers Nathaniel Fillmore and Phoebe Millard. His father obtained an apprenticeship for Millard at a textile mill. Fillmore felt he was not accomplishing anything in the apprenticeship, so he began educating himself. By clerking with local judge Walter Wood and teaching school, he was able to buy out his indenture.

He moved with his family to East Aurora, where he taught school. At 21 he moved to Buffalo, where he accepted a teaching position at the Cold Springs school, located on Main Street near West Utica – later the location of precinct #6, near the WKBW studios. Fillmore was paid $20.00 a month for teaching school and his board was paid for by the parents of his students. During this time, he also studied law at the offices of Asa Rice and Joseph Clary. Fillmore was accepted to the bar when he was 23 years old and set up practice as the only residing attorney in the Village of East Aurora. He was elected to the State Assembly as a member of the Anti-Masonic Party from 1829 to 1831.

At age 19, while he attended school in New Hope, NY in 1819, Fillmore developed a relationship with his teacher Abigail Powers, who was only two years older than him. After they married in 1826, they resided in East Aurora. Mrs. Fillmore continued to teach school in East Aurora until their son Millard Powers Fillmore was born in 1828, followed by a daughter Mary Abigail Fillmore in 1832.

Fillmore's legal practice grew and much of his business was now in Buffalo, so he moved there in 1830. When Buffalo was incorporated as a city in 1832, Fillmore assisted in drafting the city charter. He was elected to House of Representatives as an Anti-Mason in 1832, joined the Whig Party in 1834 and was again elected to the House as a Whig in 1836. In 1841, he unsuccessfully sought the Speaker of the House position but became chairman of the House Ways and Means Committee.

He was an unsuccessful candidate for New York Governor in 1844, partly because the Whig Party backed a nativist for NYC Mayor earlier that year, which resulted in Fillmore not getting the NYC immigrant vote. Fillmore blamed his defeat on foreign born Catholics. In 1847, he won the election for State Comptroller and was the vice president candidate on the Whig ticket of General Zachary Taylor in 1848.

After Taylor died in July of 1850 and Fillmore became president, the Compromise of 1850 was passed. This included a provision for new states being designated as free or slave states, along with passing the Fugitive Slave Act. The compromise and enforcement of the Fugitive Slave Act heightened the tensions between free and slave states and strengthened positions for or against slavery. Fillmore's personal position was he did not agree with slavery as an institution but did not feel the federal government could dictate policy. His position and support of the Comprise resulted in Fillmore not receiving the Whig presidential nomination in the election of 1852.

Accomplishments of the Fillmore presidency included establishing the first library in the White House with his wife and an appropriation of $2,000 from Congress. They also began the practice of inviting writers and performers to the White House. Being a former teacher, Mrs. Fillmore set the standard for the First Lady to be involved with educational programs and policies, which continues until the present day. Before leaving office, Fillmore sent Commodore Perry on the expedition to Japan, with instruction to open the Far East to world trade.

Tragedy struck Fillmore after he left office in March 1853 as his wife died on March 30 and his daughter Mary Abigail, who often served as the White House hostess, passed away at age 22 in July 1854. Fillmore came out of retirement after his daughter's death, making public appearances and speaking out on national issues. While he was traveling in Europe, Fillmore accepted the nomination of the American Party or Know Nothing Party for the presidential election of 1856. As a third-party candidate, Fillmore only won one state but received a respectable 21.5 percent of the vote. The Know Nothing Party was anti-immigrant and anti-Catholic. The people of Buffalo were against Fillmore's policies and the city remained a center for the Underground Railroad, often not enforcing the Fugitive Slave Act.

Fillmore helped build his first home in 1826 on Main Street in East Aurora. It was located near the current location of the Aurora Theatre and his office was across the street at 686 Main Street, now the location of Vidler's 5 & 10. The house fell into disrepair and was saved by Margaret Evans Price and Irving Price of Fisher Price Toys. It was moved to its current location at 24 Shearer Avenue in East Aurora and Mrs. Price used the home as her studio. The Aurora Historical Society acquired the house in 1975 and restored it to the appearance from the time of Fillmore's ownership. It is furnished with pieces that belonged to the Fillmore's from their East Aurora, White House and Buffalo homes. The home is one of ten National Historic Landmarks in Erie County.

When he moved to Buffalo in 1831, he lived at 180 Franklin Street. He rented the house out when he was governor, vice president and president. After his presidency, the home was sold because it was not grand enough for a former president. The home that Fillmore lived in at 180 Franklin Street was demolished in the early 1900s and the Buffalo YWCA was built at the address.

Fillmore married Carolyn McIntosh and purchased a house on Niagara Square in 1858, where he lived until his death in 1874. He entertained many dignitaries at the home, including John Quincy Adams, Abraham Lincoln and Commodore Perry. The house was merged with the adjacent M.S. Hawley home to became Hotel Fillmore in 1881, converted to Castle Inn in 1901 and razed in 1919 when the Hotel Statler was built on the site.

Figure 51 Fillmore Mansion on Niagara Square, later the location of the Statler Hotel

Some of the many organizations in which he was involved were:

- University of Buffalo
- Buffalo Historical Society
- Buffalo General Hospital
- Albright Art Gallery
- Buffalo Club
- Buffalo Public Schools
- Grosvenor Library
- Buffalo Science Museum
- Buffalo SPCA

Many historians felt that due to Fillmore's support of the Compromise of 1850, especially the Fugitive Slave Act, he was an ineffective president. However, his actions delayed the Civil War for a decade, during which time the North progressed in industry and was in a better position to wage war. Fillmore is possibly responsible for the North winning the Civil War and the preservation of the nation. He also devoted his life to public service and was responsible for establishing many Buffalo cultural, social and educational institutions that still exist today. In addition to the many organizations he assisted in starting, many others have been named after him and his statue stands in front of City Hall, overlooking his former mansion and the city he loved.

GEORGE FORMAN

Oil industry pioneer and one of the founders of Fidelity Trust,
which evolved into M&T Bank

George Van Syckel Forman was born in Milford, New Jersey on December 3, 1841 and graduated from Princeton at age nineteen. He practiced law in Trenton, New Jersey and moved to Oil City, Pennsylvania to become involved with the oil business.

Figure 52 Manufacturers & Traders Bank
at Main and Swan Streets

In Oil City, he partnered with Captain Vandergrift to establish Vandergrift, Forman and Company. This company was instrumental in laying pipelines for oil and gas. Eventually, Vandergrift controlled most of the pipelines in the Oil City area. This company became part of Standard Oil Company and Daniel O'Day from Buffalo, managed the Standard Oil pipelines. Forman was also involved with the Oil Exchange in Oil City and was president of the bank Oil City Trust Company. In 1879, Forman moved to Olean where he organized the Eastern Oil Company, that was incorporated in West Virginia. When Forman moved to Buffalo to be president of that company in 1891, he purchased O'Day's former house at 672 Delaware Avenue.

In 1893, George Forman, John J. Albright, John Satterfield and Franklin D. Locke founded The Fidelity Trust and Guaranty Company of Buffalo with Forman as president. E.B. Green designed the Fidelity Trust Building which was completed in 1909. It is at 284 Main Street at Swan, on the former location of The

Weed Block, where many prominent businessmen had their offices, including Millard Fillmore's Buffalo law offices. This building is now known as Swan Tower and Fidelity Trust merged with Manufacturers & Traders Trust Company to become M&T Bank.

After living at 672 Delaware for four years, Forman had Green & Wicks design a mansion at 824 Delaware Avenue. George lived at this home from 1893 to 1922. It was later purchased by Oliver F. Cabana, who owned Buffalo Specialty Company, later known as Liquid Veneer, and was a director of 35 companies, along with being a member of numerous clubs and societies. Cabana was a local benefactor of the Democratic Party, an original supporter of Franklin D Roosevelt for president and held many events at his mansion. This building is now Conners Children's Center – Child and Family Services.

George Forman's children were Howard Arter (1870), George Alfred (1875) and Mary Martha (1877). Howard was vice-president of Eastern Petroleum and during WWI was Federal Fuel Administrator for Buffalo. He married Georgia M. Green in 1892 and they divorced after the war, with Forman moving to Lexington, Kentucky. Georgia moved into 77 Oakland Place, behind the Forman mansion on Delaware and lived there until 1955. It was sold to the Catholic Diocese of Buffalo for the Bishop's residence, which the diocese put up for sale to fund the Diocese of Buffalo Independent Reconciliation & Compensation Program to assist victims of past sexual abuse by priests. George Alfred Forman was the president of Southwestern Petroleum Company. He died in 1925 and his widow Lucie Matter married Harry Blanchard Spaulding, the grandson of Elbridge G. Spaulding. Mary Martha Forman married Anson Conger Goodyear, who established the Museum of Modern Art in NYC.

Figure 53 Forman mansion at 672 Delaware Avenue

HENRY MONTGOMERY GERRANS

Made the Iroquois Hotel the premier Buffalo hotel at the end of the 19th
and beginning of the 20th centuries

Henry Montgomery Gerrans was born in Dunkirk, the son of James Gerrans who operated hotels in Detroit, Michigan and Akron, Ohio. After completing high school, Gerrans came to Buffalo and became a clerk with the Erie Railroad. By the time he was twenty years of age, he was cashier and chief clerk for the railroad. He worked as a stock broker, kerosene lamp salesman and coal salesman before becoming involved with the Iroquois Hotel.

The Iroquois Hotel was built upon the site of The Richmond Hotel, where on March 18, 1887, the Richmond Hotel along with St. James Hall, were destroyed in a deadly fire that killed 15 employees and guests. This hotel was owned by the Young Men's Association, the predecessor of the Buffalo Public Library. Since the hotel was a source of income for the subscription library, the Young Men's Association began building the Iroquois, which was advertised as absolutely fireproof. Gerrans and his partner William E. Woolley formed a company to lease the hotel.

Gerrans had the personality and connections to make the Iroquois the hotel where members of Buffalo society entertained. He was a business partner of William "Wild Bill" Cody in an irrigation canal in Wyoming and the establishment of Cody, Wyoming, with other partners being George Bleistein and Bert Rumsey. During the day, he played golf at the country clubs and participated in all night poker games. Henry Montgomery Gerrans was steward at Saratoga and Fort Erie, along with being on the board of Hialeah Racetrack. Socially, he was a member of the Buffalo, Country, Park and Saturn Clubs, and a 32nd degree Mason. Visiting celebrities went to the Iroquois and local society gathered there.

The Iroquois Hotel opened in 1889 and in anticipation of additional business from the Pan-American Exposition, in 1899 they added three more floors. It was at this hotel that barbers Morrel Howe and Robert Kideney developed the first products of the Wildroot Company. The hotel was such a focal point of the city of Buffalo's social and political interests, that E.M. Statler knew he could not divert them to his new Statler Hotel if the Iroquois was still in business. To overcome this obstacle, Statler purchased the Iroquois Hotel and closed it the day he opened the Statler Hotel in 1923. It was converted to an office building, with Bond's Clothing Store on the ground floor, and Statler renamed it the Gerrans Building in 1927. The location of the Iroquois Hotel is where One M&T Plaza has been located since 1966.

After the Iroquois closed, Gerrans retired from the hotel business and became vice president of a real estate company. In 1926, the owner of Hotel Touraine asked him to become manager and president of his hotel. Gerran moved into the Touraine and continued running the hotel until he died there in 1939 at age 86.

Figure 54 Iroquois Hotel at Main and Eagle Streets, now the location of One M&T Plaza

CHARLES W. AND FRANK H. GOODYEAR

Lumber industry pioneers who also owned railroads and steel mills

Charles and Frank Goodyear were the sons of (Jabez) Bradley Goodyear and Esther Permelia Kinne. Bradley Goodyear was born in Sempronius, NY in 1816 and his first occupation was as a tailor. After traveling through the South, while in his mid-20s, he returned to New York and his uncle Dr. Miles Goodyear, who was the president of the Cortland County Medical Society, induced him to practice medicine. Bradley graduated from Geneva Medical School in 1845, got married, settled in Cortland, NY, with Charles being born in 1846 and Frank in 1849. Dr. Goodyear moved his medical practice to Holland, NY and later to East Aurora. Charles and Frank attended the locals district school and East Aurora Academy, and as boys both brothers worked at Root & Keeting's tannery.

In 1868, Charles moved to Buffalo to study law at the firm of Laning & Miller. Continuing his studies with John C. Strong, he was admitted to the bar in 1871. He practiced individually and had separate partnerships with Major John Tyler and Henry F. Allen. Goodyear was also an Assistant District Attorney. In 1883, when Grover Cleveland stepped down from his law firm of Cleveland, Bissel & Sicard, Goodyear took his place and the firm became Bissell, Sicard & Goodyear. Charles was the first visitor to the White House in 1885 when Cleveland was president. In 1887, he stopped practicing law to form a lumber company F.H. & C.W. Goodyear with his brother.

Frank worked as a bookkeeper for Looneyville, owned by Robert Looney. In addition to a farm, sawmill, general store, feed & grain business, Looney owned vast timberlands in Pennsylvania. Frank married Josephine Looney and when her father died, she inherited the lumber land. Frank moved to Buffalo in 1872 and set up several mills in his timberlands in Pennsylvania and New York. In 1884, he purchased more land in Potter County, where he established a headquarters at a sawmill in Austin, PA. The stressful managing of the timberlands and the difficulty in the building of railroad spurs to service his holdings, resulted in a nervous breakdown which necessitated Charles joining the business.

In 1887, Frank and Charles formed the company F.H. & C.W. Goodyear. The Goodyears invested in timberland, lumber mills, coal and railroads in remote areas of Pennsylvania and New York. They bought tracts of land that were considered inaccessible for harvest because they were isolated and away from streams that could transport the logs. To access the land, they built railroad spurs and sawmills to process the trees into lumber. In many areas they built company towns for workers at isolated mills. Their railroad holdings developed into the Buffalo & Susquehanna Railroad.

The Buffalo & Susquehanna Iron Company began in 1899 when William A. Rogers, who was VP of The Iroquois Iron Company in South Chicago, invited fellow stockholders John Albright, Edmund Hayes and Stephen M. Clement to visit the property. Frank Goodyear heard about the trip and offered his private railroad car

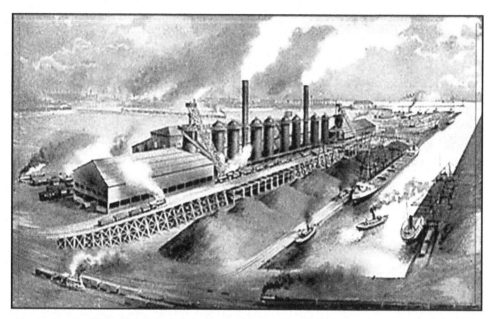

Figure 55 Buffalo & Susquehanna Iron Company and the Union Ship Canal

for the journey. He and Charles were invited to join the party and Frank was impressed with the possible tonnage it could bring to his railroad and wanted a plant that produced iron ingots at the end of his railroad line at the Buffalo Harbor. The amount of iron ore required to supply the furnaces necessitated the building of the Union Ship Canal. They also owned freighters that brought iron ore from Minnesota and Michigan to the Buffalo Harbor. The plant was later sold to the Hanna Furnace Company and later became part of National Steel Corporation. When the steel industry changed, the plant closed in 1982.

In 1901 to 1905, the brothers purchased 300,000 acres of pine timberland in southeastern Louisiana and southwestern Mississippi. They formed the Great Southern Lumber Company, the largest sawmill in the world. The city of Bogalusa was built to house the families working at the mill and the New Orleans Great Northern Railroad was established to connect the city to the national railroad network and New Orleans. The mill closed in 1938 and was the site of a bloody labor riot in 1919.

Charles Goodyear built a home at 888 Delaware Avenue, designed by E.B. Green. The house was built in 1903 at a cost of $500,000 or over 13 million in today's dollars. The Goodyear family lived there until 1940 when it was sold to Blue Cross Corporation. In 1950, it was sold to the Catholic Diocese of Buffalo and became Bishop McMahon High School. The property was sold to Kaleida Health in 1988 to be used as the Robert B. Adam Education Center and in 2005 it became the Oracle Charter School.

Frank Goodyear built a house at 762 Delaware in 1907. He and his family previously lived in homes at 443 Delaware, 652 Main Street, 671 Main Street, 267 North Street (the Bemis House) and 237 North Street (later owned by John D. Larkin). His next-door neighbor on Delaware Avenue was lumbar baron William Gratwick. Frank died shortly after moving into the home. He was constantly working, was only pleased with his successes and seldom happy, especially because even though all his businesses were a success his pet project the Buffalo & Susquehanna Railroad was not as successful as he had anticipated. Due to little exercise, at the time of his death he weighed 220 pounds but was only 5 foot 8 inches tall. His estate was valued at 10 million dollars at his death in 1907. His wife, and later his son Frank Jr., lived in the house which was razed in 1938. It is now the parking lot for the former Stephen Clement Mansion, now the American Red Cross building.

Frank made donations to parks in Buffalo and he wanted to build a zoo for the city. The Buffalo Zoo had its origin in 1871 when furrier Jacob Bergtold donated a pair of deer to the city. A fenced Deer Paddock was created in the meadow, in the current location of the zoo. Elam Jewett, who was developing the Parkside area agreed to look after the deer. During the 1880s only Civil War veterans, on the civil service list were eligible to work in the city parks. To assist in maintaining the grass of Delaware Park meadows, a flock of sheep grazed to keep the grass low and to add interest to that portion of the park. In 1895, a pair of bison and eight elk were added, with the bear pits being built in 1897. In 1900, Frank Goodyear offered one million dollars to build a new zoo which would have been located closer to the Art Gallery, near the area where Shakespeare in the Park now takes place. The City of Buffalo did not accept the proposal, but they did accept the elephant Goodyear donated. It was called Little Frank until he grew, with his name being changed to Big Frank. The elephant was chained to a tree for several years before funds could be raised to build the Elephant House.

The sons of both Frank and Charles worked in their family businesses and family members married into many of the prominent Buffalo families: Forman, Spaulding, Rumsey, Cary, Depew and Knox. Charles granddaughter married the grandson of Franklin D. Roosevelt. Charles son Anson Conger Goodyear was the founder of the Museum of Modern Art in NYC. Frank Goodyear Jr. was married to Dorothy Knox, the daughter of Seymour Knox I. Frank Jr. died in 1930 when his Rolls Royce crashed on Transit Road, between Broadway and Genesee, on the way to a dinner party in North Tonawanda. His home was Crag Burn on Davis Road in East Aurora. The grounds became Crag Burn Country Club, with the stable becoming the clubhouse.

ERASTUS GRANGER

*Postmaster, Superintendent of Indian Affairs and his farm became
Forest Lawn and part of Delaware Park*

Erastus Granger and his cousin Gideon Granger befriended Thomas Jefferson before he became president. They met him while working in Virginia and when the Grangers returned to their native New England, they supported Jefferson's presidential candidacy of 1800. The Grangers became members of the Democratic-Republican Party, formed to oppose the Federalist Party. Gideon Granger was appointed Postmaster General and to promote the party's interests, Jefferson sent Erastus to Buffalo and granted him the offices of Superintendent of Indian Affairs and Collector of Customs, and later the office of Postmaster. In 1807, Granger was appointed one of the Judges of Genesee County and when the western portion was split off, he was appointed a judge of the new county called Niagara. Granger presided over the first court held in Buffalo and was a member of the bench until 1817.

A recent widower, in 1804 he became a border at Crow's Tavern, the only accommodations that were available upon his arrival. He bought inner lot 31 in 1805 and later purchased additional outer lots in 1809 and 1810. Granger's farm was called Flint Hill and was located about four miles north of Buffalo, along Scajaquada Creek, which was then called Conjockety and later Granger's Creek. His farm eventually covered 700 acres and upon it were scattered homes of some friends and family members. In 1813, Granger married Elizabeth Sanborn, the daughter of Nathaniel Sanborn from Canandaigua and they had two sons, Reverend James Granger and Warren Granger, who was an attorney. Erastus' father Abner Granger, a Revolutionary War Captain, who was with Washington at Valley Forge, settled with his son in Buffalo.

Upon Granger's land was a site sacred to the Six Nations, as a great battle was fought there many years ago. The tribes held councils there, at a site called Councils in the Oaks of the Senecas. Granger permitted the Senecas to continue

*Figure 56 Erastus Granger homestead on Flint Hill was far enough away
from Buffalo to not be burned during War of 1812*

meeting in this location. As Superintendent of Indian Affairs, he held meetings with them in that spot. At the beginning of the War of 1812, he held a meeting with Red Jacket, Cornplanter, Farmer's Brother and other chiefs from the Seneca, Onondaga, Cayuga, Tuscarora and Oneida tribes. Upon the instruction of President Madison, Granger requested that the Six Nations remain neutral in the War of 1812. They stayed out of the conflict until the Mohawks, who fled to Canada after the American Revolution, sided with the British. In a later meeting with Granger at Flint Hill, the Six Nations announced that they were aligning with the American forces. When Granger died in December 1826, Red Jacket delivered the eulogy, in the Seneca language, a symbol of the friendship and respect shown to Granger by the Seneca Nation.

When Buffalo was burned on December 30, 1813, Granger's home was far enough away from the city and was not burned. Situated on the road to Williamsville, the house provided shelter to survivors, traveling to the safety of Williamsville and Clarence. The Buffalo-Williamsville Road, now known as Main Street, became a toll road and the first toll station from Buffalo was adjacent to Schardt's Tavern on the southeast corner of Steele and Main Street. Steele Street became Kensington Avenue, so the first toll booth was in front of the Granger's Flint Hill property.

In 1845, Warren Granger, Erastus' son, built a stone mansion on the site of the Seneca's Council in the Oaks. The home was designed by Calvin Otis and built by John Ambrose, with stone cut from the Quarry on the Granger estate. This home became the center of Buffalo society, with former President John Quincy Adams being a guest in 1849. The home was torn down and its location is marked by the large sundial in Forest Lawn Cemetery, which is still visible from Main Street.

When Erastus Granger purchased the 700 acres of land in 1806, it was not considered good farmland. The hills, lakes and oak trees resulted in few tillable parts. In 1831, the rural cemetery movement started with Mount Auburn outside of Boston. By 1849, the movement to bury people in large, parklike settings with trees and natural surroundings was established. With the Granger farm being two-and-one-half miles from downtown, a safe distance from city wells, its natural beauty met the criteria for a rural cemetery. In 1849, Forest Lawn founder attorney Charles E Clark paid Reverend James N. Granger and his brother Warren Granger $150 per acre for the 80 acres of land adjacent to Delaware Avenue and north of Scajaquada Creek. When landscape architect Frederick Law Olmstead was hired to create the Buffalo Parks System, he studied Forest Lawn. He was so impressed with the natural beauty of the cemetery that he selected the 243 acres meadow adjacent to it as the site for Delaware Park. Olmsted formed the park's 46-acre lake by damming Scajaquada Creek after it emerged from the cemetery. The land for Delaware Park came from the estates of Daniel Chapin, Washington Russell and Granger.

WILLIAM GRATWICK

Entrepreneur in the lumber and shipping industry

William Henry Gratwick was born in Albany, New York on January 25, 1839. He completed school at the Boys Academy and was hired at a lumber company as a tally boy, the lowest entry-level position in the industry. After ten years of working for the company, he owned one-half interest in the firm. Before leaving Albany, he formed his own business, William H. Gratwick & Company

In 1877, Gratwick moved to Buffalo and started Gratwick, Smith & Fryer Lumber Company, with offices in Albany, Detroit and Tonawanda. Gratwick purchased over 800 feet of frontage on the Niagara River in 1879. Docks were built extending 390 feet into the river, until they reached the depth of 13 feet required to accommodate the lumber ships. Later the river was reclaimed by filling it in with slag from Tonawanda Iron & Steel, until it reached the required water depth. In addition to Gratwick, Smith & Fryer and W. H. Gratwick, he owned White, Gratwick & Mitchell and Gratwick & Company in Michigan. In northern Michigan, the company owned 31,000 acres of pine forests, which provided 28 million feet of lumber to be shipped by barge to North Tonawanda. The lumber concerns on River Road and Tonawanda Island employed 450 men and forwarded the lumber to east coast markets by train, with the Erie and New York Central having tracks to their plant, or by Erie Canal barge, with the canal being located just over a mile from the plant. Gratwick later also owned six of the largest freighters on the Great Lakes. In addition to his business interests, Gratwick was the president of the YMCA and curator of the Buffalo Fine Arts Academy.

William H. Gratwick married Martha Ware and they had three children, Mildred M., William H. Jr. and Frederick Colman Gratwick., During the late 1870s, they lived at 414 Delaware Avenue in the Sternberg House, now Mansion on Delaware. Gratwick commissioned H.H. Richardson to design a spectacular Richardsonian Romanesque style mansion at 776 Delaware Avenue at Summer Street.

Figure 57 The Gratwick Mansion at 776 Delaware Avenue was the last property designed by architect H.H. Richardson

This house was the last commission of Richardson's career. The Richardson Olmsted Complex for the Buffalo Psychiatric Center, designed in the Kirkbridge Plan, is one of his signature buildings. That complex was designated a National Historic Landmark in 1986 and is now the location of Hotel Henry Urban Resort Conference Center. Tragically the Gratwick Mansion at 776 Delaware Avenue, was torn down in 1919.

William Gratwick suffered from colon cancer and he was treated by Dr. Roswell Park. In 1901, Martha Gratwick donated $25,000 to fund the Gratwick Research Laboratory at High and Elm Streets, across from Buffalo General Hospital. After grants were received from New York State to build a dedicated cancer hospital called the Cary Pavilion, in 1913 Martha and her sons William Jr. and Frederick Gratwick contributed in donating the funds required to purchase the land at Oak and Carlton Streets. These donations assisted in developing the research and treatment segments of Roswell Park Hospital, with William Jr. and Frederick Gratwick serving on the hospital board of trustees. Currently, Roswell Park continues to receive the philanthropic gift of the family through the Gratwick Family Endowed Fund for Cancer Research.

The Gratwicks' daughter Mildred married attorney and banker James L. Crane, for whom the Crane Branch, on Elmwood Avenue, of the Buffalo and Erie County Library is named. Their son Frederick Coleman Gratwick married Dotha Dart, the daughter of Joseph Dart who invented the grain elevator. Frederick's son Davies devoted his adult life to managing the Gratwick summer home and rental property in Muskoka, Ontario.

William Gratwick Jr. continued his father's lumber business out of an office at 881 Ellicott Square Building. He lived at 800 West Ferry, in the former Hengerer's Mansion, before the mansion was torn down and replaced by the luxury 800 West Ferry apartment building. Between 1901 and 1910, he built Linwood Gardens in Pavilion, New York, as a country home. Architect Thomas Fox designed the house and all the original garden areas.

William Gratwick III was a horticulturalist, artist and landscape architect, and in 1933, he and his family moved to Linwood Gardens. There he set up the Rare Plants Nursery and the Japanese Tree Peony as a feature of the nursery and gardens. He also contributed sculptures and new garden areas to the estate. His wife Harriet Lee Saltonstall directed the Linwood School of Music from 1947 – 1963 at the estate. Linwood Gardens is listed on the National Register of Historic Places and the New York State Register of Historic Places. It is only open to the public for the Tree Peony Festival and other special summer events.

In honor to his contributions to the lumber industry in North Tonawanda, Gratwick Park, which is on the lumber yard land filled in by slag from Tonawanda Iron & Steel, and the Gratwick section of North Tonawanda are named after William Gratwick.

ANNA KATHERINE GREEN

Considered the mother of the detective novel and was married to furniture designer Charles Rohlfs

Anna Katherine Green was born in Brooklyn in 1846, the daughter of prominent attorney James Wilson Green and Catherine Ann Whitney Green. The Green family can be traced back to The Plymouth Colony, with William Green being married to Elizabeth Warren, who was descended from the Pilgrim fathers and three barons that signed the Magna Carta. Catherine Ann Whitney Green died when Anna was three years old and her father married Grace Hollister of Buffalo. The family moved to Buffalo, with Anna growing up in the city. She received her B.A. from Ripley Female College in Poultney Vermont in 1866.

After graduating from college, Green embarked on her desired

Figure 58 Portrait of Anna Katherine Green

career as a poet. She found no success and began secretly working on the novel *The Leavenworth Case*. The book was considered the first American detective novel and the first written by a woman. Anna gained knowledge of legal and police matters from her father, who was an attorney. Yale University so highly regarded the novel for its insight into legal matters that the school used the book in law classes to show the perils of relying upon circumstantial evidence.

Leavenworth Case was the most successful book of Green's career, becoming a bestseller, with over three quarters of a million copies sold. It was made into a play and two movies. Her fans included Presidents Theodore Roosevelt and Woodrow Wilson, along with Sir Arthur Conan Doyle, who read the book ten years before he created the Sherlock Holmes character. Doyle made a trip to Buffalo to meet Green when he came to America. The book followed Green's essentials of a good detective story: a tightly constructed plot with a unique turn of events, a step-by-step revelation of the story line and a climax that did not disappoint the reader. In addition to this formula, Green created the elderly spinster detective, young female detective and many plot devices still used in the whodunit genre.

In 1884, Green married actor Charles Rohlfs in Brooklyn. Her father agreed to the marriage only after Rohlfs promised to give up his acting career, which he did with the exception of returning to the stage for a production of *Leavenworth Case*. Green and Rohlfs moved to Anna's childhood home of Buffalo in 1887, when Charles was offered a job in Buffalo. Rohlfs had studied the design and crafting of iron stoves at the Cooper Union institute for the Advancement of Science & Art in NYC. He received a number of patents for stove designs and was hired by stove manufacturers Sherman S. Jewett & Company. The Rohlfs resided at 26 Highland Avenue and, after deciding to permanently stay in Buffalo, built a Craftsman style home at 156 Park Street in the Allentown district.

Figure 59 Charles Rohlfs and furniture he designed

While in Buffalo, Charles Rohlfs began designing and building Arts & Crafts style furniture, in the same manner and type as the Roycrofters, with his work preceding that of Gustav Stickley by ten years. Rohlfs opened his furniture company in Buffalo in 1898. His work was featured at an exhibition at Marshall Field's Department Store in Chicago in 1900. He participated in the Arts & Crafts Exhibition at the National Arts Club in New York in December 1900. Stickley and Rohlfs both presented their work at the Pan-American Exposition in 1901, where Rohlfs assisted as an organizer of the Exposition. In 1902, Rohlfs was the only American to participate at the International Exposition of Decorative Art in Turin. The exposure resulted in Rohlfs being invited to become a member of the Royal Society of Arts in London and being commissioned to provide a set of chairs for Buckingham Palace. His furniture now sells in the four to five-figure range, with some pieces selling for over $100,000.

Green raised three children and during her 45-year career, she published 35 novels, 23 short stories and a volume of poetry. She died at the age of 88 on April 11, 1935 in Buffalo, NY. The new queen of detective novels, Agatha Christie, later revealed that she began writing mysteries after having been influenced by the work of Anna Katherine Green.

SETH GROSVENOR

Donated the money to start Grosvenor Library

S eth Grosvenor was only a resident of Buffalo from 1813 to 1815, but he left a bequest for the establishment of the Grosvenor Library, which still exists as the Grosvenor Room in the Downtown Buffalo Branch of the Erie County Public Library.

His older brother Abel arrived in Buffalo in 1811, establishing a store with Ruben B. Hancock on the east side of Main Street between Seneca and Swan. Seth moved to Buffalo to assist in settling the estate of Abel, who died in later 1812 or 1813. There are various versions of the cause of Abel's death. One version states the owner of Pomeroy's Tavern, at Main and Seneca, offended troops from Baltimore (stationed in Buffalo during the War of 1812) by stating he was a friend of the British. A mob of Baltimore troops attacked him, thinking he was Mr. Pomeroy. Abel died a short time later from his injuries.

During the December 30, 1813 British attack on Buffalo, Grosvenor was one of the volunteers who mounted the defense at the corner of Main and Niagara. The Cyrenius Chapin led defense was unsuccessful and Grosvenor's store was burned to the ground. Four days later, on January 4, 1814, Grosvenor advertised in the Buffalo

Figure 60 Grosvenor Library at Franklin and Edward Streets

Figure 61 *Grosvenor Library demolition in 1974 with Cyclorama Building behind the debris*
St. Louis Church is visible in the background

Gazette that his dry goods store was back in business, operating from the Harris Tavern in Clarence.

Grosvenor was a member of the brick company that worked to quickly rebuild the city of Buffalo. By May 24, 1814, there were 23 houses, three taverns, four dry goods stores, twelve grocery stores or other shops and three offices rebuilt in Buffalo. On April 25, 1814, he advertised that his store was again open in Buffalo, now located at the northwest corner of Pearl and Seneca Streets (current location of The Pearl Street Brewery). His brother Stephen joined the business in 1815 and the name was changed to S. & S.K. Grosvenor. When Ruben B. Hancock rejoined the business, Seth moved to New York City.

Upon Seth Grosvenor's death in October 1857, he bequeathed $40,000 to the city of Buffalo for the establishment of a library; $10,000 for the building and $30,000 to be invested for the purchase of books. In 1870, the original Grosvenor Library opened in the Buffalo Savings Bank Building at Broadway and Washington. In 1891, the trustees erected a library at Franklin and Edward and in 1897 it was passed to the control of the City of Buffalo who had appropriated $4,000 a year to operate the library. The Cyclorama Building, located next to the library, was annexed by the Grosvenor Library and used as a reading room by scholars, students and library patrons. In 1953, the Grosvenor Library, Erie County Public Library (founded to provide bookmobile service to outlying towns in the 1940s), and Buffalo Library (founded as the Young Men's Association in 1836), were consolidated by the New York State Legislature. All libraries were moved into the downtown library at Lafayette Square, when the new library opened in 1964. The Grosvenor Library building was demolished in 1974 and the Cyclorama is now an office building.

CICERO J. HAMLIN

Horse racing enthusiast, Hamlin Park and president of American Glucose Company

Cicero J. Hamlin was born in Hillsdale, New York, near the Massachusetts border on November 7, 1819 and moved to East Aurora in 1836. He had a general store in East Aurora and moved to Buffalo in 1846 as the junior partner in Wattles & Hamlin, a dry goods company. Hamlin was involved with other retail companies and on April 12, 1861, the day Fort Sumter was fired upon to begin the Civil War, he opened Hamlin & Mendsen, a wholesale and retail dry goods company which also sold furniture and carpets.

In 1871, Hamlin left the dry goods industry, concentrating on his other business interests and real estate development. He built the Hamlin Block at 256 to 268 Main Street, where William Hengerer started in the dry goods business as a clerk with Sherman & Barnes. After a fire in 1888, the building was rebuilt and became the home of Barnes & Hengerer, the largest store in Buffalo. When Hengerer's built a new store at 465 Main, Sweeney & Company located their department store in the building. It is now called the Sweeney Building, a six-story commercial building, leasing office space

The Hamlin family became involved with the sugar industry in 1874 when William Hamlin invested in the Buffalo Grape Sugar Company formed by Arthur W. Fox and Horace Williams. Fox and Williams operated a brewery and opened a vinegar company called A.W. Fox & Company. Realizing they needed large quantities of sugar, they opened Buffalo Grape Sugar Company at Court Street and the Erie Canal. When Fox died after a train accident in August 1874, Cicero Hamlin covered the debts of the company and became president. Buffalo Grape Sugar expanded, adding

Figure 62 Buffalo Driving Park, Horserace track and site of International Industrial Fair

two additional plants, and was reorganized as the American Glucose Company in 1883. Prior to the Hamlin's glucose venture, all glucose was imported from France and Germany. Glucose manufacturing became an important industry in Buffalo during the late 1800s, with American Glucose employing over 2,500 workers in 1888. The company was sold by the Hamlin family to a glucose combine in 1897.

The Buffalo Driving Park, located at East Ferry and Humboldt Parkway, began holding races prior to the Civil War and in 1868 Cicero J. Hamlin purchased and improved the grounds. He created one of America's premier harness racing tracks, where the first race with a $20,000 purse was held. Hamlin also presented what he called the Kentucky Derby of the North, with 40,000 people attending the park over a weekend. In 1888 and 1889, the Buffalo International Industrial Fair was held at the Driving Park. It was a predecessor to the Pan-American Exposition, featuring industrial exhibits and all kinds of entertainment; including sporting contests, concerts, livestock shows, carriage races, bicycle races, art displays and drawing up to 30,000 visitors a day. Ringling Brothers brought their circus to the grounds for several years and Buffalo Bill Cody held his Wild West Show to the Driving Park, but after several fires and years of neglect, the grounds laid dormant and the over 300 acres were vacant.

Figure 63 Advertisement for properties in the Hamlin Park Development

Beginning in 1912, developers were purchasing portions of Hamlin Park, which included the grounds of Buffalo Driving Park and was bordered by East Ferry, Humboldt Parkway and Jefferson. Toronto's John J. Cook was one of the first Canadian developers who began investing in Buffalo. Their goal for Hamlin Park was replicating the development in the Parkside area, but on a more modest scale and including two family units. Other homebuilders were Volgamore (Cook's former partner), International Building Company, Robert E. Baurer, Niederpreum & Company, F.T. Jenzen Builders and George Steinmiller. They marketed to the German and Jewish middle-class homebuyers of the early 20th century. Additional attention was brought to the development when Canisius College relocated on Main Street, at the edge of Hamlin Park, and Sears Roebuck built their store at Main and Jefferson. Hamlin Park evolved into a middle-class black neighborhood but lost its appeal when construction of the Kensington Expressway in 1958 destroyed the elegance of Humboldt Parkway and the cohesiveness of the neighborhood.

On May 1, 1855, Cicero J. Hamlin founded Village Farms in East Aurora. It was a 66-acre farm north of Main Street, between Tannery Brook and Buffalo Road. The farm featured 800 stalls for horses and cattle, a racetrack and became known as one of the greatest trotting nurseries in the Western Hemisphere, breeding more world champions than any other farm. To oversee the farm's racing department, the Hamlin's hired Edward F. (Pop) Geers, considered one of the greatest drivers in racing history, to a ten-year contract at $10,000 a year in 1892.

In 1882, Hamlin purchased a ten-year-old horse named Mambrino King for $17,000, equivalent to about $400,000 in today's money. During the next several years over 30,000 people came to see Mambrino King, who the East Aurora Advertiser called "the handsomest horse in the world." People would bring their horses to East Aurora and pay for mating time with the horse. Mambrino King died in 1899 and the East Aurora Historical Society placed a marker, where the horse was buried in a mahogany casket, on North Willow Street in East Aurora. In memory of this historic horse, there is even The Mambrino King Wine, Coffee and Chocolate bar on Main Street in East Aurora.

Hamlin's farm and racetrack brought other horse racing enthusiasts to East Aurora. Henry C. Jewett built a completely enclosed racetrack, which allowed for training year-round, at the southwest corner of Grover Road and Route 20A. Knox Farms was on Buffalo Road and it is said that Elbert Hubbard's love and ownership of horses, influenced his decision to locate the Roycroft movement in East Aurora.

Cicero Hamlin owned property at 420 to 440 Franklin Street, that backed up to Delaware Avenue. In 1865, Cicero began building an Italianate style mansion at 432 Franklin Street. He and his wife Ann Ford Hamlin lived at the home until 1898, when they moved to 1035 Delaware Avenue. The home at 432 Franklin later became the American Legion Post 665 and is now the Hamlin House, a restaurant and banquet facility. Cicero and Ann lived at 1035 Delaware Avenue until Cicero passed away in 1905. At the time of his death Cicero J. Hamlin was considered one of the richest men in NYS outside of NYC. The home at 1035 Delaware Avenue was sold to the Catholic Diocese to make room for the construction of St. Joseph's New Cathedral at Utica and Delaware.

Cicero's sons were William, Frank and Harry Hamlin. William worked with his father at American Glucose and was with the company until it was sold in 1897. He married Kate Gates, who was the daughter of George Gates, the sleeping car magnet. William had a home built at 1058 Delaware, at the southwest corner of Lexington, in which William and Kate lived until William died at age 81 in 1931. Their daughter Susan Gates Hamlin married George Armstrong Mitchell of 1040 Delaware Avenue, their next-door neighbor. Mitchell was associated with Pratt & Letchworth, the Depew Car Company, White, Gratwick & Mitchell Lumber dealers and was vice-president of Shredded Wheat of Niagara Falls.

Harry Hamlin was born in Buffalo in 1855. At 17 he entered Yale University, but left school to work with his father and brother William in the glucose business. In 1887, he built a Queen Ann residence at 1014 Delaware Avenue. During the 1890s Harry managed the glucose refining plant in Peoria and returned to Buffalo to assist his father at Village Farms in East Aurora. He shared his father's love for horses and became involved with polo. When the family sold their glucose businesses in 1897, Harry followed his father in breeding champion pacers and trotters named Cogent, Duke, the Abbott and others. He won so many trophies and ribbons that Harry hired architect George Cary to redesign the first floor of his Delaware Avenue mansion to include a Trophy Room for the many awards presented to his horses.

After Cicero Hamlin's Village Farms was sold, Harry expanded upon his love for speed formerly supplied by horse racing to automobile racing. He was the one of first to import high powered French race cars to America and raced in Central, Eastern and Mid-Western America, including the sea beaches. He was known for being a fast but reckless driver, not only on the tracks but also on the streets of WNY. On June 4, 1907, while heading east on Main Street in Eggertsville, Harry Hamlin was killed in one of the first traffic fatalities recorded in the Buffalo area. The honorary pallbearers at his funeral included the social elite of Buffalo: John J. Milburn, J.N. Scatcherd. Dr. Roswell Park, Montgomery Gerrans. George L. Williams, Dr. Charles Cary, Thomas Cary, Trumull Cary, J.H. Metcalfe, Lawrence D. Rumsey, Bronson Case Rumsey, Ansley Wilcox, George Bliestein and Harry Seymour.

The only son of Harry Hamlin was Chauncey Hamlin, who was educated at Miss Hoffman's, the Heathcote School, Nichols and the Hill School in Pottstown. In 1903, he graduated from Yale where he played football, along with being a member of Phi Beta Kappa and Skull & Bones. He graduated from UB Law School in 1905 and during law school married Martha Grey, daughter of David Gray, reporter, editor and part owner of The Courier. After graduation Chauncey clerked at the offices of Rogers, Locke & Milburn before forming a private practice in Snyder and later a partnership with John Lord O'Brian, William Donovan and Charles Goodyear. In 1910, Chauncey organized and was the first president of the Buffalo Legal Aid Bureau.

While Chauncey was serving in the Army during WWI, the home at 1014 Delaware was leased to George Rand, president of Marine Bank, and later to oil man Ellis Treat, until Chauncey moved back in during the 1920s. He retired from law in his early 40s and devoted himself to affairs for the public good. In 1920, he became president of the Buffalo Society of Natural Sciences and was a member of the City Planning Committee that choose the location of the new City Hall on Niagara Square. In 1924, President Coolidge appointed Chauncey chairman of the National Conference on Outdoor Recreation and he was credited with the creation of Allegany State Park. Chauncey is best remembered for being on the board of managers of the American Association of Museums, president of the International Council of Museums and the creation of the Museum of Science at Humboldt Park.

Chauncey's daughter Martha Visser't Hooft studied art in Europe and after returning to Buffalo in 1928, her paintings were exhibited at major galleries, including Burchfield-Penny and Albright-Knox Galleries in Buffalo. Chauncey's grandson is actor Harry Hamlin, who starred in L.A. Law, along with numerous movies and television shows. In 1987, he was voted People Magazine's "Sexiest Man Alive."

WILLIAM HENGERER

The founder of Hengerer's Department Store

William Hengerer was born in Württemberg, Germany on March 2, 1839 and began his education in Germany. When he was ten years of age his parents moved to Pittsburgh, Pennsylvania, where he completed his schooling. In March 1861, Hengerer moved to Buffalo and obtained a position with Sherman & Barnes dry goods store at 259 Main Street, receiving a salary of $6.00 per week. However, in 1861 Hengerer enlisted in the 21st New York Volunteers, the first regiment from Erie County to serve at the front during the Civil War.

After serving two years with his unit, William returned to Buffalo and his former position as clerk at Sherman & Barnes, which was succeeded by J.G. Barnes & Company and Barnes & Bancroft. In 1874, Hengerer became a partner of Barnes, Bancroft & Company at 260-266 Main Street. Upon the retirement of Bancroft in 1885, the company became Barnes, Hengerer Company. On February 1, 1888, a fire started at the store at 11:45 in the morning. There were over 500 people in the building at the time of the fire and four female clerks died. The building, owned by Cicero J. Hamlin, and the contents of the store were a complete loss. Firemen concentrated on trying to save surrounding buildings, several of which received smoke and water damage.

Barnes, Hengerer & Company rebuilt in a six-story building at 268 Main Street. When Barnes died in 1895 the company was reorganized as a corporation, the William Hengerer Company, with Hengerer as president, C.O. Howard as treasurer and E.D. Robbins as secretary. It became one of the largest and most complete department stores between NYC and Chicago, with over 600 employees. Sales increased from $300,000 in 1865 to $4,000,000 by the end of the 19th century.

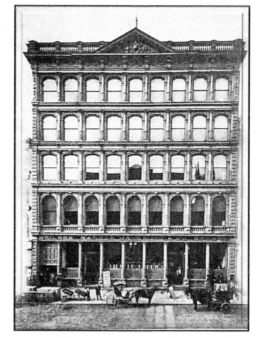

Figure 64 Barnes, Bancroft & Company store in the Hamlin Block at 260-266 Main Street in 1875, shortly after William Hengerer became a partner in the business

Figure 65 Hengerer's Store at 268 Main Street
Photo: Buffalo History Museum

In 1903, their new store was built at 465 Main Street in the former location of The Phoenix House and Tifft House. This was a nine-story neo-classical steel framed commercial building with a brick façade. The store was next to the German Insurance Company in what was then the center of the Buffalo business district. The William Hengerer Company was a founding member of Associated Dry Goods Corporation in 1916. Hengerer's opened suburban locations at Main and Eggert in Amherst (1958), Sheridan and Delaware in Tonawanda (1965), the Seneca Mall (1969) and Eastern Hills Mall (1971). Their name was changed to Sibley's, the Rochester chain also operated by Associated Dry Goods, in 1981, and in 1987 the downtown store closed. As Sibley's they opened locations in the Boulevard Mall, Walden Galleria and McKinley Mall. Eventually Sibley's merged with Kaufmann's from Pittsburgh and later became Macy's.

William Hengerer married Louise Duerr of Buffalo in 1863 and they had eight sons and one daughter. Five of his sons worked for William Hengerer Company. In 1887, William purchased the mansion of Alonzo J. Holt at 800 West Ferry Street, next to the estate of John J. Albright. The Hengerer Family lived at 800 West Ferry until 1905, when it was sold to William Gratwick Jr. In 1929, this property was sold to Darwin Reidpath Martin (son of Darwin D. Martin from the Larkin Company), who built the 11 story, 21-unit luxury apartment building, which still exists at this address. The building was subdivided into smaller apartments in 1940 and in 1980 was converted to a condominium association.

In 1896, William Hengerer organized the Lutheran Church Home for the Aged and Infirm and was president of the association. That organization continues and is now part of Greenfields Continuing Care Community in Lancaster. Hengerer was a commissioner and president of the Buffalo Parks Department and a member of the Board of Directors of the Pan-American Exposition. William Hengerer died on December 3, 1905 at age 66.

SARA HINSON

Buffalo teacher, who is credited as one of the founders of Flag Day

Sara Hinson was born on February 25, 1841, educated in the Buffalo school system and completed her education at private finishing schools. Sara began her teaching career at Buffalo Public School #13 and #4, transferring to School #31 on Emslie Street, now the Harriot Ross Tubman School at 212 Stanton Street, in 1864. Hinson remained at this school for 50 years - 30 years as a fourth-grade teacher and 20 years as the school principal.

Hinson determined that The Continental Congress accepted Betsy Ross' design of the American Flag on June 14, 1777. On June 14, 1891 she began the tradition of a formal ceremony of saluting and honoring the flag. Other teachers and schools joined in on the tradition and over the years, it began to catch on across the country. President Woodrow Wilson agreed to set aside June 14th as a day of national observance of Flag Day and President Harry Truman signed the legislation making it a national holiday in 1949.

Other teachers also lay claim to beginning the practice of Flag Day. Wisconsin teacher Bernard J. Cigrand states he recognized the observance of Flag Day in 1885. He was a prolific writer, founder of the National Flag Day Organization, and he traveled across the country campaigning to make Flag Day a national holiday. However, his 1885 claim cannot be documented. Another early Flag Day proponent was George Bloch, who claimed he started the practice in NYC in 1891. Francis Bellamy wrote the Pledge of Allegiance in 1892 and promoted Flag Day in the schools. No one can prove they were first, so Flag Day is considered a joint effort of various teachers, with those involved being listed here and others included as one of the founders.

After Hinson resigned as principal of School 31, she was appointed by Mayor Louis Fuhrmann as the first woman to serve on the Board of School Examiners, the predecessor to the Buffalo School Board, serving on the board from 1910 to 1916. She was also the chairman of the Teacher's Association Fellowship committee. In this capacity, she would visit the homes of teachers when they were ill. This was during the time when teachers were not allowed to marry, so they often did not have family members to help care for them.

Hinson died on March 20, 1926 at the age of 85. Her grave at Forest Lawn is marked by a flagpole with the American flying above her final resting place. The gravestone is engraved "Sara M. Hinson – dedicated teacher who with others gave us Flag Day."

Figure 66 Memorial plaque at Forest Lawn Cemetery

WILLIAM HODGE

One of the earliest settlers in the area and what he experienced in moving to and settling in Buffalo was an example of what other early residents of WNY encountered

William Hodge was born in Glastonbury, Connecticut on July 2, 1781. He married Sally Abbott in 1802 and for three years, he farmed during the summer and taught school during the winter in Exeter, not far from Cooperstown, NY.

In 1805, he decided to move to Buffalo, which at that time was considered the extreme western edge of civilization. With his wife and two children, Hodge traveled in an open boat with two other families, with about twenty people making the journey. And it was quite a journey. In their boat, they went up the Mohawk River, Wood Creek, Oneida Lake and Oswego River, portaging around the rapids, until they reached Lake Ontario. The lake took them to Lewiston, where their boat was taken out of the water and drawn by a team of oxen around Niagara Falls to Schlosser on the upper Niagara. They then traveled against the current of the Niagara River, with their boat being rowed, poled and towed to Buffalo Creek. The trip took twenty days.

The Hodge Family spent, June 16, 1805, their first night in Buffalo at Zenas Baker's tavern, on Terrace about 200 feet west of Main Street. Major Baker moved the family and their possessions to the log home next to the sawmill on Granger's Farm, near where Scajaquada Creek crossed Main Street. That fall they moved to a log home at farm lot #35, the northeast corner of Main and Utica, only to move again the following spring to a lot at the southeast corner of Main and Ferry, later the site of the Cold Springs Tavern. Hodge still did not yet own any land, having just his labor and work ethic to support his family.

Figure 67 Portrait of William Hodge
Photo: Courtesy Buffalo Stories
archives/Steve Cichon

Since he did not have any money to purchase land in Buffalo, Hodge acquired land in Eden and went to work building a log home so his family could establish a farm in what is now Eden Valley. After he completed the home, Hodge came back to Buffalo to bring his family to their Eden farm. Upon arrival, he found his father Benjamin Hodge had moved to Buffalo and purchased farm lot #35, where he previously lived. They traded properties with William moving back to the 50-acre lot at Main and Utica, and his father moving into the log home and farm in Eden. His wife's parents also later moved to Buffalo in 1810. Daniel Abbott, his father-in-law, moved to the lakeshore in Hamburg in June 1812 on a farm that became known as Abbott's.

To support his family Hodge made furniture and sash windows that he exchanged for produce and products from area farmers. Hodge also split logs, threshed grain, finished buildings and made coffins. There was no tavern or public houses between the village of Buffalo and the Elias Ransom/Hopkins tavern two miles west of Williamsville. The Hodge family sometimes took in travelers but in 1807, they added an addition to offer accommodations to travelers. In 1807, he also traveled to Utica, NY and paid a manufacturer of screens ten dollars to teach him how to make screens, a business he successfully continued for the next 25 years.

After he was settled with his tavern and business at lot #35, at the northeast corner of Main and Utica, Hodge became interested in purchasing farm lot #57 at the southwest corner of Main and Utica. Joseph Huesten owned that 60-acre plot. Huesten had planted a nursery of apple trees, from seed, on the lot but still had not finished paying the Holland Land Company for the land. Hodge paid Huesten $250 for the land and paid off the balance of $400 still due to the Holland Land Company. This was about double the going price of land in this vicinity and Hodge had to deed the western ten acres to Michael Hunt, the original owner of the article (title) to the lot.

The history of lot #57 is of importance because its nursery provided the beginning trees of many apple orchards in WNY and it resulted in Hodge becoming friends with Abner Bryant, the owner of adjoining lot #56. Hodge decided to move across the street to lot #57, where he built a large brick building to include his dwelling and the tavern. It was the first brick house built in Buffalo. The bricks for the building were made on Hodge's lot #35 and the lumber came from Erastus Granger's saw mill. In 1812, he moved into his new home. Since the army was camped on lots #58 and #59, owned by Christjohn Staley and William DeShay, the soldiers provided a lot of business for what became known as The Brick Tavern on the Hill. Hodge was also kept busy making coffins for the 300 soldiers that died at the Flint Hill encampment during the winter of 1812-1813.

When Buffalo was burned on December 30, 1813, Hodge and his family took refuge at the Harris Hill Tavern, three miles east of Williamsville. The British and Indians did not get down Main Street to Utica Street, so the tavern survived destruction of December 30 and 31. In fact, Hodge returned on December 31 and took additional item from his house to the Harris Hill tavern. However, on January 1 he returned to find the British or Indians came further out from the village of Buffalo and set fire to his home.

Hodge was the second person to rebuild after the burning of Buffalo, following Ralph Pomeroy who rebuilt his tavern on the northeast corner of Main and Seneca Streets. In December 1814 the entire Brick Tavern on the Hill was rebuilt, and after the War of 1812 ended, business was good, with Hodge running the tavern, tree nursery, farm, screen business, fanning mill business, brick manufacturing business and adding a store in the tavern. Soon business decreased and during the national Financial Panic of 1819 Hodge was close to losing everything. His cousin Dr. Joseph White from Cherry Valley came to Buffalo, paid off his debts and on November 6, 1819 took a note giving him possession of the 150 acres of property Hodge owned on farm lots #57, #33 and #35. Hodge made annual payments to White, but due to the scarcity of cash and lack of business, he was sometimes not even able to cover the interest. It took Hodge until December 29, 1831 to pay off the notes and again take full possession of his property. This was not the final time Hodge experienced financial difficulties. He formed a bank in the late 1830s and built a brick block of buildings at the corner of Main and Chippewa. When that bank failed, the debt incurred by Hodge was not cleared until a year before his death.

When the Erie Canal opened in 1825, Hodge and his wife Sally accompanied Governor DeWitt Clinton back to NYC on the ceremonious journey in the Seneca Chief along the entire Erie Canal, to pour water from Lake Erie into the ocean at New York harbor. Before making the return journey to Buffalo, Hodge went to nurseries on Long Island to purchase additional trees for his Buffalo nursery. This purchase included some Elm trees. That nursery was sold to Abner Bryant in 1834, with Bryant and Hodge having planted many of the Elm trees that graced Delaware Avenue and the upper west side streets.

Hodge died on September 18, 1848. He and his wife had been two of the earliest residents of Buffalo and they raised ten children. The Brick Tavern on the Hill was a Buffalo landmark and his elm trees graced the west side, until the Dutch Elm Disease decimated the population of elm trees in the 1970s.

His son William Hodge was five months old when the Hodge family moved to Buffalo in 1805. It was William, the son, who developed the land from his father's farm lot #57, which was bordered by Main, Hodge, Elmwood and Utica. He laid out Hodge Avenue and built many fine buildings upon it. He continued his father's love of Buffalo by writing many articles on the early settlement of the city and by serving as president of the Buffalo Historical Society.

BIRDSILL HOLLY

Mechanical engineer and hydraulics inventor who held many patents,
including the fire hydrant and central steam heating

Birdsill Holly was born on November 8, 1820 in Auburn, NY to Birdsill Holly, Sr. and Comfort Holly. His father was a general mechanic and millwright, who moved the family to Seneca Falls, NY due to the amount of work available in the water powered mill industry. When his father died at the age of 37, Birdsill Jr. dropped out of third grade at school, at age ten, and became an apprentice at a cabinetry shop. He then apprenticed in a machine shop and by his late teens, Birdsill was a superintendent at a machine shop in Uniontown, Pennsylvania.

He returned to Seneca Falls, where he joined the company of Silsby & Race in 1853, which later became Silsby, Race & Holly. In 1855, the fire-fighting industry was forever changed when Holly invented the Silsby steam fire engine with its rotary engine and pumps. The first fire steam engine was produced in 1856 and the company went on to sell more pumps than any other U.S. firm.

The village of Lockport realized they had the potential for water powered industries and in 1858 recognized the need to develop manufacturing. They invited Birdsill Holly to relocate to Lockport and in 1859, The Holly Manufacturing Company was organized with the initial stockholders being former NYS Governor Washington Hunt, former Congressman Thomas T. Flagler, Charles Keep, Silas H. Marks, L.F. Bowen, G.W. Bowen and Birdsill Holly. Under the supervision of Holly, the company manufactured sewing machines, a variety of pumps and various metal goods.

To power his company, Holly built a tunnel system that drew water above the Erie Canal Locks at Lockport, which ran through the hydraulic raceways, spinning a water wheel or turbine that produced 3,000 horsepower to each piece of machinery in the factory.

With the factory operating, Holly began working on improving fire protection systems and designing a more efficient water delivery system. In 1863, using Lockport as a test market, he designed the Holly Fire Protection and Water System, which used water turbine and steam engine powered pumps to distribute

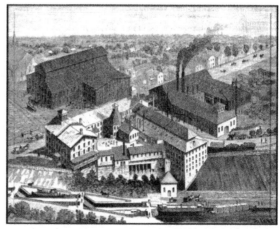

Figure 68 Holly Manufacturing Company along the Erie Canal

water under consistent pressure into the town water system. He improved upon the system and invented the fire hydrant in 1869, which looked very similar to the hydrants still in use today. Many cities across the U.S. and Europe adopted Holly's invention, with the exception of Chicago. After the Chicago Fire of 1871, the city purchased the Holly fire protection system for all of Chicago.

In 1877, Holly turned his attention to devising a steam heating system where one central plant would send heat to surrounding buildings, via a network of supply and return mains. The Holly Stream Combination Company was unable to attract sufficient investors, so he built a boiler at his home and ran a 100-foot steam line to heat a neighboring house. Holly then built a system that provided steam heat to several buildings in the central business section of Lockport. The success of these experiments resulted in central heat spreading across the U.S. and the company name being changed to American District Steam Company. By the end of the 19th Century, a number of district heating companies were formed in large cities, with Consolidated Edison, New York Steam Company, operating the largest commercial steam system in the world in lower Manhattan. Heating systems were also installed in factories, orphanages, asylums and universities. One of the earliest district heating systems in Detroit is still operational and was designated a National Landmark in 1985.

Birdsill Holly made important inventions that benefitted society and was successful in manufacturing these products for public use, however, his name is not known by many people outside of academic circles. This could be attributed to the fact that the inventions were of a mechanical nature and were not as glamorous as the phonograph, motion picture projector or telephone. It also could have been because Holly was not a good communicator and did not have an outgoing personality. Some contend it was the result of Holly divorcing his wife Elizabeth, with whom he had four sons, and marrying his adopted daughter. She was 28 years his junior and they had five children. This divorce and marriage resulted in Holly being shunned by society, his move to Chicago for several years did not remove this stigma, and his inventions were accepted without his name being associated with them.

Holly died in Lockport on April 27, 1894. The American Society of Mechanical Engineers (ASME) recognized two Mechanical Engineering Heritage Sites in Lockport – The Holly System of Fire Protection and Water Supply installed in 1863 and the Holly System of District Heating introduced in 1877. The progression from fire bucket brigades to Holly's system to deliver water hundreds of feet into a fire has saved countless buildings and lives, and central steam heating keeps many people warm during northern winters.

LUCIEN HOWE

*Ophthalmologist who initiated the use of silver nitrate drops
to prevent infant blindness*

Dr. Lucien Howe was born in Standish, Maine on September 18, 1848 and raised in New Mexico by his father, who was a military officer. He graduated from Bowdoin College and studied medicine at Harvard University and Bellevue Hospital before traveling to the medical centers of Europe for addition study. In Edinburgh, he studied with Dr. Joseph Lister, who was a pioneer in sterile surgery, and in Germany, with Dr. Hermann von Helmholz, who revolutionized the field of ophthalmology.

In 1876, he founded the Buffalo Eye and Ear Infirmary. In 1879, he became professor of ophthalmology at UB and in 1885, became an ophthalmic surgeon at Buffalo General Hospital. After working for ten years to reduce the incidence of infant blindness, in 1890 he was instrumental in getting the New York State legislature to pass the Howe

Figure 69 Dr. Lucian Howe late in his career

Law. This required the application of silver nitrate drops in the eyes of newborns as a disinfectant to prevent neonatal infection and possible blindness. In 1926, he donated $250,000 (almost five million in today's dollars) for the establishment of the Howe Laboratory of Ophthalmology at Harvard University. The American Ophthalmological Society annually awards the Lucien Howe Medal, the most celebrated award given by the society.

During his career, it is estimated that over 100,000 patients were treated at his clinics. He wrote two books and published 130 articles. He was president of the New York Medical Society, president of the American Ophthalmological Society and chair of the section on ophthalmology of the American Medical Association.

Howe was a proponent of the controversial science of Eugenics, improving the human population by controlled breeding to increase the occurrence of desirable inheritable characteristics. Eugenics was an elaboration of Charles Darwin's theory of natural selection, but Darwin did not agree that desirable human qualities were hereditary traits. Howe theorized that inherited blindness could be eradicated by sterilization of people who had hereditary blindness.

In 1890, Howe and his wife Elizabeth, who was one of the earliest graduates from Vassar College, purchased the home of George Beals at 183 Delaware Avenue. The home had an attached office, which served as Dr. Howe's office at 87 West Huron Street. Howe moved to 522 Delaware Avenue in 1912, where he had a magnificent mansion built by English architects, with his office being on the first floor of the home. When the Harvard Laboratory opened at Harvard Medical School in 1926, Howe left Buffalo to direct the facility. He died two years later at 80 on December 17, 1928.

Figure 70 Lucien Howe home and medical offices at 522 Delaware Avenue

WILLIAM BALLARD HOYT

Prominent contributor to business and politics in WNY since the early 1800s

D r. Jonathan Hoyt moved to East Aurora in 1817 from Saratoga, where he was born to Jonathan and Chloe Miller Hoyt on February 25, 1792. He was the second physician to settle in East Aurora and was one of the founding members of the Erie County Medical Society in 1821. In addition to his medical practice, he served as town supervisor from 1830 to 1834.

Jonathan married Prudence Eddy in 1813 and they had six children. Their son James M. was born in East Aurora on October 5, 1817. After he graduated from Geneva Medical College in Geneva, NY, James moved to Michigan. There he established his medical practice and served one term in the senate of the State of Michigan.

Prudence and Jonathan's son Horace was born in East Aurora on August 15, 1822. Horace graduated from the University of Buffalo Medical School in 1847 and practiced medicine with his father in East Aurora, continuing after his father's death in 1850 until his own death in 1896. In addition to practicing medicine, he was the postmaster of East Aurora and trustee of the City and County Hall for ten years. He married Josephine Ballard and had four children, including William Ballard Hoyt.

Orson Hoyt was born in East Aurora on May 20, 1825. He finished his studies at the Aurora Academy and taught school for two years in Kentucky, Mississippi and Alabama. Since his father and two older brothers were physicians, when he returned in 1849, he entered Buffalo Medical College and graduated from Rush Medical College in Chicago in 1850. After practicing medicine in Orchard Park for two years, he moved to Buffalo where he purchased a large tract of land between Main Street and North Pearl, north of Virginia Street. He built two homes on North Pearl and conducted his medical practice from one of these homes, walking distance to both Buffalo Medical School and Buffalo General Hospital.

During the 1850s and 1860s, Orson began purchasing real estate and in 1862 he opened a dry goods store at Main and Eagle Streets. In 1868, he discontinued his medical practice and concentrated on his store and various real estate holdings. He acquired sufficient wealth to build the Hoyt Mansion at 878 Main Street, behind the two homes he owned on North Pearl Street. Orson died on April 19, 1893 and this home remained in the Hoyt family until the 1920s. The home has been renovated and preserved and is currently the corporate offices for ZeptoMetrix in the medical corridor.

William Ballard Hoyt, the son of Dr. Horace Hoyt, was born in East Aurora on April 20, 1858. He was educated at Aurora Academy and Buffalo High School. He graduated from Cornell University in 1881 and was admitted to the bar in March. The law firm where he clerked became Humphrey, Lockwood & Hoyt shortly afterwards. Attorneys William C. Greene and George D. Yeomans were associated with the firm, which continued until he formed Hoyt and Spratt with Maurice C. Spratt.

In 1886, he was appointed Assistant United States District Attorney for the Northern District of New York and, in 1894, Assistant Attorney General for the United States Inter-State Commerce Commission for the States of New York and Ohio. His legal practice concentrated on business and corporate law, with clients including New York Central, other Vanderbilt Properties, Western Union Telegraph, Aetna Life Insurance, Western Transit, George N. Pierce Automobile, Buffalo Dredging, German Rock Asphalt, Buffalo Sanitary and M.H. Birge & Sons.

The Glenny House was purchased by William B. Hoyt in 1910. This house was originally built by Joseph Ellicott for his niece Sara Evans Lyon and was located at Main and High Streets. In 1831, it was purchased by Colonel Guy H. Goodrich who finished the construction and sold it to brewer Charles Gerber who lived there until 1892. The Main and High Streets area changed from a residential to an area dominated by industry, especially breweries, with Empire Brewing Company and German American Brewing Company located nearby. This was becoming the medical area, as Buffalo General Hospital was a couple blocks away. The home and its lot were sold to the University of Buffalo for construction of its medical school, with John C. Glenny purchasing the building for $300. He wanted to move the house, but City of Buffalo officials denied his request, so he had the house broken down into several sections and moved down High Street, to Humboldt Parkway, across Delaware Park to 1150 Amherst Street. The move in 1891 cost $10,000.

After the house was moved and reassembled, Glenny hired architect Charles Cary to design an addition. With the house being near the grounds of the Pan-American Exposition, Glenny entertained many distinguished guests during the Expo. During the existence of the home on Main and High and Amherst Streets, many members of Buffalo's elite society, including Presidents Van Buren, Fillmore and Cleveland, were entertained at the mansion. John Glenny died in 1906 and his wife sold the home to Hoyt in 1910.

When the Hoyt family purchased the home, they again hired architect Charles Cary to design another addition. Once completed, the mansion was reminiscent of a southern plantation mansion house. After William B. Hoyt died in 1915, his widow Esther lived there until 1945. She offered to donate the home to the Buffalo Historical Society, but the annual maintenance costs were too high. The home was sold to the Church Home of the German Evangelical Churches of Buffalo who demolished the mansion and opened the United Church Home in 1956. That facility closed in 2003 and the grounds were purchased by the adjacent Nichols School, who demolished the building and expanded their athletic fields. United Church Home continues today in Orchard Park as Fox Run Lifecare Community.

William B. Hoyt married Esther Lapham Hill, the daughter of Dr. John D. Hill, in 1887. They had five children - John, Josephine, Esther, Albertine and Hilda. Their son John was president of the Buffalo Niagara Association of Realters and joined the U.S. Army Air Corps during WWII. He was a captain, and there were no survivors when his plane, with nine other crew members, crashed off the coast of the Hawaiian Islands in 1943.

William B. Hoyt II was the son of Captain John Davidson Hill Hoyt and grandson of William B. Hoyt. He was born in Buffalo on June 20, 1937, was a member of the Buffalo Common Council from 1970 to 1974 and a member of the NYS Assembly from 1974 until his death in 1992. Hoyt II was interested in the environment and while he was a member of the Common Council, he proposed a plan to clean up Delaware Park Lake. Upon his death, the lake was named Hoyt Lake in his honor. In 1992, William B. Hoyt III (known as Sam Hoyt), won a special election to continue in his father's NYS Assembly seat, in which he served until 2011.

Figure 72 Hoyt Lake plaque honoring William Ballard Hoyt II

ELAM JEWETT

Newspaper owner that developed the Parkside Neighborhood

Elam Jewett was not related to the family of Sherman and John Jewett. He was raised in Vermont, wrote for several papers there before moving to Buffalo in 1838. He purchased the Buffalo Journal and Advertiser to form the Commercial Advertiser. The paper was published by E.R. Jewett & Company, with offices at 161 Main Street in Buffalo.

Jewett became one of Buffalo's leading citizens and he travelled with former President Millard Fillmore on a tour of Europe in 1856. After Colonel William Chapin died in 1852, Jewett purchased the Willow Lawn Estate on Main Street in 1864.

Elam Jewett's Willow Lawn property comprised the southern two-thirds of the Parkside area. He sold much of his farm to the city of Buffalo for the creation of Delaware Park and most of the rest to companies that were developing the Parkside neighborhood. The main developer was Parkside Improvement Company, owned by Elam Jewett, Dr. J. White and Washington Russell.

Washington Adams Russell purchased the land of Captain Rowland Cotton next to the Chapin farm. The 300 soldiers who died at Flint Hill during the War of 1812 were buried by Chapin and Cotton on their property line. Russell arrived in Buffalo in 1825, running the Cold Springs Tavern at Main and Ferry before he purchased the 200-acre Cotton estate in 1826, when Cotton moved to Lancaster. Four streets in Parkside are attributed to the Russell Family. Russell Avenue was the cow path where they led their cattle to the Delaware Park Meadow, Fairfield and Greenfield were the

Figure 73 Willow Lawn estate that Elam Jewett purchased from the Daniel Chapin family

Figure 74 Jewett's Willowlawn Estate 1901 - the day after the fall of the great willow tree

names of their pastures and Orchard Place was the Russell Farm fruit tree orchard. In 1841, Russell built the first brick home in the area, which still stands at 2540 Main Street. For many years it was the McKendry-Dengler and Roberts-Dengler Funeral Home.

The development of the Parkside neighborhood was aided by the New York Central Belt Line Railroad, which opened in 1883. The Belt Line was a 15-mile route that circled the city of Buffalo. It had 19 stops, each about a mile apart, providing access to all parts of the city. For a nickel you could get to the East Side, West Side, North Buffalo, South Buffalo, Riverside/Black Rock and Downtown, where the Exchange Street Station was located. The Belt Line helped establish commercial areas, with factories being built along the tracks, and residential developments in Black Rock, Broadway/Memorial, Kensington/Grider and the upper middle class, suburban setting of the Parkside neighborhood.

Before Elam died in 1887, he donated the land and most of the construction costs to the Episcopal Church of the Good Shepherd at 96 Jewett Parkway. His widow Caroline Wheeler Jewett continued living at the corner of Main and Jewett until her death in 1901. In 1892, she donated the land for the building of Buffalo Public School #54 at 2358 Main Street. After her death in 1905, her heirs sold the southern-most portion of the remaining Jewett property to Willow Lawn Development, where the last home was completed in 1917.

In 1913, the Park School opened in the former Chapin and Jewett Willow Lawn estate. The school became nationally known for its progressive education. When the Park School moved to its current location on Harlem Road in Snyder in 1922, the property was torn down. In its location the Main Jewett Apartments opened in 1927.

SHERMAN S. JEWETT & FAMILY

Owner Jewett & Root, bank president, railroad president, civic leader and philanthropist

T hree members of the Jewett Family arrived in America from Rowley, England in 1638 and were among the first settlers of Rowley, Massachusetts. A fourth-generation member of the family, Captain Joseph Jewett participated in the siege of Boston and died of a bayonet wound at the Battle of Long Island. His son Josiah was born in Lyme, Connecticut and moved to Moravia, New York in 1814. There Josiah Jewett raised a large family of nine children with his first wife Elizabeth Smith and six children with his second wife Sophia Skinner.

Sherman Skinner Jewett was born on January 17, 1818 in Moravia, New York, a small town in the Finger Lakes region of New York State. Moravia was also the birthplace of President Millard Fillmore and boyhood home of industrialist John D. Rockefeller. The eldest son in the family, Sherman worked at his father's farm and received a limited formal education during the winter months. After working as a clerk at a relative's store, he moved to Buffalo at age sixteen in 1834. Later in life, Jewett claimed he arrived in Buffalo with fifty cents in his pocket.

Jewett's uncle Isaac Watts Jewett owned a small foundry in Buffalo. He gave Sherman a job, where he learned the business from the bottom up. He became proficient in the moulders trade, his uncle provided him with some administrative training, and he furthered his education by attending a semester at Silas Kingsley's High School.

In September 1836, Jewett became a partner with Franklin Day and Francis H. Root in Root, Day & Company, a small foundry on Mississippi Street near South Park Avenue. A new firm was formed with Thomas Dudley a couple years later. After Dudley left, Jewett operated the company

Figure 75 Portrait of Sherman S. Jewett

on his own, until Root rejoined him in 1843. That company of Jewett & Root remained in business for 35 years and their primary business became the manufacturing of stoves. The Buffalo plant expanding to five acres of manufacturing, wholesale and retail activity, with branches in Chicago, Detroit, Milwaukee and San Francisco. In 1878, Sherman's sons Henry and Josiah joined the company and it became Sherman S. Jewett & Company.

In addition to his manufacturing company, Jewett was active in banking and railroads. The Bank of Buffalo was originated by Jewett and some of his associates. Jewett served as bank president from its inception until 1892. Jewett was also a director of M&T Bank for over 30 years, a director of Marine Bank for over 20 years, a director of Niagara Falls Bank and a director of Columbia National Bank from its formation until his death in 1897. Being a friend of Cornelius Vanderbilt, he was a director of the New York Central Railroad and was also president of the Western Transit Company and the Buffalo, New York and Philadelphia Railroad. The latter railroad was near bankruptcy, but he guided it to profitability and the $700,000 in bonds held by the City of Buffalo, were paid back to the city in full.

Jewett was active in various civic institutions, especially the Young Men's Association. In 1863, when the Association discussed purchasing St. James Hall and St. James Hotel to improve their facilities, Jewett subscribed $3,000. He also headed the list of subscribers for their erection of a fireproof library building. In addition, Jewett was one of the founders of the Buffalo Fine Arts Academy, creating a permanent $10,000 endowment, which became known as the Jewett Fund.

However, Jewett is best remembered for his involvement with Frederick Law Olmsted and the Buffalo Parks Department. On August 25, 1868, William Dorsheimer invited Olmsted to tour Buffalo and a meeting was held at Jewett's mansion at 256 Delaware to discuss a plan for the parks. Jewett was a member of the committee which reviewed Olmsted's plans and Mayor William Rogers appointed him to the Board of Parks Commissioners. When Pascal Paoli Pratt resigned as President of the Board in 1879, Jewett succeed him and served as president until his death on February 28, 1897 at age 79.

Figure 76 Jewett stove from 1871

Sherman Skinner Jewett's sons were Henry and Josiah. Henry Clay Jewett loved horses, trotters in particular, and built a totally covered one-mile track near East Aurora. Horses could train year-round at this facility which was heated during the winter. Josiah graduated from Yale in 1863 and went to work with his father. He was the president of the Buffalo Bisons baseball team from 1880 to 1885. Josiah was married to Grace Hall, daughter of Nathan Kelsey Hall, who was U.S. Postmaster General under President Millard Fillmore and later U.S. District Court Judge in Buffalo. After selling the baseball team, Josiah returned to his banking and manufacturing interests.

John Cotton Jewett was Sherman S. Jewett's brother. John left Moravia in 1820 to work with his other brother Samuel at his mercantile business in Ann Arbor, Michigan. In 1849, he relocated to Buffalo to open John C. Jewett Manufacturing, a small manufacturing concern. That company grew into a major manufacturer of refrigerators, shipping their products to all section of the U.S. and many foreign countries. After his sons Edgar and Frederick joined the company, John retired and died in Los Angeles in 1904.

Edgar B. Jewett was born on December 14, 1843 in Ann Arbor, Michigan, the first son of John Cotton and Priscilla Boardman Jewett. Moving to Buffalo when he was five, Edgar was educated in Buffalo schools and started working for his father's company in 1860. When the Civil War began, he enlisted as private, climbing through the enlisted and officer ranks until he was promoted to Brigadier General in 1884. He became President of John C. Jewett Manufacturing in December 1885, was appointed Buffalo Police Commissioner in March 1894 and was elected Mayor of Buffalo in November 1894. As mayor he implemented contract, public welfare and civil service reforms, and a began a school construction program, which included the building of Masten Park High School.

Frederick A. Jewett was the youngest son of John and Priscilla Jewett, born in Buffalo on November 10, 1859. He was educated at DeVeaux College in Niagara Falls, graduating in 1878. After graduation, he started working for his father's company, being promoted to Treasurer of the John C. Jewett Manufacturing Company in 1881, a position he held until his death in 1906.

EBENEZER JOHNSON

Successful businessman who was the first mayor of the City of Buffalo

Ebenezer Johnson was born in Connecticut on November 7, 1786 and relocated to Cherry Valley, NY, where he studied medicine with Dr. Joseph White. In 1809, Ebenezer Johnson came to Buffalo to practice medicine, not realizing Dr. Cyrenius Chapin had already established a practice in WNY.

When Buffalo was burned by the British in 1813, he fled to Williamsville where he treated wounded soldiers. Upon returning to Buffalo, he opened a drug store, invested in real estate, built a grain elevator and established a bank.

He became associated in business activities with Samuel Wilkeson, teaming with him to help build the Buffalo Harbor. Johnson and Wilkeson were given a contract by the Canal Commission to construct a dam across Tonawanda Creek, near where it joined with the Erie

Figure 77 Portrait of Ebenezer Johnson - the first Mayor of Buffalo

Canal. As part of this project they built a toll bridge over the creek, which led to the development of Tonawanda village. Later they were partners in shipping and real estate ventures. Through these enterprises, Johnson became one of the richest citizens of Buffalo.

When Buffalo became a city in 1832, Johnson was chosen as the first mayor, serving two terms. His salary as mayor was $250 per year and the total Buffalo annual budget was $8,000. That budget included the cost to cover street lighting, the night watch, road repairs, building bridges and other city expenses. The fact that Ebenezer Johnson was a physician became important when a cholera epidemic affected the city in the summer of 1832. Johnson created the Board of Health and McHose House, a hospital in an abandoned tavern. He and the Common Council issued a decree requiring the immediate burial of all dead and placed a quarantine on the city, closing all lake and canal traffic. He refused reappointment as mayor in 1833 but accepted a second term in 1834. During that term the amount of money that could be collected to cover the budget of the city was increased to $12,000.

Figure 78 Johnson Cottage built in 1832 was one of the first Delaware Avenue estates

In 1832, he built Johnson Cottage located on Delaware Avenue and extending from Chippewa to Tracy Streets. This 25-acre estate extended to a triangle of Carolina and Whitney Place, including the portion where Elmwood now traverses the property. The grounds were a large park, enclosed with a high picket fence, and included walkways and waterfalls. Many garden parties were held at the house during the summer and elegant balls during the winter. These parties featured live music and tables of food, and people were invited from the village of Buffalo and surrounding towns. The house burned in 1840 and since Johnson lost much of his wealth in the Panic of 1837, it was rebuilt on a less grand scale.

Johnson left Buffalo in 1843, moving to Tellico Valley, Tennessee and taking $83,000 to invest in mining. There he operated an iron ore mine with his brother Elisha Johnson, who was the former mayor of Rochester, NY. He died in Tennessee in 1849 at age 62.

After Johnson's death, his estate was split up. His house was purchased to create an academy for girls in 1851, originally called the Female Academy. The Academy changed its name to Buffalo Seminary in 1889. In 1908, the school moved to its current location on Bidwell Parkway. The rear portion of the estate was donated to Buffalo and in 1851 became Johnson Park, the first public park in the city. Elegant brick homes were built on either side of Johnson Park and it remains one of the oldest residential neighborhoods in Buffalo.

WILLIAM JOHNSTON

Buffalo's first settler

Johnston can be considered the first land owner in Buffalo. During the Revolutionary War, he was a lieutenant in the British Army stationed at Fort Niagara, where he served in the Indian Department. As an official for the British government, he first visited Buffalo in 1780 or 1781. In this position he gained the respect of the Seneca (Haudenosaunee), and when the British vacated Fort Niagara, although he had been promoted to Captain, he decided not to withdraw with the rest of the military but to remain in Buffalo. Johnston married a member of the Seneca tribe and in 1794, he built a home, north of Exchange Street and east of Washington Street. It was next to the store of Cornelius Winney, who erected the first building in Buffalo.

Due to Johnston's influence with the Seneca, they gave him two square miles of land, which included most of what became the original city of Buffalo. The Seneca included the land given to Johnston as part of the purchase agreement with the Holland Land Company. This resulted in the mouth of the Buffalo River being in the Holland Land Purchase territory and not part of the Seneca Buffalo Creek reservation. In consideration for Johnston surrendering his land claim, the Holland Land Company gave him a deed for 640 acres of land about six miles from the mouth of Buffalo Creek and 45½ acres that included the land upon which Johnston had already made improvements. Part of the land was the four acres next to Johnston's

Figure 79 Drawing of first houses at Buffalo Creek in 1798

house, bounded by Main Street and Buffalo Creek. Other than Joseph Ellicott, Johnston was the largest property owner in early Buffalo.

When Ellicott began his survey in 1798, Johnston was the most respected member of the community, by both the white settlers and Indians. He died in 1807 when he was about 65 years old. His son John was educated at Yale University and was considered one of the most accomplished young men in the settlement. John Johnston was employed by Captain Pratt at his store on Exchange Street and in 1808 married Ruth Barker, daughter of Judge Zenus Barker. He died in 1811, without any children, and his wife married Elisha Foster.

Captain William Johnston was not related to Sir William Johnson. Both were British Army officers who worked with the American Indians in New York State and were associated with Fort Niagara. However, Sir William Johnson fought in the French & Indian War and was the British Superintendent of Indian Affairs of the northern colonies. After his death in 1774, he was succeeded by his nephew Guy Johnson.

Their names are similar, Johnston and Johnson, but their individual accomplishments should not be confused.

Figure 80 The earliest known drawing of Buffalo by Edward Walsh of the 49th British Regiment Drawing depicts Fort Erie across the mouth of the Niagara River

JONCAIRE

The first white settler in Western New York and the first non-Native American
to settle within the current limits of the city of Buffalo

The name Joncaire refers to three separate people, Thomas Louis De Joncaire (the father, 1670-1739), Phillippe Thomas de Joncaire (eldest son, 1707-1766) and Daniel de Joncaire (younger son, 1716-late 1770s). The accomplishments of each member of the family are often confused, which is further complicated by each also being referred to by the name of Chabert.

Thomas was born in France and came to North America in 1687. Soon after his arrival, he was captured by Seneca Indians of the Iroquois Nation. When he was about to be tortured by his captors, Thomas broke his restraints and punched a Seneca chief, breaking his nose. The Seneca admired Joncaire's bravery, he was adopted into the tribe and married a member of the Seneca. Joncaire also had a French wife in Montreal, with whom he fathered many children. Marie-Madeleine Le Gay of Montreal is considered the mother of Phillippe and Daniel, but some records refer to Daniel as having a Seneca mother. This may be true because he was considered an Indian by the Seneca and membership in the Seneca tribe is inherited from the mother.

In 1719, Thomas Joncaire was given permission from the Seneca to build a trading post, which was one of the first structures in Lewiston. It was located on the current site of Artpark's painted parking lot, just east of the main theater, where a historic plaque is placed. The building stood until 1741, when it was destroyed in a fire. The 30 by 40-foot building was enclosed within a stockade and was later called Joncaire's Blockhouse or Magazin' Royal.

Thomas also used his influence with the Seneca to get permission for the French to build a trading post at the mouth of the Niagara River at Lake Ontario. This was in the location of what LaSalle called Fort Conti in 1679 and was later Fort Denonville. In 1726, The French Castle was built and called the "House of Peace" but it was actually a fort known as Fort Niagara. Thomas Joncaire became the portage master around the Falls and died at Fort Niagara on June 29, 1739.

In 1750, Daniel Joncaire was given his father's post as portage master and built Little Fort Niagara at the upper portage above Niagara Falls. It was constructed at Frenchman's

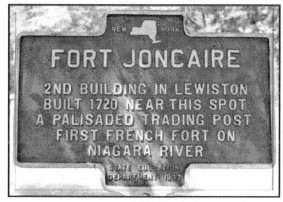

Figure 81 Plaque of Lewiston trading post

Landing, where a storehouse and blockhouse had been erected in 1745. Little Fort Niagara was abandoned by the French in 1759 and rebuilt by the British as Fort Schlosser in 1760, with a British shipyard across the Niagara on Navy Island. The Old Stone Chimney was part of Joncaire's Little Fort Niagara and was incorporated as part of Fort Schlosser. It still stands, at a new location, between the Niagara River and the highway leading to Niagara Falls State Park.

Figure 82 Plaque commemorating first settlement in Buffalo
Photo: Credit Angela Keppel

Daniel Joncaire was instructed by the Governor of French Canada to establish a trading post at the Riviere aux Chevaux (now called Buffalo Creek), because the French had plans to construct a fort at the Lake Erie entrance to the Niagara River. In 1758, Joncaire built a 100-foot-long pine shed, a 100-foot-long cedar barn, a 45-foot-long dwelling, a 20-foot-long blacksmith shop, a 25-foot-long storehouse, a stable and second barn. He plowed fields where he cultivated corn, tobacco and hay in an area one half mile by three quarters of a mile. The settlement was in the current location of the General Mills plant on Ganson Street but was only in existence for one and a half years.

In 1759, Daniel Joncaire dug a channel to divert water from the Niagara River to power mills he built between Little Fort Niagara and the brink of Niagara Falls. This made him the first person to make use of the Niagara River for water power. The diversion channel at the upper Niagara rapids created the man-made Willow Island, which remained until the channel was filled in during the 1960s to build the Robert Moses Parkway.

During the French and Indian War, the British attacked Fort Niagara in 1759. The Buffalo Creek settlement and Little Fort Niagara were abandoned and both Joncaire sons participated in the Battle of LaBelle Famille, just outside of Fort Niagara. In this battle French forces were attempting to aid the besieged Fort Niagara but were defeated. Fort Niagara fell to the British, with both Joncaire brothers being taken prisoner and returned to Europe.

Phillippe remained in Europe, but Daniel went to court claiming the Iroquois gave his father land on the Eastern shores of the Niagara River and at Buffalo Creek. He was not successful in his legal battle to claim title to the lands, but he later returned to America, settling in Detroit, where he died in the late 1700s.

JESSE KETCHUM

Businessman, landowner and benefactor to schools

The Ketchum family is of Welsh origin and can be traced back in America to 1635 when brothers Edward, John and Samuel Ketchum arrived at Ipswich, Massachusetts. John was a member of the Massachusetts Legislature and moved to New Town, Long Island in 1648. Edward moved to Southwold, Long Island in 1654 and Samuel relocated to Norwalk, Connecticut. Samuel's side of the family remained British loyalists and Jesse is related to this faction of the family.

Jesse Ketchum was born on March 31, 1782 in Spencerport, NY, in Columbia County, south of Albany. He was the fifth of eleven children. His mother was the educated and refined daughter of Judge Zubulon Robbins. She instilled her personality upon her son, but Molly Robbins Ketchum died when Jesse was only six years old. His father was a drinker, an attribute Jesse despised throughout his life. After his mother's death, he and his siblings were placed in the homes of family members and neighbors. Jesse was taken into the home of a William Johnson, a farmer and tanner. He learned the tanning trade but came into conflict with his foster parents because he wanted to obtain a proper school education. Eventually at age 17, he left home and walked to join his brother in Canada.

Seneca Ketchum, with his elderly uncles Joseph and James Ketchum arrived with friends from Columbia County and planned to reside in Kingston Ontario. However, when Governor Simco announced in 1794 that the capital was being moved from Newark (Niagara-on-the-Lake) to York (Toronto), they felt there would be more opportunities at the capital. In 1796, Joseph and James were among the first settlers of Scarborough, east of York, and Seneca settled on a new road opened from York to Lake Simco called Younge Street. After leaving his foster parents' home, Jesse walked from Spencerport to Lake Ontario, worked his way across the lake on a boat headed to Kingston, where he found work on a boat to York. He arrived at his brother's farm in 1799. Two other Ketchum brothers also relocated to Canada.

Zebulon Ketchum arrived in York a couple years after Jesse, bringing their father with him. Henry Ketchum also came to York before he decided to move to Buffalo in 1807. In Buffalo, he purchased property and built a home at the corner of Main and Chippewa. After his home and the city of Buffalo were burned down during the war of 1812, Henry moved to Holley, outside of Rochester, where he married Elizabeth Powers, a relative of Millard Fillmore's wife. Zebulon, who had also moved to Buffalo, remained in the city until his death in 1854. When his brothers moved to Buffalo, Jesse visited the city and purchased property. He frequently came to Buffalo and when the First Presbyterian Church was built in 1828, he contributed to the expense of the building and purchased a pew.

Widow Ann Love, who had a young daughter, was the housekeeper for Seneca and Jesse Ketchum. They both wanted to marry Ann so they drew lots to determine who would ask for her hand in marriage. Jesse won and that was in line with Ann's wishes because she favored the younger brother. They married on January 24, 1804 and Jesse built a home near his brothers Younge Street homestead. In 1812, when Jesse was 30, he moved to York and purchased a tannery from an American who moved back to the U.S. when the War of 1812 was declared. There Jesse then built a home at Yonge St. and Newgate, across from the tannery, which flourished during the War of 1812 as Jesse made shoes for Canadian and British soldiers.

Since Jesse was born in New York and his two brothers had moved to Buffalo, Jesse's loyalty to the British was questioned, but he joined the local militia and took part in the Battle of Fort York, where he was captured by the Americans and later paroled. When the war ended, Ketchum helped fund the rebuilding of bridges over the Don River in Canada and contributed to the building of the first common school in York.

After he became a successful merchant and landowner in York, Jesse donated his time and money to benevolent and relief societies and assisted in building or starting schools, churches, Sunday schools and bible societies. He assisted in establishing the York Mechanics Institute, which had a goal of teaching workers about the applied technology behind new methods of manufacture and craftsmanship. It offered lectures, held classes and operated a lending library.

Ketchum was an opponent of the Family Compact, which was an attempt to rule Upper Canada by an elite group of wealthy individuals who wanted to create family dynasties to solidify their positions of power in government, business and society. He helped organize reform committees and associations and was a member of the House of Assembly from 1828 to 1834. Although he supported William Lyon Mackenzie in the Assembly, Ketchum did not take part in the Upper Canada Rebellion.

When the Patriot War broke out in 1837, Americans in Canada were again looked upon with suspicion. Ketchum purchased land on Main Street between Allen and High to build a tannery in Buffalo. His first wife Ann had died in 1829 and they had six children. In 1845, Ketchum and his new wife, Mary Ann Rubergall, moved to Buffalo where he built a home on North Street near Elmwood, and Jesse left his York holdings to the children from his first marriage.

Establishing himself as a successful businessman and property owner in Buffalo, he decided to devote the rest of his life to giving his money away for the good of the community, rather than working to accumulate more wealth. Ketchum donated significant amounts of money to assist those in need during the cholera epidemic of 1849 and during the Civil War, he funded the care of enlisted soldier's families. He also would rent homes to deserving tenants and apply the rent they paid to the eventual purchase of the property, allowing people to own land that they otherwise would not have been able to afford.

In addition to helping individuals and families, he worked with religious institutions. Ketchum funded Sunday Schools at various churches and donated $5,000 to the building fund for Westminster Church. He also donated five acres for the building of the State Normal School. When the Normal School moved to 1300 Elmwood Avenue and became Buffalo State College, Ketchum Hall was named in his honor. The original site of the Normal School became Grover Cleveland High School.

The public schools of Buffalo received the most of Ketchum's interest. He would go to every school, urging the students to abstain from tobacco and liquor, rewarding the students that did well with prizes. Annually, Ketchum

Figure 83 Jesse Ketchum Homestead

visited every room in every school, delivering books to the students and teachers. This earned him the name of Father Ketchum. On his way to visit a school on September 7, 1867 Ketchum felt ill and returned home, where he died the next day. His funeral was one of the largest seen in Buffalo up to that time and the Buffalo schools were closed as a tribute to their benefactor.

William Ketchum wrote about Jesse Ketchum, he does not appear to be related to him, but there were several similarities. William became Mayor of Buffalo in 1844, beating Oliver G. Steele, the father of the Buffalo Public School system in the election. He worked in the fur and hat business and was also involved in the Buffalo School system, serving as a common school trustee in the 1830s. William lived at 109 Delaware Avenue and retired from business and political life in 1857. After retiring he took an interest in the early history of Buffalo and published *History of Buffalo and the Senecas* and *An Authentic and Comprehensive History of Buffalo*.

When Jesse Ketchum died his son-in-law Barnabas H. Brennan inherited the Ketchum estate and donated $10,000 to the Buffalo Public School System for the awarding of medals to be presented to students achieving academic excellence. The first medals were awarded in 1873 and until 1949 were minted by the U.S. Mint. One side featured a portrait of Jesse Ketchum and they were originally awarded to high school seniors and students in the last two grades of grammar school. The awards are still presented today, now awarded to eighth grade students.

Recipients of the medal today reflect the racial, ethnic and religious diversity of Buffalo. However, in 1884 Grace Celia Taylor was the first black recipient of the Jesse Ketchum gold medal. She won a small silver medal in 1879, large silver medal in 1880 and the large gold medal in 1884. Grace was the first black student admitted to Buffalo Central High School, the only public high school in Buffalo prior to 1897. When she won the award, she was the top academic student and only black student in the graduation class. Her father Benjamin C. Taylor was the second black physician in Buffalo. Although the top graduate in her class, Grace did not attend college. She worked as a musician and was the organist at St. Philip's Episcopal Church.

The Buffalo Public School System shares a distinction with the Jesse Ketchum medal, as it is the longest running medal awarded for academic excellence in the entire country. Since 1873, over 15,000 medals have been presented.

GERHARD LANG

*Owned the largest brewery in Buffalo, a city known for its
numerous quality breweries*

The first beer was brewed in Buffalo at the Cold Springs Tavern. This was
followed by small breweries, including the 1811 Joseph Webb's brewery in Black
Rock and in 1826 a strong lager brewed by Rudolph Baer. In 1830, the Jacob Roos
Brewing Company opened in the area called Sandytown, between Church and York
Streets. Roos purchased land on Pratt Street between Broadway and William, where
the brewery operated until Leonard Burgwerger purchased it and the name was
changed to Iroquois Brewing Company. In 1840, Joseph Friedman opened a brewery
on Oak near Tupper Street, which was purchased by Jacob Baumgartner and Mangus
Beck. Baumgartner moved to Exchange and Van Rensselaer, while Beck moved
Friedman's operations to Oak near Genesee and later to North Division and Spruce,
to form the Mangus Beck Brewery, which remained in business until 1956.

In 1842, Phillip Born started the Born Brewery at 581 Genesee Street at Jefferson.
Born operated the brewery until he passed away in 1848. His daughter Barbara Born
and Jacob Weppner ran the company until 1862, when Gerhard Lang bought out
Weppner's shares.

Gerhard Lang was born in Germany in 1834 and his father Jacob Lang brought
him to Buffalo in 1848, at which time Gerhard did not speak any English. Jacob was
a butcher and Gerhard quickly learned English while assisting his father at the shop.
While working for his father, he also learned proper business principles. After he
married Barbara Born in 1860, he began working with his wife at the brewery. The
business was already one of prominence and good repute, with Lang increasing and
expanding the company. They continued operating as a partnership of Born & Lang
until 1876 when the company became Gerhard Lang Brewery. An indication of the
importance of the brewery was exemplified when the Buffalo Brewers Association
was formed. At their first meeting in 1873, Gerhard Lang was elected president, with
Mangus Beck being elected vice-president.

Lang visited and inspected most of the prominent breweries in the country to
obtain information for further expansion of the business. He purchased 34 acres of
land on Jefferson Avenue between Best and Dodge Streets to build the largest
brewery that ever existed in Buffalo. People referred to the brewery as the "Palace
Brewery" because of its opulent Victorian design and quality of its operations. Lang
implemented the best features and machinery observed during his travels and
designed a building that looked more like a public institution than a factory. The
entrance featured a landscaped semi-circular drive, with a fountain in the middle. The
immense building was entered through a large lobby, with polished stairs leading to
the manufacturing space. Beer was made in vats covered with black walnut and ash,
bound with wide hoops of brass.

Figure 84 Gerhard Lang Brewery on Jefferson Avenue

Historically, Buffalo was known as the city that seemed to have "a bar on every corner." This was because Buffalo had one of the highest number per capita of bars and taverns of any city in the country. One factor contributing to the number of bars was the number of European immigrants that populated the city. Another factor was that local breweries financed or bought many of the corner bars that served their beer. This allowed the brewery to exclusively provide their product to the tavern and control where their beer was sold. Lang Brewing Company, at one time, owned 80 taverns, a contributing factor to it becoming the largest brewery in NYS outside of NYC.

In 1884, Edwin G.S. Miller, a former partner in George Urban & Sons, became a manager of Gerhard Lang Brewery and married Lang's daughter. After the death of Gerhard Lang, Miller became president of the brewery and ran it with Lang's son Jacob Gerhard Lang. Miller was also president of the German American Bank and president of The Buffalo Traction Company, a company that constructed expanded railway streetcar lines.

During Prohibition the company survived by producing cereal beverages and soft drinks, with names like AA Near Beer and Hyan-Dry Ginger Ale. They reopened immediately after the repeal of Prohibition and picked up with production levels where they left off prior to Prohibition. Due to competition from national brands, local breweries began going out of business and the Gerhard Lang Brewery closed in 1949. The former site of the business is now the Stanley Makowski Early Childhood Center, Buffalo Public School #99. That school is across the street from Johnnie B. Wiley Sports Pavilion, the former location of War Memorial Stadium (prior to that the site of the New Prospect Reservoir) and near Masten Park, Fosdick-Masten Park High School and the Masten Avenue Armory.

JOHN D. LARKIN

*President of the Larkin Company and a pioneer in
the mail order catalogue business*

John Durrant Larkin was born in his parent's home at 13 Clinton Street on
September 29, 1845. His father Levi Larkin moved to Buffalo from Sussex County,
England, after his sister Mary relocated here with her husband, brickyard owner
Edmund Ralph. Levi apprenticed as a blacksmith in England and worked for George
Jones until he opened Levi H. Larkin Manufacturing at the 13 Clinton Street address,
across from the current location of the Downtown Buffalo Library. His mother Mary
Ann Durrant was raised on her parent's farm in Guelph, Ontario.

Levi Larkin was considered a hero for extinguishing sparks in the belfry of the old
Court House on Washington Street during the Eagle Tavern fire of November 14,
1848, but he later contracted pneumonia while fighting another fire. He died on June
27, 1852, leaving Mary Ann Larkin a widow at 33 years of age, with seven children
ranging in age from three months to thirteen years. With the help of her husband's
foreman Robert Bingham, she continued the iron works until 1856, when it was sold
to Daniel S. Forbes and Stephen M. Newton. On November 20, 1865 John's mother
married Henry Hoag of East Hamburg and moved to his farm.

After his father's death John Larkin left PS #15 and at age twelve obtained a job
as a messenger for Western Union Telegraph. He then worked for William H.
Woodward, a wholesale and retail dealer in straw goods, artificial flowers, ribbons,
silks, satins, velvets and millinery articles. Larkin continued in Woodward's
employment for four years. His sister Mary married Justus Weller in 1861 and John
began working for him at his soap company. Over the next several years John lived
and worked with Justus Weller, lived and worked at his mother's farm in Hamburg,
took a course at Bryant & Stratton in 1865 and sold soap on the road for his brother-
in-law in New Jersey and Brooklyn. He also spent time at his mother's relatives farm
in Ontario and worked for Philo C. Balcom, who married his aunt Mary, at their brick
company store located at Main and Ferry, where he received $25.00 a month plus
room and board.

In 1869, Larkin returned to work full time for Justus Weller with their factory
being located at 964 Seneca Street in Buffalo. Weller sold that business to the Harris
Soap Company and they relocated to 913 South Halstead Street on the west side of
Chicago, opening J. Weller & Company, Manufacturers of Staple and Fancy Soaps.
John became a partner in the business and on May 10, 1874 he married the daughter
of Dr. Silas and Juliana Hubbard, Frances "Frank" Hubbard in Hudson, Illinois.

In 1875, John Larkin and Justus Weller dissolved their business partnership. John
received $9,579.06 for his interest in the company, $8,345.57 in cash and the balance
in soap already in the hands of agents in New York. John considered relocating his
business to Boston, Albany, Syracuse or Cleveland, but decided to move to Buffalo.
On April 9, 1875 he signed a lease with E.B. Holmes for a 3,000 square foot factory

at 196-198 Chicago Street in Buffalo. Elbert Hubbard, who was a salesman with J. Weller & Company, decided to relocate and work with his brother-in-law. The Larkins rented their first house in Buffalo at 213 Eagle Street.

Elbert Hubbard was on the road selling, while John remained in Buffalo operating the factory. He was always looking for good men to work with the company and in 1875 Hubbard found William Henry Coss and Daniel John Coss in Philadelphia and Frank Martin in Columbus, Ohio. The Coss Brothers began as outside salesman, moving to Buffalo in

Figure 85 Original Larkin factory at 196-198 Chicago Street
Photo: Courtesy Larkin Gallery

1880. William became the superintendent of the factory and Daniel in charge of shipping. They became stockholders in 1892 and served as Directors until their retirement in 1909. Frank Martin was responsible for bringing his thirteen-year old brother into the company. Darwin D. Martin began as a salesman and on August 7, 1879 was the first office employee of J.D. Larkin & Company, an association that would last for 45 years.

The business outgrew their Chicago Street plant and in 1877 John purchased two 30 by 150-foot lots at 663-667 Seneca Street. He built a 50 by 80-foot factory, powered by a six horse power motor, which became the first building of a complex that would eventually spread over many acres. The Larkins had also outgrown their rented home and in April, they purchased 218 Swan Street from Frances and Delia Root, where they would live for the next eight years and where four of their seven children would be born.

The first partnership agreement between John Larkin and Elbert Hubbard was in 1878, capitalized at $18,000 and the profit/loss of the J.D. Larkin Company shared two thirds to John and one third to Elbert. That was rewritten in 1885 with capital of $77,000 and the profits shared fifty-fifty, so Hubbard would spend more time in Buffalo and devote all his efforts to the company.

While on the road, Hubbard found that direct sales under the Larkin Company name to households were becoming more successful than large quantity sales to merchants under custom labels. Bert and John began offering enticements to attract direct mail orders, soliciting referrals from customers and advertising in local newspapers. Their first promotion was in 1880, the offering of "The People's Pets"

Figure 86 Larkin Administration Building designed by Frank Lloyd Wright
Photo: Courtesy Larkin Gallery

large chromo cards, provided with the purchase of Boraxine and Sweet Home Soap. In 1885, they introduced the Great Combination Box, followed by the Mammoth Christmas Box, which offered soap products along with premium gifts. These promotions worked so well that by 1887 all salesmen had been eliminated and the company depended entirely on the advertising and mailings.

In 1885, the company began using the slogan "Factory to Family", and expanded by constructing a five-story building. In 1886, the Larkin Company began offering Modjeska toilet soap, perfume, tooth powder and sachet, named after actress Madame Helena Modjeska, whose performances at the Academy of Music were enjoyed by John and Frank Larkin. Premiums expanded to include silver spoons and "Little Journeys" biographical sketches of statesmen and authors, which were later published by the Roycroft Press. Premiums later included furniture and the popular Chautauqua Premiums. In 1892, The Chautauqua Desk/Combination Box ad in the *Ladies Home Journal* exploded sales between 1892 and 1900. The desk was so popular it was included in the Larkin Catalog until 1920 and accounted for an average annual profit of $87,378.

The Larkin Secretary program began in 1890, where groups of ten housewives formed a club, each contributing a dollar to obtain a combination box every month. They shared the products and took turns getting the premiums. The members were called secretaries and club size eventually ranged from five to twenty members. The concept expanded to having local events, regional conferences, a national annual picnic for all secretaries and a periodical called *The Larkin Idea,* which gave details on Larkin products, premiums, info on how to form clubs and suggestions for social activities.

Elbert Hubbard was a pioneer in creating the idea of mail-order merchandising. By 1925 the Larkin Company manufactured most of their 900 catalog items, ranging from their core soap products to a very large assortment of premium products. One premium manufacturer, formed as Buffalo Pottery in 1903, was one of the largest fireproof pottery factories in the world and the only one completely operated by electricity. It continued after the Larkin Company closed, becoming Buffalo China, one of the largest manufacturers of commercial chinaware in the U.S. The Larkin Catalogue competed with Sears and Montgomery Ward; however, Sears was ten times larger.

On January 6, 1893 Elbert Hubbard resigned from the company and sold his 13,000 shares of stock to John Larkin. Hubbard started the Roycroft Press in East Aurora in 1895, which grew into an Arts & Crafts movement haven for artists, writers and philosophers. He died in the torpedoing of the Lusitania in 1915.

After the departure of Hubbard, the Larkin Company became more of a family affair. Charlie Larkin became a director in 1893, while sons John Jr., and Harry became directors in 1896. The boys all attended LaFayette College, before becoming full time employees, John Jr. in 1898, Charles in 1899 and Harry in 1903. Harold Esty, who married John's daughter Daisy Larkin, joined the company in 1897. Brother-in-law William Heath moved to Buffalo in 1898 to head up the legal department.

The company continued to grow and in 1895 John Larkin received board approval to build the first six story brick, steel and concrete building in the Larkin Complex. In 1906, Frank Lloyd Wright designed the Larkin Office Building, which accommodated 1800 corresponding secretaries, clerks and executives. It was considered the most modern office building in the world and it marked the beginning of Wright's association with Larkin employees and the building of signature homes for them in Buffalo. In 1912, warehouses R, S and T were constructed and by 1914, the floor space of the factories, warehouses and offices covered 64 acres. Employee satisfaction, health and welfare was very important to the Larkin Company. The buildings and benefits featured modern ventilation systems, fireproof structures, nine-hour workdays began in 1900, break rooms, lunchrooms, free coffee, social clubs, company bands, a YWCA, a library, school, dental office, doctor's office and company outings. The company reached its peak in 1920 with 23 million dollars in sales, 4,900 employees, 2,000,000 customers and 90,000 clubs.

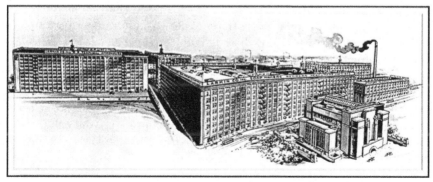

Figure 87 Larkin factory and warehouse complex in 1920
Photo: Courtesy Larkin Gallery

John worked hard but also devoted as much time as possible to his family. In 1882, he purchased property in the Idlewood Association formed by retailer J.N. Adam. It was an exclusive parkland along Lake Erie just east of the mouth of 18 Mile Creek in North Evans. A who's who of Buffalo businessmen and professionals had camps at Idlewood. In 1899, an attempt to purchase a property in Niagara-on-the-Lake fell through but in 1900, the property Glencaim in Queenston, Ontario became available from the Rumsey family. The property was built, on the site of a War of 1812 battery, by a member of the Hamilton family, after whom Hamilton, Ontario was named. All Larkin family members would stay at Glencaim during the summer and John purchased an additional 1,900 acres of farmland nearby, which he called Larkin Farms. Over time the family members moved their summer residences to the U.S. Lake Erie shoreline, purchasing or building estates in Derby, Sturgeon Point and Eden.

Larkin became more successful in business and with his growing family, on February 23, 1884, he purchased 125 Hodge Street, near Elmwood, from Charles J. Hodge. In 1901, the Larkins purchased 237 North Street from Frank Goodyear. The Larkins always loved Delaware Park and in 1909, John purchased the property known as Rumsey's Woods, bordered by Lincoln Parkway, Rumsey Road, Windsor Avenue and Forest Avenue. John called the property Larkland and built homes at 107 and 75 Lincoln Parkway, and 160, 175 and 176 Windsor Avenue for himself and his children, deeding the homes to his children after construction was completed. The Junior League of Buffalo Decorators Show House series began in 1981 at the Larkin House at 75 Lincoln Parkway, and other Larkin homes have been featured in the program.

John Larkin celebrated the 50th Anniversary of the company on May 1, 1925, and passed away on February 15, 1926. Sales of the company began to decline in 1921, with other sales from grocery stores, retail stores, gas stations and leases offsetting the main soap product and premium sales. The depression further reduced sales and changed how people purchased their products. Soap manufacturing stopped in 1939 and all other manufacturing was halted in 1941. However, there was so much inventory that the last Larkin mail order was shipped in 1962.

The Larkin Buildings were sold, with 726 Exchange Street becoming the Graphic Controls building and other buildings offering office, manufacturing and warehousing space. 716 Exchange Street is now The Larkin Terminal Warehouse housing Key Bank in the former First Niagara Financial Headquarters. 701 Seneca Street is The Larkin Center of Commerce, housing over 100 businesses and the Larkin Gallery. Over 2,000 people again work in Larkinville, and during the summer Larkin Square features Food Truck Tuesdays and live music concerts on Wednesday. The buildings that housed the Larkin Company are again alive with businesses and cultural events.

John Larkin, Elbert Hubbard and Darwin Martin made the Larkin Company one of the most successful companies in Buffalo. The Larkin Company may be gone but its name and spirit live on as part of the fabric of the WNY community.

LASALLE

French explorer who built Le Griffon on the Niagara River

Lewiston was the first European settlement in Western New York. The first French explorer, Etienne Brule arrived in 1615 and in 1626, Joseph de la Roche-Dallion preached to the native Indians at various villages. This was shortly after Samuel de Champlain was the first European explorer to navigate Lake Ontario in 1604. Champlain wrote about but never visited Niagara Falls, basing his reports upon information provided to him by the Indians.

The WNY area was the territory of The Five Nation Indian Alliance established by the Mohawk, Seneca, Onondaga, Oneida and Cayuga tribes. The confederacy was given the common name of The Iroquois, but preferred to be called Haudenosaunee, meaning "People of the Longhouse". The Peacemaker formed the confederacy in 1142. At the peak of its power, their influence extended from the St. Lawrence and Hudson Rivers, into Canada, along the Great Lakes and on both sides of the Allegheny Mountains into present day Virginia, Kentucky and into the Ohio Valley. Each Nation had its own language, territory and function. The Seneca were the protectors of the land and waterways of the Niagara River, Lake Erie and Lake Ontario and were known as the "Keepers of the Western Door." When the Tuscarora were admitted to the confederacy in 1722, they became known as the Six Nations.

Figure 88 Painting of Le Griffon at the Buffalo History Museum

Rene-Robert Chevalier, Sieur de LaSalle briefly visited the east bank of the Niagara River in 1669. He returned on December 6, 1678 and docked in Lewiston. The next day Father Hennepin walked to Niagara Falls and was the first European to write about seeing the Falls. At the time, there was twice as much water going over the Falls. Today half the natural water flow has been diverted to hydroelectric plants in both the U.S. and Canada.

In early 1679, LaSalle began building a ship on the Upper Niagara River at the mouth of Cayuga Creek at Cayuga Island, in the area now known as LaSalle. The vessel, was called *Le Griffon*, was built to trade with the Indians in the Western Lakes and was like a floating fort. It had a burden of 60 tons, had a crew of 34 men and seven cannons. The ship was launched prior to being completed in early May because they heard the Seneca planned on burning it. *Le Griffon* was towed through the Niagara rapids and sailed upstream to Black Rock, but the current and weather conditions prevented the ship from sailing any further. Finally, on August 7 favorable winds allowed the ship to enter Lake Erie.

On August 11, 1679 it arrived at the mouth of the Detroit River, sailed up to Lake St. Clair, entered Lake Huron, Lake Saginaw and Lake Michigan to the mouth of the Green Bay. LaSalle decided to remain behind to explore Lake Michigan. On *Le Griffon's* return voyage, loaded with over 12,000 pounds of furs, it was lost at sea with all on board.

After attacking Seneca villages in Central New York, in 1687 Marquis de Denonville sailed on Lake Ontario to the mouth of the Niagara River and constructed Fort Denonville, at the site LaSalle named Fort Conti in 1679, and later known as Fort Niagara. In 1689, Denonville sent Baron La Hontan to escort Indian allies to their western home. La Hontan found a large Indian village at the Eastern end of Lake Erie, which later became the site of Buffalo. La Hontan wrote to a minister of French King Louis XIV that a fort should be constructed at this site. The Baron wrote "rest assured that at the mouth of this creek there will be a settlement which will rival the speculation in favor of Niagara (which the French considered the key to Western New York); as the latter is at the head of Ontario, so this is at the foot of Erie."

The land around Niagara Falls was known as the portage and Lewiston was called "the carrying place." Indians were employed to carry goods from the lower landing at Lewiston up the Niagara Escarpment. In 1754, French soldiers cut a narrow road from the river to the top of the escarpment. A series of capstans and booms were installed to assist the oxen to pull wagons up the zigzag road. In 1757, the Seneca complained to the French Governor, but after the British won the French & Indian War in 1763, they expanded upon and improved the portage trails. Fighting over control of the portage led to the Devils Hole Massacre on September 14, 1763, about two miles south of Lewiston.

Their defeat in the French & Indian War ended French influence in the Niagara Frontier. If the French had concentrated on settlement, rather than just trading posts and forts, there possibly would have been more French history in the WNY area.

WILLIAM PRYOR LETCHWORTH

Founder of Pratt & Letchworth, created Letchworth State Park and humanitarian for children's welfare

William Pryor Letchworth was born in Brownville, New York on May 26, 1823 to Josiah and Ann Hance Letchworth. He was the fourth of eight children and grew up in a Quaker family that valued hard work, charity and the development of the intellect. When he was fifteen, he began working as a clerk in the saddlery and hardware business of Hayden and Holmes in Auburn, New York. By the time he was twenty-five years old, he was a partner in Pratt & Letchworth, which he founded in 1848 with Samuel Fletcher Pratt and Pascal Paoli Pratt.

The original business of Pratt & Letchworth was the manufacture and jobbing of saddlery and carriage hardware. Pratt & Letchworth continually expanded and became one of the largest manufacturers of malleable steel and iron castings, and material for locomotive and car builders. Their plant in Brantford, Ontario furnished nearly all the parts for cars made in Canada and the Buffalo plant supplied complete fittings for many railway systems in the U.S. The plants were renowned for the company's contribution to the comfort, health and general welfare of their employees. The grounds were landscaped with lawns and flower beds, while the company offered employees excursions and field days at Niagara River parks.

Letchworth's brothers were involved with Pratt & Letchworth since its inception, and members of the Letchworth family were the chief executives and managers of the firm throughout its existence. George became involved with his brother's company as a junior partner in 1848. William's younger brother Josiah Letchworth joined the company in 1856. Ogden Pearl Letchworth worked at the saddlery manufacturing company of his father George Letchworth in Auburn and was employed by Hayden, Letchworth & Smith in Auburn. Ogden moved to Buffalo in 1876 to join Pratt & Letchworth, working his way up through various positions in the company and becoming a partner in 1886, when his father passed away. When the company became a corporation in 1896, Ogden Pearl Letchworth was named president and Josiah became secretary/treasurer.

Letchworth worked hard and he was looking for a refuge from the business world. As a tourist he stepped off a train to gaze at the great Portage Bridge of the Genesee and fell in love with the valley created by the Genesee River. In 1859, he purchased land near Portage Falls, NY and began work on his estate named, Glen Iris. He hired landscape architect William Webster to design winding paths and roadways, glistening lakes and a sparkling fountain

After purchasing Glen Iris, Letchworth became fascinated by the native heritage of the Genesee Valley. He had a life-long interest in history and invited fellow members of the Buffalo Historical Society to the archaeological sites in the valley, where they collected many native relics. Over time, his interest continued to grow, and he purchased the Council House from the Caneadea Reservation, moving it to his estate. Letchworth built a museum to house his artifacts and allowed Mary Jamison to be buried on the Council Grounds, erecting a statue in her honor. For his contributions, the Seneca People named Letchworth Hai-wa-ye-is-tah, "he who does the right thing."

Letchworth retired from the business world at age 48 in 1871 but due to his Quaker heritage and desire to help his fellow man, he accepted an appointment to the New York State Board of Charities in 1873. Using his own funds, Letchworth traveled Europe and the U.S. to study the treatment of epilepsy and children. He wrote extensively on the treatment of epileptics, poor children and the creating of institutions to care for the helpless members of society. Letchworth retired from the State Board of Charities in 1896 and is credited with the development of epileptic centers and the foster care system.

In 1898, the Genesee River Company was formed with the objective of building a dam south of the Portage Bridge to profit off the power of the Genesee River by generating electricity. Letchworth's plan was to turn Glen Iris into an orphanage, but that would not be protected if the dam project proceeded. In 1906, he offered Glen Iris and his thousand acres to the State of New York for use as a public park. In 1907, Letchworth State Park was born, resulting in the dam never being built and the land being preserved for future generations.

William Pryor Letchworth never married and lived in his beloved valley until his death on December 1, 1910. He was buried in Forest Lawn Cemetery and a plain slab of stone from the Lower Falls of the Genesee River in Letchworth State Park marks his memorial.

Figure 89 Letchworth's home, Glen Iris, in 1896

JENNY LIND

*The Swedish Nightingale, who was considered the first
Entertainment Superstar*

Jenny Lind was born Johanna Maria Lind on October 6, 1820 in Stockholm, Sweden. She was raised by her single mother and inherited her musical gifts from her absent father, who was a traveling tavern musician. A lonely child, she entertained herself by singing alone in her room. One day an attendant to a Stockholm ballet dancer heard her singing and after the dancer heard Jenny's voice, she presented her to the director of Sweden's Royal Opera. He was so impressed, that although she was only nine years old, he enrolled Lind in the opera's training program. Jenny's mother also began giving her piano lessons and teaching her French.

Lind made her operatic debut at age seventeen and moved into the household

Figure 90 Portrait of Jenny Lind

of Adolf Fredrik Lindlad, one of Stockholm's leading composers. This introduced her to the artistic community, and she gained popularity in her home country of Sweden. In 1841, she moved to Paris where vocal teacher Manuel Garcia explained that since she was basically a self-taught singer, the way she was singing and breathing, was ruining her voice. He convinced her to take several months off, during which time he properly retrained her as a vocalist, increasing her range and vocal quality.

While touring Denmark, Lind attracted the romantic attention of writer Hans Christian Andersen. He wrote a story called, "The Nightingale" (Lind's nickname) and after she rejected Andersen as a suitor, it is theorized that he portrayed her as the

Snow Queen, with a heart of ice, in his fairy tales. Alternative rock performer Elvis Costello wrote an opera about the relationship between Andersen and Lind, along with Lind's association with P.T. Barnum.

Jenny Lind moved to Germany where she cultivated an image of respectability, performing concerts for charity, rather than depict the persona of illicit sexuality often portrayed by nineteenth century opera singers and stage stars. In 1846, she received demands for encores from the tough audiences of Vienna, the home of Mozart and Beethoven. In 1847, Lind and Felix Mendelssohn, one of Europe's greatest composers of the era, gave three concerts in the German city of Aachen, which inaugurated the celebrity status of Jenny Lind. However, that fame and public attention came to fruition in England where a dangerously packed in crowd was called a "Jenny Lind Crush"; a London & Brighton Railway locomotive was named after her, her image appeared on candy wrappers, handkerchiefs, snuff boxes and other paraphernalia, along with songs and dances being named after her.

Although Lind was relatively unknown in America, P.T. Barnum was certain that with proper promotion, she would be a huge success in the U.S. Lind personally handled the negotiations of the contract for the tour, with the terms surpassing any previous entertainment contract. Lind's contract called for $1,000 per night plus expenses for up to 150 concerts plus $25,000 for her conductor Julius Benedict and $12,500 for assisting artist the Italian baritone Giovanni Belletti. Barnum was accustomed to paying artists as a tour progressed, but Lind demanded $187,500 (over five million current dollars) be deposited in advance to her bank account. Barnum's faith in her resulted in him mortgaging all of his properties and borrowing additional money to make the deposit. However, Barnum's gamble was a solid investment as he eventually profited over $500,000 or 15 million current dollars.

Barnum's promotion of Jenny Lind for the tour was relentless. The promotion made Lind a star before she stepped foot in America. When her ship docked in NYC on September 1, 1850 there were over 30,000 people waiting to greet her. The demand for tickets at her first concert on September 11 was so great, that the tickets were raffled off. Lind realized the amount of money Barnum was going to make on the tour and renegotiated her contract even before performing her first show. Her admiration by American audiences was heightened when at the end of her first concert P.T. Barnum went on stage and announced that Lind was donating her entire $10,000 fee for the concert to local NYC charities. Lindmania was born, over 100 years before Beatlemania followed in the 1960s.

As the tour progressed, the crowd response and public admiration did not diminish. To provide privacy while traveling to concert dates, the first private railroad car was designed for her use by P.T. Barnum. In New Orleans, the demand for tickets to her 13 concerts was so great that an admission was charged just to attend the auction for available tickets. The commercial marketing of Lind's name and image resulted in the manufacture of Jenny Lind shirts, cravats, gloves, handkerchiefs, coats, hats and even sausages. All items were made without any merchandising agreement to share any of the profits with Jenny Lind. Additional use of the Jenny Lind name included the first Singer Sewing Machine being called the Jenny Lind; Jenny Lind Furniture, a cottage style spindled furniture, especially cribs and beds, being manufactured (they are still sold); Mammoth Caves in Kentucky named a cave feature the Jenny Lind's Armchair after she visited the site; and the community of Jenny Lind, California was named after her.

Lind performed 93 concerts with Barnum, and she netted $350,000, while Barnum netted $500,000. In current dollars is this approximately $10 million to Lind and $15 to Barnum. Prior to the concert tour Lind expressed that she planned to donate her earnings to charity, with her primary beneficiary being free schools in her native Sweden. She fulfilled this promise, and also donated money to local charities in the cities where she performed.

The association with Barnum was amicably terminated after a concert in Philadelphia on June 9, 1851. Lind self-managed the balance of her dates in North America and, shortly after the split, she gave a concert at the North Presbyterian Church in Buffalo in July 1851. After this concert Lind decided to take an extended vacation in the Niagara Falls region. During this time off Otto Goldschmidt, whom she would marry in Boston on February 5, 1852, joined as her new music director. The Cataract House in Niagara Falls and Frontier House in Lewiston were two of the locations where she stayed while in WNY. One of the two trains operating between Niagara Falls and Lewiston was renamed The Jenny Lind.

During her stay in WNY, in September 1851 a large section of Canal Street in Buffalo was destroyed by a fire. Keeping with her tradition of charitable contributions, Lind organized a charity concert for the victims of the fire at the Washington Street Baptist Church on October 15, 1851. Tickets sold for $2.00. $3.00 and $4.00, with scalpers getting $20.00 a ticket. A second show was scheduled two days later, with these concerts marking Lind's return to touring in the U.S. One of these shows was a performance in Washington, DC, and since Mrs. Fillmore had seen Lind perform at her Buffalo concert, President and Abigail Fillmore entertained Lind at the White House. The tour continued until May 1852 when she played her final concert in NYC, including a song written by Goldschmidt called "Farewell to America."

Jenny Lind is remembered as the first musical superstar to tour America. Buffalo was an important part of that tour as she performed a benefit concert for the people of Canal Street and made WNY her vacation home.

MARIA LOVE

Maria Love was the founder of the first daycare center in the U.S. and the last member of the Cary Family to live in the Delaware Avenue mansion known as Cary Castle

Maria Love was born January 26, 1840 on a farm in Clarence, attended Buffalo PS #10 and Central High School. Her father Judge Thomas C. Love was wounded and captured at the Battle of Fort Erie during the War of 1812. Judge Love was the attorney that defended the Thayer Brothers, who were convicted of the murder of Johnny Love (no relation) in Boston, New York. They were hung in Niagara Square on June 17, 1825, near the current location of the front doors to City Hall. The population of Buffalo was only about 2,000 people but over 20,000 to 30,000 witnessed the hanging. Maria Love's brother George Malthy Love was awarded the Congressional Medal of Honor for capturing the South Carolina flag after General Daniel Bidwell was killed at the Battle of Cedar Creek in the Civil War.

After her father's death in 1853, she and her younger sister Elizabeth moved from the Love home at Mohawk and Franklin to the Cary Castle at 184 Delaware. Her older sister Julia had married Dr. Walter Cary, who was the son of Trumbull Cary and Margaret Brisbane. Trumbull Cary was an agent for the Holland Land Company, which sold all their land in Chautauqua County to him and two of his associates. Walter Cary was very wealthy (his holdings included the Genesee House, a hotel at

Figure 91 Cary Castle at 184 Delaware Avenue
Photo: Courtesy David Rumsey

Main and Genesee Streets) and politically connected, with three presidents dining at the Cary Mansion. He remained a close friend of William Henry Seward, who was his father's attorney in purchasing and defending him in lawsuits for the Chautauqua county lands. Seward was Governor of New York from 1839 to 1842, the U.S. Senator from New York from 1849 to 1861, and Secretary of State for Lincoln and Johnson from 1861 to 1869 when he negotiated the purchase of Alaska from Russia.

Love traveled extensively with Dr. Walter Cary and her sister, crossing the Atlantic 14 times and visiting South America, the Middle East and the Far East. She believed that travel was the best means of education. During a visit to France she became aware of the plight of working women. Upon returning to Buffalo, Benjamin Fitch donated his former dry goods store at 159 Swan Street to be used as a daycare for children, while their mothers worked. The mothers were charged for the service but told they could pay when their financial conditions permitted. The center was called Fitch Creche and opened on January 6, 1881, with Love directing its operations for 50 years. In addition to operating the first daycare center in the U.S., she was a benefactor of the Red Cross. She also worked with William Pryor Letchworth in allowing orphans the opportunity to stay at Glen Iris for two weeks during the summer.

Maria Love was an amateur actress and starred in productions by local thespians. She also sang in the choir at Central Presbyterian and Trinity Church. After her sister Julia died in 1917, she took her place in society and as mistress of 184 Delaware Avenue. She retained her love of horses throughout life, was a member of riding clubs and kept a horse, carriage and sleigh until 1929. When Maria died in 1931 her estate was only valued at $120,000, much less than it had been before the stock market crash of 1929.

The Maria M. Love Convalescent Fund annually provides over $100,000 in grants to WNY residents that have medical requirements and funds to not-for-profit agencies that assist Erie County residents. Their biggest fundraiser is the annual Maria M. Love Charity Ball, which has been held since 1903.

After her death on July 20, 1931 Cary Castle became a rooming house and later the Normandy, an upscale restaurant and steak house. The property was sold to the federal government in 1964 and the Government Services Administration Building was constructed on Delaware Avenue between Huron and Cary Streets.

STEELE MACKAYE

Actor, director, innovator and inventor who started the first acting school in America

James Steele MacKaye was born on June 6, 1842 to James Morrison MacKaye and Emily Steele MacKaye, the sister of Oliver G. Steele, the builder of the Buffalo public school system. His father returned to his hometown in 1829 and opened the first private high school in Buffalo, the Western Literary & Scientific Academy, on the Pearl Block. When the school closed in 1846, the building became the first location of Sisters Hospital. After closing the school, he studied law and was a junior partner in a law practice with Millard Fillmore. Colonel MacKaye became a successful businessman, working with William Fargo as an organizer of Wells Fargo and with Samuel F.B. Morse in building the telegraph industry. He was instrumental in founding the American Telegraph Company and became one of the richest citizens of Buffalo. James MacKaye was active in the antislavery movement and was personal friends with William Lloyd Garrison, Ralph Waldo Emerson, Henry Clay and Abraham Lincoln. Colonel MacKaye worked with President Lincoln on the writing of the Emancipation Proclamation.

Figure 92 Portrait of Steele MacKaye age about 27

When Steele MacKaye was born his parents lived in a home called the Old Castle. This house was built in 1837 and it was sold to the government to become the Commandant's House at Fort Porter on Niagara Street, in the current location of the Peace Bridge. His father built two other houses, The Seminary on Delaware Avenue and The Tuscany House on Pearl Street. The family also lived in Johnson's Cottage. In 1832, Colonel MacKaye was one of the six founders of the Unitarian Church and he built the first church for the congregation.

While Steele was a child, he would visit Belmont, Massachusetts to stay with his aunt. There he became friends with his cousin, Winslow Homer, who was later considered one of the foremost painters in 19th Century America. In 1853, Colonel MacKaye became

Figure 93 Castle at Fort Porter – the birthplace of Steele MacKaye

president of the United States Express Company and moved to Brooklyn, with a summer home in Newport, Rhode Island. Steele was sent to Roe's Military Academy at age 14 but after two years ran away from the camp to study art under William Hunt in Newport. His father found him, and in 1858 they relocated to Paris where he studied under various masters at Ecole des Beaux Arts and studied his thespian love at Theatre Francais. As a teenager Steele was given unlimited credit at banks by his father, which resulted in him having little regard and even less command of money as an adult.

After two years in Paris, he returned to NYC and taught art, becoming acquainted with Henry David Thoreau, Walt Whitman, Horace Greeley, Henry Alden of Harpers and Wendell Phillips. While serving in the army during the Civil War, he passed the time by putting on theatrical plays. He married Jennie Spring, who he divorced, and then married Mary Medbury, a direct descendant of Roger Williams, the founder of Rhode Island. In 1869, his father persuaded Steele and his family to join him in Paris, where he first met Francois Delsarte, the actor and teacher.

MacKaye began his career as an actor and appeared in productions of *Hamlet* in Paris and London. He was the first American actor to perform this role in London. However, more time was devoted to his playwriting than acting. The majority of his twenty-five plays were successful, and in 1880 the play *Hazel Kirke* ran for 486 performances at the Madison Square Theatre, a record long run that stood for forty years. Utilizing MacKaye's concept of multiple companies, within the next five years the play was staged at various NYC theatres over 3,500 times.

After studying in Europe, MacKaye brought the Delsarte system to America. Francois Delsarte devised a system of actors portraying their emotions in bodily movement, expression and gestures. Delsarte taught this method in Europe and his sole American student was MacKaye. Neither Delsarte nor his protégé MacKaye wrote a book on the Delsarte system, but MacKaye's student Genevieve Stebbins wrote *The Delsarte System of Expression*, which was innovative in expanding theatrical and dance movements, along with influencing speech education and elocution.

When giving lectures on the Delsarte system, MacKaye expressed the need for acting schools. He proclaimed that if all other professions have schools, acting should be taught by experienced actors, sharing their experience to teach new actors. MacKaye organized five acting schools, including the Lyceum School of Acting. That school was taken over by one of MacKaye's students, Franklin Haven Sargent, and in 1888 became the American Academy of Dramatic Art, which is still in existence today. It is considered the first, oldest and one of the most respected acting schools in America, with campuses in NYC and LA.

Steele MacKaye and producer Gustave Frohman built up the Lyceum Theater on Park Avenue South between 23rd and 24th Streets in Manhattan, with it being the base for the Lyceum School in 1885. The theater was the first entirely lit by electricity, with reportedly Thomas Edison personally working on the project, and Louis Comfort Tiffany designing the interior of the theater. With Gustave Frohman as General Manager and MacKaye as Stage Manager, they presented productions of high moral quality and utilized MacKaye's innovations of his draw curtain, elevator orchestra platform and elevator traps. The theater was demolished in 1902 and in November 1903 Gustave's brother Daniel Frohman opened the new Lyceum Theatre on Broadway at 149 West 45th Street. It remains the oldest continuously operating legitimate theater in NYC, which is now owned by the Shubert Organization.

In the fall of 1886 Steele MacKaye joined Nate Salsbury and Buffalo Bill Cody to direct the indoor production of *Buffalo Bill's Wild West* at Madison Square Garden. MacKaye transformed Madison Square Garden into a huge theatre and since the show featured visual effects, he devised a pantomime for each actor. Reviewers praised the productions and high panoramas, considering the indoor Wild West superior to the outdoor version. It was a success as it attracted 10,000 to 18,000 people a day for more than 100 performances. The show then moved to London where it ran for six months drawing an average daily attendance of over 35,000 people.

In May of 1887 MacKaye returned to Buffalo to produce his independent play *Anarchy* at The Academy of Music on Main Street, between Swan and Seneca. An invitation was sent to MacKaye by 1,200 leading citizens of Buffalo, requesting that the play premier in Buffalo. After opening night, a grand banquet was held at the Genesee Hotel. The play depicted a mob of anarchists so well-rehearsed that it simulated reality. For political reasons the play was renamed *Paul Kauvar* and premiered in NYC with its cast increasing from 50 to 118 actors. As director, MacKaye coordinated all rehearsals and could assume the part of any member of the large cast. The culmination of Steele MacKaye's theatrical extravagance would have been at the Chicago Exposition in 1893. A Spectatorium or super theater with stage appliances to create illusions never before seen and a seating capacity of 10,000 people was conceived but never completed due to the Panic of 1892. MacKaye died in 1894 shortly after the smaller scale Scenitorium opened and before MacKaye could prove its effectiveness at the Chicago World's Fair.

It was reported Steele MacKaye had about 100 inventions that benefited theater but only fourteen patents were issued to him by the U.S. Patent Office. MacKaye's main concern was fire safety in theaters. He almost lost his life in a fire at the Brooklyn Theatre in NYC in December 1876, where between 175 and 300 people died. It was reported that during the sixty years that gas lighting was in use, basically from the first use of gas at the Chestnut Street Theatre in Philadelphia in 1816 until Edison invented the electric light bulb in 1879, there were 385 disastrous fires in England, France and America.

MacKaye designed a mixture of papier-mâché with clay and powdered asbestos, that could be folded into sheets to cover the stationary woodwork of the scenery, which made it fireproof. He devised a system where a series of trap doors would open and the area of the stage would serve as a chimney, with all the smoke and fire traveling upwards and not into the auditorium. The curtains were treated with the papier-mâché mixture or treated with zinc so they would not burn. Finally solder softened with bismuth secured the roof traps and curtains. It would melt at 160 degrees, automatically opening the drafts and dropping the curtains.

The folding chair was invented as a fire safety feature. With permanent seats, theater patrons were trapped between seats until they could get to the aisle which was clogged with people entering from many rows of seats. With the folding chair, multiple aisles could quickly be formed to exit the theatre.

MacKaye's next inventions were dedicated to reducing the time required for scene changes and he advertised that set changes only took 55 seconds. This reduced time span allowed theaters to open later and drew time conscious patrons to the theatre. These inventions included the double stage, over stage orchestra, elevator stage for orchestra, sliding stage, telescopic stage and floating stage. When one stage was in use, the next stage was set up and moved into place at the completion of the act. MacKaye was also responsible for air cooling devices (blowing air over ice), playbills and various effects.

Steele MacKaye is not a household name and he did not obtain financial prosperity from his work, but he was responsible for starting the first acting school in America and his inventions-innovations changed the face of theatres.

OTHNIEL CHARLES MARSH

Paleontologist who popularized the study of dinosaurs and was responsible for identifying and naming hundreds of species and fossil animals, including Brontosaurus, Pterosaur, Ichthyornis, Stegosaurus, Triceratops and Allosaurus

Othniel Charles Marsh, the son of Caleb and Mary Peabody Marsh, was born on October 29, 1831 on a farm on Chestnut Ridge Road in Lockport. When his mother died of cholera when he was three years old, his father moved the family back to Danvers, Massachusetts. After his father returned to the Lockport farm, Marsh remained in Danvers and lived with his aunts. At thirteen years of age Marsh moved back to Lockport, where he lived in a stone house near the Lockport Gulf and Deep Cut of the Erie Canal.

In 1844, Marsh befriended Colonel Ezekiel Jewett, a veteran of the War of 1812 and the commander of Fort Niagara, from 1826 to 1843. Jewett just retired from the military and enjoyed collecting minerals and marine fossils known as trilobites. That year the Erie Canal was being expanded and the exposed rock strata revealed vast mineral deposits and trilobite fossils. Jewett and Marsh, with pickaxes in hand, searched the digs for specimens. It was from this experience that Marsh gained his love and obsessive compulsion for collecting fossil treasures. Jewett's fossil collection was sold to Cornell University in 1868, his collection said to be one of the largest private collections in the country. In addition to influencing Marsh, Jewett was also a mentor to Charles Doolittle Walcott of the Smithsonian Institution.

Like most youths in agricultural communities, Marsh attended school during the winter and worked at the family farm during the summer. He attended the Lockport schools and at 16 years of age entered the Collegiate Institute in Wilson for two winter terms. At 19 years of age he entered the Lockport Union School and took a teaching position in Millersport (now part of Amherst), for $16.00 per month. He only continued teaching until he earned sufficient funds to travel to his aunt's home in Danvers.

While in Danvers, Marsh's Peabody family connections came into fruition. His Aunt Judith, in addition to his mother Mary, were sisters of entrepreneur George Peabody, who was also born in Danvers. Peabody began his career in the dry good business and became the most important American banker and financier in London. His business partner was Junius Spencer Morgan, the father of J.P. Morgan, with J.P. continuing the business after Peabody and Junius Morgan retired. Peabody devoted his later life to giving away his fortune and is considered the father of modern philanthropy. On April 30, 1868, the town of Danvers, adjacent to Salem, one of the earliest settled towns in America, changed its name to Peabody in honor of George Peabody.

Figure 94 Othniel Marsh (upper center) with his associates on an expedition

At age twenty Marsh received a $1,200 endowment from his Uncle George Peabody, which he used to attend Phillips Academy, a college prep school in Andover, Massachusetts. Marsh dedicated more time to hunting and rock gathering than academics during his first year at Phillips. However, after the death of his sister Mary in 1851, he applied himself and became an academic and student leader. George Peabody was impressed with Marsh's progress and agreed to support his undergraduate and graduate studies in geology and minerology at Yale University.

After graduating from Yale in 1863, Marsh studied at European Universities and at the British Museum. While in London he met with his Uncle George Peabody and on Marsh's recommendation he donated $150,000 to Yale University, to create the Peabody Museum of Natural History, now one of the oldest, largest and most prolific university natural history museums in the world. The grant delegated Othniel Marsh as a trustee and when Yale established a chair of paleontology, Marsh was appointed the first professor of paleontology in the U.S.

When the tracks were being built by the railroads across Kansas, Nebraska, Colorado and Wyoming, they began finding unusual bones and other fossils that they sent back to East Coast experts to identify and preserve. Marsh personally financed expeditions to the dinosaur sites and established a persona as a cowboy scientist. His expeditions and discoveries were chronicled in scientific journals and major newspapers.

Future adversary, Edward Drinker Cope was the son of a wealthy Philadelphia merchant and a self-taught naturalist. He submitted a paper to the Philadelphia Academy of Natural Sciences and University of Pennsylvania while still in his teens, which began his acceptance in the academic community. Cope set up a workshop and study in the brownstone adjacent to his home in Philadelphia. However, Cope never had the funding provided to Marsh by his uncle George Peabody or the Yale University Peabody Museum of Natural History.

In 1863, Cope met Marsh when Marsh was studying at the University of Berlin and Cope was touring Europe. Marsh had Ivy League degrees and Cope did not have any formal education, but Cope had published 37 scientific papers compared to only two produced by Marsh. However, they had similar interests and became friends. They even named dinosaurs after each other. That changed when Marsh paid a New Jersey site manager to send him shipments of fossils from a dig being performed by Cope. Their relationship totally deteriorated when Marsh attended a Philadelphia Academy of Natural Sciences exhibit and pointed out that the head of a marine dinosaur named Elasmosaurus was placed on its tail rather than its neck. Marsh was correct and Cope unsuccessfully tried to recall and buy back the scientific paper he published with the incorrect assemblage.

Bone Wars was the name given to the conflict between competing paleontologists Edward Drinker Cope and Othniel Charles Marsh. Their competition to be the first to identify and name new dinosaurs resulted in rushed publications, attempts to destroy each other's reputations, along with allegations of spying, bribery, stealing employees, treaty violations and events including the accused dynamiting by Marsh of a Cope fossil site. Their rivalry and contempt for each other became more important than their scientific work. During his life Cope published over 1,400 scientific papers, with a large number of them dedicated to discrediting Marsh. The competition and their continual attacks against each other in scientific journals even resulting in reduced funding to U.S. Geological Survey headed by John Wesley Powell.

The competition between Marsh and Cope was continued by their associates after Cope's death in 1896 and Marsh's death in 1899. Even until the present day, there are opposing schools of paleontology that side with either Marsh or Cope. Regardless of the controversies, they brought attention to the study of fossils; it was Lockport's Othniel Charles Marsh that was one of the first paleontologists that made a connection between dinosaurs and birds, a theory which is expounded by current day scientists.

Othniel Charles Marsh was president of The National Academy of Sciences from 1883 to 1895. Since he never married, he left his estate to Yale University, with his former home, now Marsh House, housing the Yale School of Forestry and Environmental Studies and being declared a National Historic Landmark in 1965.

If you are wondering who won Bone Wars? The final tally of identified dinosaurs was Cope 56 and Marsh 80.

JOSEPH GRIFFITHS MASTEN

Judge, Mayor of Buffalo and purchaser of Poinsett Barracks

Joseph Masten was born in Red Hook, New York on June 24, 1809. After attending school in Granby, Connecticut he graduated from Union College in Schenectady, NY at age nineteen. Masten studied law in Kingston, NY at the offices of A.B. Hasbrouch and Judge Ruggles, and in Oxford, NY at the office of Henry Vanderlyn.

After being admitted to the bar, Masten worked at the office of Henry W. Rogers in Bath, NY. After he moved to Buffalo, he again partnered with Rogers in 1836. He later formed law partnerships with Evert Van Buren and Thomas Dudley, but although he was devoted to the law, Masten was more interested in politics.

In 1843, Masten was elected the eleventh mayor of Buffalo at age 34 and was the first member of the Democratic Party elected mayor of the city. The emphasis during the first term of his administration was the school system. Salaries were set for the Superintendent of Schools at $500 per year, male teachers not to exceed $600 per year and female teachers not to exceed $200 per year. Also, during his term, the first St. Patrick's Day was celebrated by the growing Irish population in Buffalo, with a dinner at the Mansion House. On April 5, 1843 an ordinance was passed that owners of buildings and vacant lots had to keep the sidewalks and gutters in front of their property free from snow and mud. Masten did not seek re-election in 1844 but was elected to a second term in 1845.

When he moved to Buffalo, he and his wife Christina Cameron, of the prosperous Cameron family from Bath, NY, lived in a home on Swan Street. Then for $3,500 he purchased the former Poinsett Barracks on September 22, 1847 from Ebenezer Walden. Only the home of the commandant and post surgeon remained on the property. The house was a duplex, with quarters for the officer and his family on each side. In 1848, Masten had architect Thomas Tilden remodel the duplex into a single-family home and expand the former officer's quarters. The first floor of the former house became the present library and exhibit room, and rooms above became the bedrooms. The entrance had

Figure 95 Portrait of Joseph Masten

originally faced the parade grounds, but Masten had a porch built and entrance changed to face Delaware Avenue and extra rooms added to the new back of the home. He called the property Chestnut Lawn, after the many chestnuts that fell from trees on the estate. After he sold the Delaware Avenue property, he lived in a stone home at the southwest corner of Elmwood Avenue and North Street.

The Poinsett Barracks came into existence due to tense American and Canadian relations during the Patriot War. In 1837, William Lyon MacKenzie led Canadian patriots in the Patriot War, attempting to obtain self-rule from the British. The patriot forces tried to capture arms that were stored in Toronto, but they were disbursed by British forces and Canadian militia. MacKenzie crossed the border and escaped to Buffalo, where he found sympathetic Americans and Canadians that joined him. They created an independent provisional government on British Navy Island, off Grand Island and above Niagara Falls. This allowed MacKenzie to have a base on Canadian soil and easy access for supplies from the Americans. The British considered the encampment on Navy Island an illegal invasion of Canadian territory. Canadian Loyalist Colonel Sir Allen MacNab ordered Canadian Militia to cross the Niagara River on December 19, 1837 and seize the ship the *Caroline* that was taking supplies to Navy Island. The *Caroline* was docked on U.S. soil at Fort Schlosser; the Canadian militia towed her into the current, set the ship on fire and cast her adrift to go over Niagara Falls. There was one confirmed American casualty - Amos Durfee.

To relieve the tensions between Canada and the U.S., President Martin Van Buren ordered General Winfield Scott to Buffalo to assume command of U.S. regular army and local militia. The troops stayed in various places in the Buffalo area until they leased land from former Buffalo Mayor, Ebenezer Walden, for the Buffalo Barracks bordered by Main, Allen, Delaware and North Streets. It was renamed Poinsett Barracks after Van Buren's secretary of war, Joel Robert Poinsett. Poinsett was the ambassador to Mexico and his interest in botany led him to send clippings of a wild growing plant with green and red leaves to his greenhouse in the U.S. in 1825. This native growing plant was associated with Christmas in Mexico dating back to the 16th century. When introduced to the U.S., it was called the Poinsettia and became widely used in Christmas floral displays.

The barracks were dedicated by President Van Buren on May 6, 1839 and many other presidents were future guests. Zackary Taylor visited in 1840 because his daughter was the wife of the post surgeon and she lived in the officer's quarters which later became Masten's house. John Tyler visited in 1841 and John Quincey Adams in 1843. Being from Buffalo, Millard Fillmore was there on a number of occasions and Grover Cleveland visited because the house was later owned by Albert Pierce Laning, one of his law firm partners. Other visitors to the barracks or the Masten/Wilcox house included Abraham Lincoln, Ulysses S. Grant, William McKinley, William Howard Taft, Woodrow Wilson and Franklin D. Roosevelt. Theodore Roosevelt was inaugurated President in the home when it was owned by Ansley Wilcox. The barracks closed in 1845 and the army base in Buffalo became Fort Porter on the Niagara River.

After Masten served as Mayor of Buffalo, in 1847 he was elected City Recorder, a post he held from 1848 to 1862. From 1856 until his death on April 14, 1871 Masten held the office of Superior Court Judge, serving with George W. Clinton and Isaac Verplanck. He was involved as a council member in establishing the medical school in Buffalo and the University of Buffalo. Masten also was a trustee of Grosvenor Library and a lecturer on Commercial Law at Bryant & Stratton.

Prior to Masten moving to Buffalo, in 1832 a new cemetery had to be selected to replace the Franklin Square Cemetery. The site chosen extended from East North to Best Street and Michigan to Cemetery Street. That cemetery fell into disuse and it was closed in 1886, with the graves being moved to Forest Lawn. After it closed, the cemetery grounds became a park, (part of Frederick Law Olmsted's city plans), named Masten Park and in 1897, Cemetery Street was renamed Masten Avenue. Masten Park High School was built within the park in 1897. It was destroyed by a fire on March 27, 1912; the principal, Frank Fosdick, was almost killed when he went back into the school to make certain all the students and staff were out of the building. Rumor spread that the site was cursed because it was built upon a cemetery. The school was rebuilt at 186 East North Street as Fosdick-Masten High School, became Fosdick-Masten Vocational High School and is now the home of City Honors School. In addition to the street, school and park, the Masten Avenue Armory and the Masten District of the City of Buffalo were named after Joseph Masten.

Figure 96 Original Masten Park High School

JOHN G. MILBURN

*Attorney, President of the Pan-American Exposition and owner of the
Delaware Avenue mansion where President McKinley died*

John G. Milburn was born in Newcastle-on-Tyne, England in 1851 and at 18 years of age emigrated to America to join his sister-in-law who had moved to Batavia. There he taught school and studied law at the Batavia offices of Wakeman & Watson. When he was admitted to the bar in 1874, an exception had to be made because he was not yet a citizen. The following year he married Mary Patty Stocking, from Pike in Wyoming County, and he became a U.S. Citizen.

In 1876, John and Mary Patty Milburn moved to Buffalo with Milburn setting up a solo practice before forming a partnership with E. Carlton Sprague and Henry W. Sprague in 1879. Milburn moved to Denver, Colorado for a year to practice with former Senator Edward Wolcott, returning to Buffalo in 1883 to form a partnership with Sherman S. Rogers and Franklin D. Locke. John and his wife Mary Patty were proponents of establishing free kindergartens in Buffalo, and during his residence in Buffalo, Milburn was the president of the Buffalo Free Kindergarten Association. The Milburns had three sons, John George Jr., Devereux and Ralph, who were raised at the Milburn Home at 1168 Delaware.

The Milburn boys grew up in the affluent Delaware Avenue neighborhood, where they enjoyed playing sports. After Dr. Cary introduced polo to Buffalo, the city was considered one of the homes of American polo. The Milburns, Carys, Rumseys, along with Jack Scatcherd, Harry Hamlin and Dr. Hopkins put a team together at the Country Club, that competed in Newport, Rhode Island during one of the first polo matches in America. If not riding the boys were playing baseball, with the Milburns attending Heathcote School and the Rumseys, Laveracks and Hal Morvis attending Nichols. These two teams had a bitter baseball rivalry. The boys from the Delaware Avenue families could also be found swimming during the summer or playing hockey during the winter at Rumsey Park, behind the Rumsey family mansions on Delaware. Later in life, sports took a toll on the Milburn boys. John Jr. died in 1932 of internal hemorrhaging, believed to be attributed to the many injuries received while playing polo. Devereux died of a heart attack in 1942; however, was considered the greatest polo player in America, leading his team the Big Four in international competitions and winning the Westchester Cup six times.

President McKinley had fond memories of his trip to Buffalo on August 24-26, 1897 for the National Grand Army of the Republic Convention and a visit to the intended site of the Pan-Am on Cayuga Island in Niagara Falls. He was scheduled to give the opening speech at the Pan-American Exposition in May, but his wife became ill during a trip to the West Coast, so the Buffalo visit, speech and Presidents Day were rescheduled for September 5, 1901.

Figure 97 Milburn mansion in 1901 – home where President McKinley died

McKinley arrived in Buffalo on September 4, 1901 and the visit got off to an auspicious start when a cannon, which fired a salute to welcome the president, was placed too close to the tracks and blew out several windows of the train. This shook up the First Lady, and people in the crowd, thinking a bomb exploded, began shouting anarchists. Ironically, Leon Czolgosz, who would shoot McKinley two days later, was in the welcoming crowd at the train station but could not get close to the president. The President's personal secretary, George B. Cortelyou, was worried about the President's security at the Pan-Am, especially the reception at the Temple of Music, and tried to convince McKinley to remove the event from his schedule. McKinley refused because he enjoyed meeting the people, wanted to help the Pan-Am and did not fear potential assassins. The discouraged and concerned Cortelyou telegraphed Buffalo authorities to arrange for additional security.

The President's speech on September 5 went well, attended by an estimated 50,000 people, and on the morning of September 6, McKinley visited Lewiston and Niagara Falls. He returned to the Pan-Am and a reception was held in the Temple of Music. Leon Czolgosz attempted to get close to McKinley during his speech but returned early the following day to obtain a place in the reception line to shake the President's hand. Czolgosz had a handkerchief wrapped around his right hand, as if it was injured, and McKinley reached to shake his left hand. The moment their hands met, Czolgosz fired two point-blank shots into McKinley's abdomen from the gun concealed under the handkerchief.

McKinley was operated on under less than ideal conditions by Dr. Matthew D. Mann, a noted gynecologist but not an experienced gunshot or abdominal wound surgeon. Dr. Roswell Park, the best surgeon in Buffalo and medical director of the Pan-Am, was not available as he was performing an operation in Niagara Falls. When Dr. Mann's operation was completed McKinley was taken to the Milburn house, where he died, eight days later, on September 14, 1901. During these eight days, the Milburn home was filled with politicians, dignitaries, relatives and doctors, the stables were converted to executive offices with telegraph equipment and security of the grounds was provided by police and Army infantry. The Milburns moved out of their home, staying at a local hotel, and their four household servants were assisted by staff from neighboring mansions.

After the Pan-American Exposition ended John Milburn announced that the event had lost over six million dollars and would have to default on over three and a half million dollars in bonds. He denied that the money spent on the exposition was a foolish expenditure because millions of dollars poured into the city and Buffalo received worldwide attention.

In 1904, Milburn moved to New York City where he helped form one of the most prestigious law firms in the country, Carter, Ledyard & Milburn. Carter was the prosecutor of Boss Tweed from Tammany Hall and defended the constitutionality of the U.S. federal income tax. Ledyard was J.P. Morgan's closest advisor and a trustee for many large estates. In New York, the Milburns resided in an estate called Groombridge in Manhasset on Long Island. While living in NYC, Milburn was counsel to many important clients, which included the New York Stock Exchange; he was awarded an honorary Doctor of Law from Harvard University in 1922 and in 1924 he was elected head of the New York State Bar Association. Milburn died while visiting England in 1930 at age 79.

When John Milburn moved to NYC in 1904, the house at 1168 Delaware was sold to oilman Philip Mark Shannon. His daughter converted the home into luxury apartments, with George Rand Jr. and his sisters living at the home while their mansion next door at 1180 Delaware was being completed. In 1928, Conrad Wettlauger purchased the home turning it into eight apartments, and in 1948, it was purchased by the Jesuit community of Canisius High School as a cloistered home. It was torn down in 1957, and the location where President McKinley died is now a parking lot in front of Canisius High School.

MAJOR LUDOWICK MORGAN

Major Morgan was the hero of The Battle of Conjocta Creek

After the Battle of Lundy's Lane, the American forces fell back to their defensive stronghold – Fort Erie. The British felt the best way to stop the American supply to the fort was by attacking Black Rock and Buffalo. British forces crossed the Niagara River and landed north of Conjocta, now Scajaquada Creek. They had to travel upstream because the creek was deep near the Niagara River and the closest bridge was near the current Grant Street bridge. Major Ludowick Morgan was the commander of 240 members of the 1st and 4th Regiments, ordered to protect this crossing. American forces dug in on the south side of the bridge and every evening removed planks of the bridge so it could not be crossed.

On the morning of August 3, 1814, the British attacked the bridge and not knowing the planks had been removed, attempted to cross. The British troops either fell into the creek or were bottlenecked on the bridge, easy targets for the Kentucky sharpshooters on the American side. The British then tried to cross further upstream, in the current vicinity of Forest Lawn Cemetery, but were again repelled. After these defeats, the British crossed the Niagara River back into Canada and the battle became the last hostile movement towards Buffalo during the War of 1812. Unfortunately, Major Morgan was killed by a sniper, less than ten days later, on August 12 during the siege of Fort Erie.

The Americans were outnumbered by a 5 to 1 disadvantage but were victorious. If the Americans had not been successful at the Battle of Conjocta Creek, Buffalo may have again been burned and Fort Erie could have fallen. Fort Erie was besieged from August 4 to September 21, 1814 but the Americans held the fort until it was abandoned and demolished on November 5, 1814. This little-known battle or two-and-a-half-hour skirmish was one of the decisive battles of the war. If the British had won, they could have gained a foothold in WNY.

Figure 98 Battle of Scajaquada Creek Bridge
Painting: Courtesy Doreen Boyer DeBoth © 2016

CHARLOTTE MULLIGAN

Social advocate and the founder of the Twentieth Century Club

Charlotte Mulligan was born on September 25, 1844 to the socially active family of Henry and Sally Mulligan. She was the only daughter in a family which included five brothers.

Figure 99 Portrait of Charlotte Mulligan, President Twentieth Century Club 1894 – 1897 Photo: Courtesy Twentieth Century Club

At seventeen years of age, Charlotte was teaching Sunday School at the Wells Street Chapel of the First Presbyterian Church of Buffalo. Instead of enjoying teas and dances with her Buffalo Female Academy graduates, she obtained satisfaction instilling Christian values, giving instruction to the poor and helping those who were not fortunate to come from her wealthy and privileged class.

Her great grandfather was General Israel Chapin. He served in the American Revolution and was the General Agent for Indian Affairs of the United States who oversaw the signing of the Treaty of Canandaigua with the Six Nations. Chapin was respected by the Iroquois and Seneca Chief Red Jacket was one of the speakers at his funeral in 1795.

When the Civil War started, being a patriotic and peacemaking family, her two older brothers James and Grieg enlisted in the army. Both of her brothers died during the war and Charlotte made a vow in 1863 that she would never marry and devote herself to the care of young men devastated by the war, many of whom were wandering the streets, hungry and homeless. She founded a shelter on Washington Street, across from the Chippewa Market, for Civil War veterans and instituted an honor system that she called the Guard of Honor. This system awarded the veterans privileges if they furthered their education, obtained a job or participated in social activities like the musical band she created. The band performed in churches, the penitentiary, insane asylum and at the Twentieth Century Club. Charlotte also purchased a cemetery plot at Forest Lawn Cemetery for the Guard of Honor, where deceased members were interred, and a memorial erected to honor them.

Through her activities, Mulligan became a representative of the State Charities Aid Association. She spoke before state legislative committees and advocated and achieved more favorable conditions for the indigent insane.

In addition, Charlotte Mulligan was an educator, musician and vocalist, who performed and taught violin and voice at her home and studio on Johnson Park. For twenty years she was music critic for the *Buffalo Courier*, being one of the first female newspaper writers in Buffalo. She was the founder and president of The Scribblers, a club to advance literary accomplishments of women. Courtesy of Miss Maria Love and Thomas Cary, The Scribblers were furnished with rooms in The Genesee until space was available at the Twentieth Century Club, where The Scribblers subsequently rented rooms for many years.

Charlotte and other graduates of the Buffalo Female Academy, later known as Buffalo Seminary, formed the Graduates Association. They met in a lecture hall, at 95 Johnson Park, on land originally deeded to the Buffalo Female Academy by Buffalo's first mayor Ebenezer Johnson. That building, built in 1884, is now the New Phoenix Theatre on the Park. The Graduates Club wanted to become an independent women's club, including more than just individuals who graduated from the Buffalo Female Academy. They named their club the Twentieth Century Club in 1894 and purchased the former Delaware Avenue Baptist Church at 595 Delaware Avenue. Charlotte was the president of the Twentieth Century Club during its first four years, but she passed away at age 55 on June 20, 1900.

The grand opening of the new Twentieth Century Club took place on November 20, 1894. The several additions were designed by the architectural firm of E.B. Green and W.S. Wicks, with their creation of the elegant façade on Delaware Avenue being constructed in 1895. The members looked forward to hosting dignitaries who would be attending the Pan-American Exposition, when they held receptions for Vice President and Mrs. Theodore Roosevelt and their daughter Alice; Governor and Mrs. Benjamin Odell; Mr. and Mrs. Booker T. Washington and the Chinese Minister, Wu Ting Fang. Mrs. Roosevelt and Mrs. McKinley were extended membership privileges during their time in Buffalo for the Pan-Am.

The women's club movement of the late 19th century began as cultural organizations to provide middle and upper-class women with an outlet for their intellectual energies. To this extent the avowed purpose of the Twentieth Century Club is to advance the interests of education, literature and art. Miss Mulligan set a tradition of holding musical events and lectures on Wednesdays. This continues until the present day with noted writers, speakers and international personalities presenting talks on a wide range of subjects. Mrs. Franklin D. Roosevelt and violinist Isaac Stern, along with many other notable speakers and musicians have been featured at the Wednesday luncheons.

The Twentieth Century was the first club run by women, for women, in the U.S. and is the second oldest women's club in the country, only preceded by the Acorn Club in Philadelphia. The building was listed on the National Register of Historic Places in 2011. When you enter the building, a painting by Evelyn Rumsey of the club's founder, Charlotte Mulligan, greets you in the lobby.

Figure 100 Twentieth Century Club with original Temple Beth Zion to the left
Photo: Courtesy Twentieth Century Club

SAINT JOHN NEUMANN

The First U.S. Male Saint

John Neumann was born on March 28, 1811 in Prachatice in the Kingdom of Bohemia, then part of the Austrian Empire and now in the Czech Republic. Neumann was part German and part Czech. He attended a school operated by the Piarist Fathers in Ceske Budejovice, before he transferred to Charles University in Prague

Figure 101 Portrait of St. John Neumann

Upon graduation, he wanted to be ordained a priest, but there was an abundance of priests in that portion of Europe. Since he spoke eight languages, including English, it was recommended that he should relocate to the U.S., where there was a shortage of Catholic Priests.

When he arrived in NYC, Neumann had one suit of clothes and one dollar in his pocket. After meeting with Bishop John Dubois, he was ordained at Old St. Patrick's Cathedral in June 1836. Bishop Dubois assigned Neumann to minister the recent German immigrants in the Niagara Falls area, where there were no established churches. His ability to speak Spanish, French, Italian, and Dutch was an asset when hearing confessions. When the Irish immigration started, he even taught himself Gaelic.

Neumann traveled to Buffalo on the Erie Canal. When he arrived there were two churches, St. Louis in the city of Buffalo and St. Peter and Paul in Williamsville. He decided to establish his base at St. Peter & Paul, but there was no rectory, so he lived in the home of parishioner Philip Wirtz, who lived across from the church. It was also rumored that he lived in a room at the Eagle Inn in Williamsville, now the Eagle House Restaurant. In addition to saying Mass and performing other pastoral duties at the church, Neumann taught school for four hours a day. From this central point he also traveled on foot or by horseback to cover his congregation that ranged from Lake Ontario on the north, Batavia to the East and the Pennsylvania border to the south. He traveled from village to village visiting the sick, staying at people's homes or taverns, teaching and saying Mass at kitchen tables.

When he first arrived at North Bush (now part of Tonawanda) on July 20, 1836, the log Chapel of Saint John the Baptist existed, built by German settlers in 1833. He stayed in the home of John Schmitt until a two-room log rectory was built. Neumann was the pastor at St. John the Baptist from 1836 to 1840; when he moved into that rectory on November 4, 1838, it was also used as a school and clinic. Father Neumann left the Buffalo area in 1840 but returned for a short period of time the following year to assist when Father Pax at Lamb of God Church (now St. Louis on Main and Edward Streets) was ill.

After joining the Redemptorist order, Neumann was appointed Bishop of Philadelphia in 1852. While in Philadelphia, Bishop Neumann created the first Catholic School System because he believed Catholics should be educated by Catholics and most school systems were run by Protestants, who attempted to impart Protestant beliefs. During his time as bishop in Philadelphia the number of schools increased from one to 200. In 1855, he assisted in the founding of the Sisters of St. Francis of Philadelphia to minister to the Italian, German and Irish communities in New York and Philadelphia that did not speak English.

The beatification of John Neumann was announced in 1963 and he was canonized on June 19, 1977 as the first male Saint from the U.S. Bishop Neumann High School, formerly on Park Club Lane in Williamsville, was named in his honor.

Figure 102 St. John Neumann shrine and museum
Photo: Courtesy St. John the Baptist Church

MORDECAI MANUEL NOAH

Jewish refuge of Ararat on Grand Island

In 1825, Mordecai Manuel Noah attempted to establish the city of Ararat on Grand Island as a refuge for the oppressed Jewish people who were scattered across the world. Noah petitioned the State of New York to purchase Grand Island in 1820. The bill was favorably received by the legislature and Noah began five years of promoting the concept and attempting to raise funds to purchase the land.

Figure 103 Original Ararat stone at Buffalo History Museum and never placed in Grand Island Photo: Buffalo History Museum

Samuel Leggett, acting on Noah's behalf but using his own funds, purchased 2,555 acres of Grand Island in 1825. Noah decided to schedule an event announcing the city of Ararat and had a cornerstone made that read "Hear, O' Israel, The Lord is our God – The Lord is One. ARARAT, a City of Refuge for the Jews, founded by Mordecai Manuel Noah, in the Month of Tizzi 5586, September 1825, and in the 50th year of American Independence."

An adequate number of boats could not be obtained to transport all the participants to Grand Island, so the ceremony was held at St. Paul's Episcopal Church in Buffalo. A parade of city officials, bands and members of the Masonic Lodge marched down Main Street from the Court House to St. Paul's. Noah was dressed in rich judicial robes of crimson silk, trimmed with ermine, wearing a glistening gold medal around his neck. The rear honor guard of the Royal Arch Masons and Knights Templar completed the parade participants.

At the ceremony the cornerstone was consecrated in both Hebrew and Episcopal ceremonies. Noah proclaimed the Jewish community open and levied a capitalization tax of three Shekels (one dollar) a year upon every Jew throughout the world to assist in defraying the costs of establishing the settlement. After the ceremony, a reception was held at the Eagle Tavern. Noah never stepped foot on Grand Island and the 300-pound cornerstone remained propped against the outer rear wall of the cathedral.

Noah was not an official Zionist representative and people of the Jewish faith in America did not heed Noah's call to settle in Grand Island. Foreign rabbis did not support the settlement and the concept caused a firestorm of protest and ridicule. The project was soon forgotten and by the end of 1825 Noah was advising friends not to invest in Ararat. By 1833 Noah sold his holdings in Grand Island to timber investors.

Ararat would have been built on land adjacent to the intersection of Whitehaven and East River Roads. A plaque was erected across from Whitehaven Cemetery on

East River Road in Grand Island. In 2016 the Grand Island Town Board issued a proclamation establishing September 2 as Mordecai Manuel Noah Day, the anniversary of the original ceremony on September 2, 1825.

In addition to Noah's endeavors on Grand Island, Navy Island also holds historical significance.

Navy Island is currently an uninhabited half a square mile island between Grand Island and Niagara

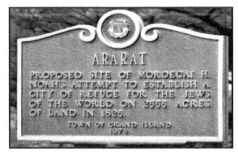

Figure 104 Historic plaque in Grand Island at proposed site of city Photo: Courtesy Grand Island Historical Society

Falls. In 1837, William Lyon Mackenzie rebelled against the government of Canada and proclaimed the Republic of Canada. He and his rebel forces captured and settled on the island, which they declared a separate and independent country, only to be routed by Canadian forces on January 13, 1838. The American steamer the *Caroline* supplied the encampment of the Republic of Canada and on December 29, 1837, Canadian militiamen crossed the Niagara River to capture the *Caroline* while it was docked on the American shore. The ship was set adrift and afire going over Niagara Falls killing one American onboard.

When the United Nations was being formed, it was determined that the headquarters would be in the United States. Many cities submitted proposals to be considered as the world peace capital. A proposal by the cities of Niagara Falls (U.S. and Canada) was submitted with the location of the capital as Navy Island, which could be deeded as neutral land between the U.S. and Canada. With the large airport in Niagara Falls and plans to build a separate airport on Grand Island, the location would be easily accessible by air to all countries. There was an abundance of reasonably priced land available, bridges would be built connecting to Canada and the U.S., and Grand Island could be included in the plan if more land was necessary.

The Niagara Falls committee included the mayors of both cities, Harry M. Hooker of Hooker Electro-chemical company, Welland, Ontario historian Blake Duff, Arthur A. Schmon of Ontario Power, Edward H. Butler of the *Buffalo News* and WBEN Radio, Larry Bell of Bell Aircraft and Paul Schoellkopf, representing the power companies. The presentation of the Navy Island plan was given by John A. Williamson of the Niagara Falls Chamber of Commerce, historian R.H. Davis and Buffalo businessman Chauncey J. Hamlin. Unfortunately, New York City won the rights to the location when John D. Rockefeller Jr. offered 8.5 million dollars of land as a gift for the United Nations site.

Noah had a unique idea but did not have the finances or influence to make it become a reality. However, WNY could be totally different today if Grand Island did become the Jewish State of Ararat, if Navy Island was the capital of the Republic of Canada or if Navy Island was selected as the Headquarters of the United Nations.

CHANCELLOR JOHN OLCOTT

Chancellor John Olcott, better known as Chauncey Olcott was an entertainer and composer, who wrote the songs "When Irish Eyes are Smiling" and "My Wild Irish Rose"

Chauncey Olcott's mother emigrated from County Cork Ireland, with her family originally settling in Montreal, Canada. In the 1840s they moved to Lockport, where she met and married Mellon Whitney Olcott. Olcott was born on July 21, 1858 and lived in what was called the "Irish chanty", located on West Genesee Street next to the Clifford Lumber Company lumberyard. Lockport residents recalled that when he was young, Olcott would sing Irish ballads on top of a table at the Washington Hose firehouse on Church Street.

Figure 105 Portrait of Chauncey Olcott

When Olcott's father died, his mother moved to Buffalo where Chauncey attended public schools. During summer vacations he lived with his maternal grandmother on West Genesee Street in Lockport. In 1879, at age 19, Olcott performed with Emerson and Hooley's Minstrel Company in Chicago and the following year joined Haverly's United Mastodon Minstrels in Buffalo. That group toured the U.S. and due to his tenor voice, Olcott was encouraged to sing Irish ballads. Olcott progressed to singing in plays, operas and operettas and in March 1886 he made his NYC debut at the Union Square Theatre in *Pepita*, with Lillian Russell as his co-star.

After studying voice in London, Olcott returned to Broadway theaters in NYC, replacing Irish singer W.J. Scanlan in the play *Mavourneen*. He continued as a star on Broadway in twenty productions that he created, for which he wrote hit songs including "My Wild Irish Rose" in 1897 for *A Romance of Athlone* and "When Irish

Eyes are Smiling" in 1912 for *The Isle of Dreams*. Olcott also wrote "Mother Machree" and "I Love the Name of Mary" and introduced the song "Too-Ra-Loo-Ra-Loo-Ral, (That's an Irish Lullaby)." In addition to his own productions he appeared in musicals by George M. Cohen. Mary Pickford got her start in the Olcott production of *Edmund Burke*. Olcott toured with his productions and returned to WNY to appear on a regular basis in Buffalo at The Academy of Music and in Lockport at Hodge Opera House.

Figure 106 My Wild Irish Rose promotion

Due to health reasons Olcott retired in 1925 and moved to Monte Carlo, Monaco where he died on March 18, 1932, which ironically was still St. Patrick's Day in NYC. His funeral was attended by over 3,000 people and a portion of 5th Avenue had to be closed due to the number of mourners. The funeral was at St. Patrick's Cathedral in NYC and the honorary pallbearers included: NYC Mayor Jimmy Walker, NYS Governor Alfred E. Smith, George M. Cohen and other personalities from the entertainment world.

Chauncey Olcott was the foremost Irish tenor of the late 1800s and early 1900s. He was one of the founding members of the American Society of Composers Authors and Publishers (ASCAP) in 1915. His widow Rita wrote his biography *A song in His Heart* in 1939 and it was produced as the Academy Award nominated movie *My Wild Irish Rose* in 1947.

FREDERICK LAW OLMSTED

The Father of American Landscape Architecture who
created the public park system of Buffalo

Frederick Law Olmsted was born in Hartford, Connecticut on April 26, 1822, the son of John Olmsted, who was a successful merchant that had a love of nature. Frederick operated a farm in Staten Island before he became a journalist. In 1850, he traveled to England where he visited the public gardens publishing *Walks and Talks of an American Farmer in England* in 1852. This book heightened his interest in landscape architecture and resulted in Olmsted securing additional work as a journalist.

Figure 107 Fredrick Law Olmsted portrait

He was interested in social issues and was commissioned by the *New York Daily Times*, now the *New York Times*, to journey through the American South from 1852 to 1857, writing about life and the effect of slavery on the economic and social conditions in the South. The Times dispatches were later published as three volumes, and an abridgement was published at the start of the Civil War in 1861.

Upon returning to NYC, Olmsted and architect Calvert Vaux submitted a proposal, in a design competition, to create Central Park. Olmsted had never previously executed a landscape design but under the guidance of the experienced Vaux, their design for the park was accepted. The design of Central Park embodied Olmsted's egalitarian social ideals. It featured common green space accessible to all citizens, creating the idea of a public park. This concept was paramount in all of Olmstead's designs, including his public park system for Buffalo.

William Dorsheimer met Frederick Law Olmsted while he was Executive Secretary of the U.S. Sanitary Commission, an organization that as a precursor to the Red Cross assisted in treating wounded Union Soldiers during the Civil War. Dorsheimer discussed Olmsted's work in creating Central Park and in 1866 wrote to him regarding the possibility of creating a park system for the City of Buffalo.

In August 1868, when Olmsted was returning to NYC from the suburban Riverside park project that he and Calvert Vaux were working on in Chicago, Olmsted visited Buffalo to attend a meeting regarding the Buffalo Municipal Parks system. They met at the home of Sherman S. Jewett, with other parks commission members William Dorsheimer, Pascal Paoli Pratt, Joseph Warren and Richard Flach. This meeting began an association between Olmsted and the City of Buffalo that lasted from 1868 to 1896. After Olmsted's retirement in 1897, the association continued with Olmsted's company, headed by his son, until 1915, when the Independent Board of Park Commissioners was dissolved.

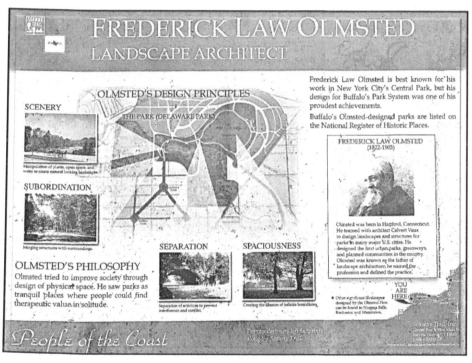

Figure 108 Olmsted signage at Delaware Park

The concept of the Buffalo parks was inspired by the parklands, boulevards and squares of Paris, France. The parks included in the system included Cazenovia, Days, The Park (now Delaware), The Front (now Front), The Parade (later Humboldt and now Martin Luther King), Riverside and South Park. Parks that were included but are no longer in existence were Bennett Park, Masten Place and The Terrace. Olmsted and the Conservancy also added three smaller parks called Pocket Parks, which are Days Park, Heacock Place and Prospect Hill Parks (Columbus and Prospect Park).

The Parkways in the system were Bidwell, Chapin, Humboldt, Lincoln, South Side (now McKinley), Porter Avenue, Red Jacket and The Avenue (now Richmond Avenue). Parkways were designed as wide medians, lined with shade trees, connecting the parks so you could travel throughout the system without leaving the park-like atmosphere. The circles, that correlated to the Paris squares, were Agassiz, Bidwell Place (now Colonial Circle), Ferry, Chapin Place (now Gates Circle), Woodside (now McClellan), McKinley, Soldiers and The Circle (now Symphony Circle). The plans also included the Buffalo and Erie County Botanical gardens in South Park. The Olmsted Conservancy maintains special gardens in the major parks, which are; Bog Garden in South Park, Japanese Garden in Delaware Park, River Rock Garden in Riverside Park and the Rose Garden in Delaware Park.

Olmsted and Vaux also worked with architect H.H. Richardson in the design of the gardens for the Buffalo State Hospital, to create a pleasing environment for people who suffer from mental illness. Originally there were farms extending from the complex to Scajaquada Creek, with Buffalo State College being built in that area starting in 1927. Today the complex is called the Richardson Olmsted Campus and it is one of the largest historic preservation projects in the country.

Beginning in the 1860s Olmsted advocated for the preservation of Niagara Falls. Olmsted and a band of early environmentalists founded the Free Niagara movement, to protect the Falls from commercial interests and maintain free access to the general public. In 1879, Olmsted and State Surveyor James T. Gardner assisted in preparing a report on the condition of Niagara Falls which argued for increased public access and recommended the state purchase the lands surrounding it. Olmsted and others formed the Niagara Falls Association in 1883, and a bill authorizing the selection, location and appropriation of lands in Niagara Falls to create a state reservation was signed by then NYS Governor Grover Cleveland. The Niagara Reservation was created in 1885; it is recognized as the oldest state park in the U.S. Olmsted's vision of a network of footpaths throughout wooded areas, the maintaining of native vegetation, and unparalleled public access for Niagara Falls has been preserved for present and future generations.

Olmsted transformed the landscape of the City of Buffalo by creating its urban park system, the first and oldest coordinated system of public parks and parkways in the country. When he completed the park system, Olmsted proclaimed "Buffalo to be the best planned city in the United States, if not the world."

ROSWELL PARK

Physician that created the first cancer research center in the country

R oswell Park was born on May 4, 1852 in Pomfret, Connecticut to Reverend Roswell Park and Mary Baldwin Park. The family moved to Wisconsin where his father took a job as the first president of Racine College. When Roswell was two years old his mother died in childbirth, and a year later his older sister and younger brother died. Park moved back to Connecticut to be raised by his mother's sister Clarissa and her husband, physician Lewis Williams. He lived with his aunt and uncle for the next six years and often accompanied his uncle on medical rounds.

At nine years old Roswell joined his father, who was then teaching at a college in Chicago and he sometimes assisted his father in preparing classes for his chemistry labs. In 1872, he received his BA, and in 1875, an MA from Racine College. He received a Medical degree at Northwestern University in 1876. This was substantially more preliminary education than most doctors received during this era. His internship was completed in 1879 at Cook County Hospital in Chicago, where he specialized in gunshot wounds.

Figure 109 Portrait of Dr. Roswell Park

Beginning in 1879, he started teaching at Women's Medical College in Chicago and at Northwestern University medical school. He married Prudence Dukee of Chicago in 1880. To further his education, he resigned his teaching positions and in 1882 went to study at notable medical schools and hospitals in Berlin, Vienna and Prague. His studies were cut short when he was offered a position in 1883 as Chairman and Professor of Surgery at the UB Medical School. Park accepted the position because he was originally impressed with Buffalo after attending the American Medical Association (AMA) Conference held in the city in 1878.

Upon arrival in Buffalo, members of the medical community initially thought he was too young for the positions of responsibility that he was granted. He won them over with his knowledge and quickly became surgeon-in-chief at Buffalo General Hospital. Park developed a national and international reputation for his scientific approach to medical problems. In addition to teaching, he published over 150 articles and several books including *History of Medicine* in 1897 and *Brain Surgery* in 1905.

In 1892, the city of Chicago offered Park a position as an attempt to lure him back to the city. Charles and Frank Goodyear, John Albright and other businessmen lobbied to keep Park in Buffalo and assisted in building a new medical school on High Street, which opened in 1893. The medical school remained there until 1953 when it was relocated to the South UB Campus.

Park believed that medical doctors should have a liberal arts background. The AMA agreed with him and passed college requirements in 1913. Initially UB was a medical and law school but with Park's insistence it became a full-fledged college offering a Liberal Arts Degree program. His son Julian Park was the first Dean of Arts & Sciences at UB, serving from 1919 to 1954. He was also the university's first historian.

Figure 110 Gratwick Laboratory – the first lab devoted to the study of cancer

Park was active in Buffalo Civic life, at various times serving as president of Buffalo Academy of Medicine, Buffalo Society of Natural Sciences, Red Cross Association, Buffalo Club, Philharmonic Society, Saturn Club, Liberal Club and the Good Government Club. The Park home at 510 Delaware Avenue hosted many receptions where Dr. Park often entertained with his original musical compositions.

In 1897, Dr. Park lobbied New York State to fund cancer research. A $10,000 grant was approved by both houses of the legislature, but Governor Black vetoed the bill. Edward Butler, publisher of the *Buffalo News*, recruited other newspaper editors across NYS to support the bill and in 1898 it was passed and signed by the governor. The research center was called the New York State Pathological Laboratory of the University of Buffalo. Five years later Dr. Willian M. Osler, the founder of John Hopkins Hospital of Baltimore, wrote to Park stating that as far as he knew, the only laboratory devoted to systematic work on cancer was the clinic Park organized. The grant was also the first cancer research laboratory supported by the government.

In 1898, the center was the first laboratory in the world devoted solely to the study of cancer. Due to the support of Mrs. William Gratwick, who was the major donor of building funds for the laboratory, it became known as the Gratwick Laboratory. In 1911, it was named the State Institute for the Study of Malignant Diseases. In 1946, it was renamed the Roswell Park Memorial Institute. The institute also had an experimental biological station in Springville in 1913. A West Seneca animal breeding facility was built for raising germ free mice and in 1940 a 78-bed hospital was added to the Buffalo campus.

When Dr. Park started the research center his main questions were: What is cancer? Why does it develop? What are the most effective treatments? Why are some cancers treatable in some patients and not in others? … These remain the main questions in cancer research.

When President McKinley was shot at the Pan-American Exposition, Dr. Park was performing an operation in Niagara Falls and he refused to leave that patient until the procedure was completed. He was rushed to the Pan-Am Hospital, but another doctor had already performed the operation in an attempt to remove the bullet.

Although Roswell Park was known as the founder of the world's first cancer research institute, he made other contributions to medicine. He was a pioneer in neurosurgery and was one of the first American surgeons to treat the serious birth defect spina bifida. When there was little knowledge of the link between bacteria and infection he campaigned for a sterile operating environment; and long before federal laws to protect patient privacy, he insisted that all patients should be treated with courtesy and privacy.

When he died in 1914, his institution served as the model for 12 cancer research centers in the U.S. and 8 internationally. Dr. Park said his biggest regret in life was not being present to operate on President McKinley.

ELY PARKER

Seneca attorney and tribal diplomat, who wrote the final draft of the Confederate Army surrender terms in the Civil War

Ely Samuel Parker was born, as Hasanoanda and later known as Donehogawa, in 1828 to William and Elizabeth Parker at Indian Falls, NY, which was part of the Tonawanda Reservation. He was the sixth of seven children in the family and his father was a Baptist Minister. In a consultation with Native seers, his mother had a vision of a rainbow with Indian culture at one end and White Man's culture at the other. This was interpreted to mean Ely would be a great man or warrior in both worlds. In his first step toward achieving this vision, Ely received a classical education at the Baptist Mission School and became fluent in both the Seneca and English languages.

In 1844, Anthropologist Lewis Henry Morgan was in Albany to research old U.S.-Native American treaties. A Seneca delegation was also in Albany to gather information to support their land claims. The Seneca delegation was led by Jemmy Johnson, a nephew of Red Jacket, who brought his grandson Ely Parker to Albany as an interpreter. Morgan and Parker established a friendship and Parker assisted him in the writing of "The League of the Haudenosaunee," a history of the Iroquois people. Parker provided Morgan with information that preserved a lot of history and culture of the Iroquois.

Morgan repaid Parker for his assistance by sponsoring him for admission to Morgan's alma mater, The Cayuga Academy, an elite school in Aurora, Cayuga County. Parker's fluency in English improved to the point that he became one of the best debaters and orators at the school. After three years at Cayuga Academy he became a translator, scribe and interpreter for the Seneca elders during their meetings and for their correspondence with the U.S. government. In this position, he went to Washington, DC to lobby for the rights of the Seneca to remain at the Tonawanda Reservation.

At the age of 18, Parker moved to Ellicottville where he studied law for three years at the offices of Nagel & Rice. When he applied to take the bar examination, his request was refused because he was not an American citizen. Native Americans were not considered American citizens until the Indian Citizenship Act of 1924.

Morgan again came to the assistance of Parker, when he helped him get accepted at Rensselaer Polytechnic Institute in Troy, NY. When he graduated as an engineer, Parker received an appointment as resident engineer in Rochester, NY for a project to extend the Erie Canal. While working on this project, he became involved with the Seneca Nation lawsuits against the Ogden Land Company and their grantees. He worked with attorney John Martindale to reverse the Treaty of 1842 and, in the cases of Fellows v Blacksmith and Cutler v Dibble, 7,549 acres were returned to the Tonawanda. Parker's abilities were recognized by the Seneca people when he was made a Sachem (Chief) in 1852.

When these lawsuits were settled Parker returned to the engineering profession and became an engineer for the U.S. Treasury Department. He went to Galena, Illinois to supervise the construction of the U.S. Customs Building. Here he befriended Ulysses S. Grant, who would have a lasting influence on Parker's future.

At the start of the U.S. Civil War Parker tried to raise a regiment of Iroquois volunteers to fight for the Union but was turned down. He then tried to enlist as an engineer but was told since he was an Indian, he could not join the military. Parker approached his friend Ulysses S. Grant, who had become a general in the Union Army. Grant's forces lacked sufficient engineers, so he personally approved Parker's commission in his command as a captain. Parker served with Grant from Vicksburg to Appomattox Court House, eventually becoming one of his aides. Remaining in the military after the Civil War, Parker served as military secretary to Grant and was a member of the Southern Treaty Commission, that negotiated treaties with Indian tribes who sided with the Confederate Army. Parker rose to the rank of Brigadier General, one of only two Native Americans to attain the rank of general during the Civil War era; the other was a confederate general.

At Appomattox Court House, Virginia, when the terms of the surrender of Robert E. Lee's Confederate Army to Ulysses S. Grant were agreed, Ely Parker was asked to write a draft for approval. Parker then rewrote the official copy of the official terms of surrender in ink and his handwritten document was signed by Grant and Lee.

Figure 111 Staff of General U.S. Grant – Parker seated at left

Figure 112 Parker memorial gravesite at Forest Lawn Cemetery

It was reported, General Lee asked to meet the members of General Grant's staff and requested to shake the hand of each officer. When Lee approached Parker, he noticed he was darker than the other staff officers and it took Lee a few moments to determine Parker's racial status. However, after realizing he was an Indian, he supposedly remarked, "Glad to meet one real American here." To which Parker replied, "We're all Americans here."

After the Civil War, President Grant appointed Parker to the Cabinet Level office of the Commissioner of Indian Affairs, the first Native American to hold that post. He was the chief architect of President Grant's Indian Peace Policy and helped reduce military actions against Indians in the West, along with supporting the tribes on their transition to resettling on the reservations. The government bureaucracy encountered in the Office of Indian Affairs, along with the corruption and racial bias, resulted in Parker's resignation.

When Parker left the government, he moved to New York City and worked for the NYC Police Department. He made and lost a fortune in the stock market, living his final years in poverty. Parker died on August 30, 1895 and was buried with full military honors in Connecticut. In 1897, he was exhumed and buried at his final resting place in Forest Lawn Cemetery next to his ancestor, Red Jacket. His mother's vision was fulfilled, as Parker was successful and affected both the Indian and White Man worlds.

WILLIAM PEACOCK

Surveyor of Buffalo and Holland Land Company Agent in Chautauqua County

Ancestors of William Peacock accompanied William the Conqueror from Normandy in 1088. Reginald Peacock was Bishop of Chinchester, England in 1449, but since he denied the doctrine of transubstantiation, he was banished, and his books were burned. During the reign of Henry VIII, Sir Stephen Peacock was the Lord Mayor of London and had the honor of accompanying Ann Boleyn from the Tower of London to her coronation at Westminster Abbey.

Thomas Peacock was the first family member in America, and he served in the Revolution with George Washington, during his retreat through New Jersey and at the crossing of the Delaware. He married Margaret Anderson, from Scotland, in 1777. After his wife's death in 1816, Thomas lived with his son John on a farm in Lyons, Wayne County and later moved to Mayville, NY to live with his son William.

William Peacock was born near New York City on February 22, 1780. When he was young his parents moved to Newburgh and then to a farm near Geneva, New York, where he received a good education and was taught surveying. In 1799, he traveled by horseback on the French trails to Fort Duquesne (present day Pittsburgh), at the confluence of the Allegheny and Monongahela Rivers. During this trip he visited Lake Chautauqua and took the Indian trails along Lake Erie to Buffalo. He was impressed by the view of Lake Erie from the higher ground, which is now the Terrace, between Franklin and Pearl Streets.

In 1803, Peacock stopped in Batavia, NY on his way to relocate in New Orleans. Joseph Ellicott convinced him to agree to employment with the Holland Land Company as a surveyor. One of his assignments was the laying out of the city Ellicott called New Amsterdam, now Buffalo. Peacock selected several tracts of land in Buffalo which he purchased. One parcel was bounded by Main, Niagara, Pearl and Eagle Streets, which became known as the Kremlin Block. The other was outer lots 7, 8 and 9 which contained 21 acres, which extended from the Terrace to Lake Erie, between Erie and Genesee Streets, including waterfront property of the Erie Basin.

Joseph Ellicott's niece Alice Evans, the daughter of his sister Ann and Joseph Evans, accompanied him from Maryland to Batavia in 1805. She journeyed to Buffalo for the wedding of her cousin Rachel Evans to Chauncey Loomis. At this wedding, she met William Peacock whom she married in 1807. The couple lived in Batavia until they moved to Mayville in 1810, where Peacock was a clerk for the Holland Land Company.

Peacock was appointed agent for the disposal of Holland Land Company property in Chautauqua County. He purchased tracts of land in Chautauqua County, including 21 acres on the south western shore of Lake Chautauqua, which became Fair Point Resort and later the Chautauqua Institution. The governor assigned Peacock as one of the judges of Chautauqua County and he was one of the commissioners that built the courthouse in Mayville. Peacock was also appointed to survey and locate portions of the Erie Canal, assisting in selecting the Western terminus by creating a report on construction of the Buffalo Harbor.

In 1836, Peacock's Holland Land Office in Mayville was destroyed by a discontented mob who objected to the manner in which the company disposed of its unsold property in Chautauqua County and the unpaid portions of previous sales. All was sold to persons outside of the county and the mob thought they would take advantage of the indebtedness of residents. Their destruction of the paperwork in the building was in vain because all transactions were reported to the Batavia office. It is interesting, no charges were placed, or legal inquiry made against the mob who destroyed the building. However, this action ended the employment of Judge Peacock with the Holland Land Company.

Judge Peacock built a large brick addition to his frame home on Main Street in Mayville in 1846. The home was high above Lake Chautauqua and afforded a view of the lake and surrounding hills. Facing the west, it was 726 feet above Lake Erie, presenting additional beautiful views of the lake and countryside. Next to his home, there was a 50-acre farm and at the bottom of the incline from Westfield to Mayville, he had an additional 120-acre farm.

Long terms leases of his Chautauqua County and Buffalo waterfront properties became very valuable. Peacock was also the executor of the estates of Benjamin Ellicott and his mother-in-law Ann Evans. With the investments made from his property income, Peacock became one of the richest residents of Western New York. His wife Alice died at 79 on April 19, 1859, after more than 50 years of marriage. William Peacock lived another eighteen years, passing away on February 21, 1877 at age 97. A Mason since 1803, after a ceremony of Masonic ritual, William was buried next to his wife in Mayville. They had no children and left no will, so his estate was distributed among his nieces and nephews.

Figure 113 Drawing of one of the Peacock family homes in Westfield

Figure 114 Map of Buffalo showing original street names and the inner, outer and water lots, as surveyed by William Peacock for Joseph Ellicott of the Holland Land Company

COMMODORE OLIVER HAZARD PERRY

Triumphant commander at the Battle of Lake Erie

At the beginning of the War of 1812, Commodore Perry supervised the building of a fleet of ships in Erie, Pennsylvania at Presque Isle. He then began building ships at the Scajaquada Creek Naval Yard at Black Rock.

The natural harbor of Black Rock, where the Scajaquada Creek enters the Niagara River, was a safe and sheltered place to build ships. At this yard, during the winter of 1812-3, five ships were built or refitted as gunboats: *Trippe, Caledonia, Sommers, Amelia* and *Ohio*. The first three ships participated in the Battle of Lake Erie. Under Perry's command, the Americans decisively won this battle, which ensured American control of the Lake Erie for the remainder of The War of 1812.

The ships refitted at Black Rock could not leave the Niagara River because the British controlled Fort Erie. They joined the American fleet after the Americans took control of the fort in May 1813. Perry had the ships towed up the Niagara River by oxen, which took six days. In July 1813, a British force of 250 men rowed up the Niagara River from Chippewa and overwhelmed the Americans at Black Rock. The British burned the Navy Yard at Scajaquada Creek and moved south along the Niagara, where they captured and burned the gun batteries, including those at Fort Tompkins. American militia from Buffalo arrived and drove the invaders back across the Niagara River. However, the ships the British hoped to destroy were safe as they had already been removed from the Naval Yard and were available for the Battle of Lake Erie, which took place on September 10, 1813 off the coast of Ohio at Put-In Bay near Sandusky. Unfortunately, the *Ariel, Little Belt, Chippewa* and *Trippe*, ships that participated in the Battle of Lake Erie were destroyed when the British burned Black Rock on December 30, 1813.

The ships that Commander Perry refitted at Black Rock Harbor assisted in the American victory at the Battle of Lake Erie which was instrumental in the outcome of the War of 1812.

Figure 115 Scajaquada Creek Naval Yard in Black Rock 1812
Painting: Courtesy Doreen Boyer DeBoth © 2013

DOCTOR RAY VAUGHN PIERCE

Manufacturer of patent medicine and owner of Invalid's Hotel

D r. Ray Vaughn Pierce was born at Stark, New York, in Herkimer County in 1840. He graduated from the Eclectic Medical Institute in Cincinnati which was only a five-month course. While practicing medicine in Pennsylvania, he sold his first bottle of elixir and created the *Medical Gazette* before moving to Buffalo in 1867.

Pierce's patent medicines were called Doctor Pierce's Favorite Prescription, Smart Weed and Dr. Pierce's Pleasant Pellets. They were manufactured at 664 Washington St., which was called The World's Dispensary. The office for The World's Dispensary Medical Association was located at 651-661 Main Street, which still exists as the Pierce Building. During the late 1880s, the Dispensary took in over half a million dollars a year and they were one of the country's largest manufacturers of patent medicines. In this time period, with exception of William G. Fargo, Pierce was possibly the most renowned person from Buffalo and one of the wealthiest.

In 1875, he published *The People's Common Sense Medical Advisor in Plain English* which sold over four million copies from 1875 to 1935 and ran to 100 editions. Pierce was elected to the State Assembly in 1876 and House of Representatives in 1878, resigning due to ill health in 1880.

Pierce's Palace, also known as Pierce's Invalid's Hotel, was built in 1876. It was a luxury hotel with 250 rooms, fireplaces in the rooms, 15-foot ceilings and included one of the first telephones and elevators in Buffalo. It was built for both tourists and invalids, and it was in the location of the current D'Youville College.

The hotel was only open for four years before it was destroyed by fire in 1881. Since Pierce took out insurance policies on Invalid's Hotel just prior to it burning down, arson charges were presumed but never proven.

In 1881, the Invalid's Hotel, was replaced by a less extravagant Invalid's Hotel and Surgical Institute at 663 Main Street, next door to the Dispensary. This was later managed by Dr. Pierce's son Doctor Valentine Mott Pierce and grandson Ray Vaughn. It was considered one of the best sanitariums of its kind in the country - prominent patients from across North America came to stay at the facility. An additional facility was built in London, England.

Pierce advertised in newspapers across the country and sold his products through the mail. He lobbied against the U.S. government requests to disclose the ingredients of his elixirs. The components were not revealed during his lifetime, but tests of the products confirmed the elixirs did not include the rumored opium and alcohol it was thought they contained.

In 1870, his home was at 138 Delaware, a block away from Niagara Square. He moved to an even larger home at 1040 Delaware between West Utica and Lexington in 1880. After losing money in gold and coal mining, by the turn of the century Pierce was living with his son, next door to the Dispensary. Pierce was called a fraud by the *Ladies Home Journal* in 1904, but he sued and won the court case. The downward spiral continued, when in 1906 the Federal Pure Food and Drug Act was passed reforming patent medicine advertising and the American Medical Association began criticizing patent medicine. Pierce saw the writing on the wall and retired to Saint Vincent's Island in Florida, where he died in 1914.

Figure 116 Pierce Palace Hotel at the current location of D'Youville College

JOHN PITASS

*Father John Pitass founded Saint Stanislaus Church and helped
develop the Polish East Side of Buffalo*

John Pitass was born on July 7, 1844 in Piekary in Northern Silesia, Poland which at that time was part of Germany. He studied for the priesthood in Rome, Italy and arrived at Our Lady of Angels Seminary (Niagara University) on May 12, 1873. Pitass received his minor orders and became a deacon in the beginning of June. On June 7, 1873, he was ordained into the priesthood by Buffalo's Bishop Stephen Ryan.

The day after his ordination, Father Pitass held his first Mass at St. Michaels Church with the Polish community in attendance. Later that day he attended a St. Stanislaus Society meeting, during which he organized St. Stanislaus Parish and 82 Polish American families enrolled.

Joseph Bork was a member of St. Mary's parish and owned large tracts of land behind St. Ann's Church on Broadway at Emslie, on the East Side of Buffalo. He noticed that in the early 1800s large numbers of Polish immigrants passed through Buffalo on their way to settle in the West. The rector of St. Mary's suggested that if there was a church with a priest of Polish nationality, Polish immigrants may be attracted to settle in Buffalo. Bork donated land on Peckham Street for the site of a church for Polish people. It was here that Father Pitass built St. Stanislaus church, school and rectory.

*Figure 117 Memorial grave site of Father John Pitass
and his nephews*

It was more difficult for Polish immigrants to assimilate in America because the Slavic Polish language was more distant from English than the Germanic or romantic language immigrants. Also, Poles were familiar with close knit peasant farming communities, not crowded multi-nationality industrial neighborhoods, so they bypassed Buffalo because there was not any community into which they could bond.

That changed when Father Pitass formed St. Stanislaus Church and the surrounding Polish community. In addition to the church, school and cemetery (purchased in 1889 on Pine Ridge in Cheektowaga), Pitass started a Polish language newspaper, *Polak w Ameryce (Pole in America)*, of which he was the publisher until his death. Prior to the arrival of Pitass, Mass at Buffalo churches was said in Latin and the sermon was in English. The Polish immigrants needed a church with the sermon and ministry in their native tongue, which Father Pitass provided. The school was bilingual, with students learning in both Polish and English. This provided a better education than most of the Poles received in their native country. To teach at St. Stanislaus School, Father Pitass invited the Felician Sisters to the city of Buffalo.

Homeownership was important to the Poles. Father Pitass became involved in the development of real estate near his parish. Small wood frame cottages were built on inexpensive lots on the East Side. With a down payment of only $25.00, even the poorest family could afford a home. In 1886, he built 300 homes and sold 600 lots. The following year he tripled those figures.

Within ten years from the founding of St. Stanislaus Church there were 1,000 families in the parish. In 1890, there were 20,000 Poles in Buffalo, and in 1894, Father Pitass was named Dean of all the churches of Polish settlers for the Diocese of Buffalo. In 1910, St. Stanislaus was baptizing over 1,200 infants a year, and in 1920, one quarter of the population of the city of Buffalo was Polish. The establishment of St. Stanislaus parish and the East Side Polish community by Father Pitass changed the complexion and character of the City of Buffalo.

Father John Pitass died on December 11, 1913 after serving as pastor of St. Stanislaus Church for over 40 years. More than 20,000 parishioners and area residents paid their respects while passing his coffin, and he was given the honorary title of the Founder and Patriarch of the Polish colony in the Diocese of Buffalo and the neighboring dioceses of Rochester and Erie.

After the death of Father John Pitass, his nephew Father Alexander Pitass, who had founded St. John Gualbert Parish, replaced him as pastor at St. Stanislaus, serving until his death in 1944. Father Peter Pitass, Alexander's older brother, began assisting his uncle at St. Stanislaus in 1893 and later served at St. John Kanty Church, Saints Peter & Paul and churches in Niagara Falls, Albion and Batavia. He concluded his priesthood as chaplain at the Felician Sisters Immaculate Heart of Mary Orphan's Home on William Street in Cheektowaga.

These three priests from the Pitass family of Poland served the Polish Americans in the WNY Catholic community and are buried next to each other at St. Stanislaus Roman Catholic Cemetery in Cheektowaga.

PETER BUELL PORTER

Peter Porter was a politician, War of 1812 General, proponent of Black Rock as the Western Terminus of the Erie Canal and with his brother owned the portage rights around Niagara Falls

The Porter family can be traced back to William de la Grande, a Norman Knight who fought with William the Conqueror and acquired land near Kenilworth, England. William's son was Grand Porteur to King Henry I and from that office the name Porter is derived.

The founder of the Porter family in America can be traced to John Porter, who arrived in 1637 and was the sixteenth in descent from William de la Grande. His great-great grandson was Colonel Joshua Porter, who graduated from Yale University in 1754 and settled in Salisbury, Connecticut. During the American Revolution he served in numerous battles, including the Battle of Saratoga Springs. At Saratoga, he was one of the officers who accepted the surrender of General John Burgoyne and his 6,000 troops. Colonel Porter later served in more than forty sessions of the State Legislature and was a Probate Judge for 37 years.

General Peter Buell Porter was born in Salisbury, Connecticut on August 14, 1773, to Joshua Porter and Abigail Buell Porter. He graduated from Yale and studied law under Judge Tapping Reeve, who also taught Aaron Burr and James C. Calhoun. Peter Porter moved to Canandaigua in 1795 to practice law, and was elected a member of the New York State Assembly. His older brother, Augustus, was a surveyor who worked for Robert Morris and Joseph Ellicott in Western New York becoming familiar with that area, especially the state lands near the Niagara River.

Peter Porter unsuccessfully inquired about purchasing large tracts of land from Joseph Ellicott and the Holland Land Company, so he looked into purchasing NYS lands. The Milestrip was a one-mile wide strip of land along the bank of the Niagara River, owned by New York State. It was surveyed in 1803 and 1804, and in 1805 it was put up for

Figure 118 Portrait of Peter Buell Porter

Figure 119 Drawing of Augustus Porter home at 101 Buffalo Street in Niagara Falls

auction. The docks and warehouses at Lewiston and Schlosser would remain the property of NYS, but be leased for 13 years to the winning bidder. Peter Porter, his brother Augustus, Benjamin Barton and Joseph Annin, who did the survey of the Milestrip, formed a partnership to purchase the property and lease the NYS land. Peter Buell Porter also formed a partnership with John McDonald, Archibald McIntyre, Benjamin Barber and Birdsey Norton to purchase lots 104 to 107, between what was designated as the village of Black Rock and Scajaquada Creek.

The Porters, Barton and Annin were successful in purchasing much of the land, including the lands above and below Niagara Falls. Augustus moved to the area of the Falls and called the property Manchester, a name it retained until 1840. Augustus opened a general store and a mill in Manchester, was the first judge in Niagara County and first postmaster in Niagara Falls. In 1816, Peter and Augustus purchased Goat Island, started the development of the tourist trade to the Falls and built the first bridge to the island. The Porter brothers also promoted the use of the rapids for powering businesses along the Niagara River and on Goat Island.

By winning the bid for the lands at Lewiston and Schlosser, they formed the portage company Porter, Barton and Company, a freight forwarding company from Lake Erie to Lake Ontario, via the Portage Road around the Falls. The company established ports at Lewiston, Niagara Falls and Black Rock. Peter Porter moved to Black Rock in 1809, where he was elected to the House of Representative from 1809 to 1813. Upon arrival in Washington, Peter Porter proposed to move the customs houses in the Niagara Frontier, to Lewiston and Black Rock, where Porter's company enjoyed a virtual freight forwarding monopoly. No one objected to moving customs from Fort Niagara to Lewiston but even the Collector of Customs, Erastus Granger, objected to moving the customs house from Buffalo to Black Rock. On March 16,

1811, President James Madison settled the location by compromise. During the shipping season of April 1 to December 1, Black Rock would be the point of entry, while Buffalo would be the point of entry the balance of the year. This would be argued in the future, but the declaration of war in 1812, put the port issue on the back burner.

With the outbreak of the War of 1812, Porter was named assistant quartermaster general of the New York State Militia. He was later a brigadier general, and fought in numerous battles, commanding the militia and 500 Senecas. Following a battle on the Canadian side of the Niagara River between Fort Erie and Chippewa, Porter was upset with Brigadier General Alexander Smyth's command of American troops. Most American soldiers agreed with Porter's assessment of Smyth's command, and Porter called Smyth a coward. The egotistical, bombastic and grandiose Smyth challenged Porter to a duel, which took place on Grand Island. Both generals' pistol shots missed their opponents, so they got into their boats and went to Dayton's Tavern near the current location of Tonawanda where they drank and dined into the evening. At the end of the war, Porter was given command of American forces on the Niagara Frontier by President Madison. He was considered a war hero by the people of WNY, and Fort Porter was later named in his honor.

Porter was assigned to the Erie Canal Commission in 1810 and argued for Black Rock to become the Western Terminus of the Canal. He represented Black Rock and Samuel Wilkeson represented Buffalo in the historic arguments as to which would be the western terminus of the Canal. Before the Canal opened in 1825, Buffalo won the designation, but a stop was made in Black Rock on DeWitt Clinton's inaugural voyage on the *Seneca Chief* packet boat, from Buffalo to New York City, where they carried and emptied two casks of water from Lake Erie into the New York Harbor. Porter later served as Secretary of War under President John Quincy Adams from 1828 to 1829.

In 1818, Peter Buell Porter married Letitia Breckinridge. When she moved to Buffalo, she brought several slaves with her from the South, being one of the few slave owners in WNY. Porter's original home was destroyed during the burning of Black Rock during the War of 1812. He built a house in Black Rock in 1816 on Niagara Street near West Ferry, which was sold to Lewis Allen in 1836 when Porter moved to Niagara Falls. Porter died in 1844 but it is ironic that the house he built in Niagara Falls and the Cataract House, which his family later owned, were stops on the underground railroad.

In 1833, the Buffalo and Black Rock Railroad was chartered, and opened in 1834. It was owned by Porter and his nephew William A. Bird. This was a horse drawn railroad that ran between downtown Buffalo and Black Rock. The Buffalo and Niagara Railroad was chartered in 1834, with construction beginning in 1836. The low-quality horse drawn tracks were replaced, and in 1837 the line was completed to Tonawanda, and around 1840 to Niagara Falls. These were the first horse drawn and locomotive railroads in Buffalo.

Figure 120 Porter house on Niagara Street in Black Rock
Rebuilt in 1816 and sold to Lewis Allen in 1836

Peter Buell Porter's son, Colonel Peter Augustus Porter, was born in Black Rock on July 14, 1827. His mother, Letitia Breckinridge, was the daughter of John Breckinridge, Senator from Kentucky during 1801 to 1805 and Attorney General under Thomas Jefferson in 1805 and 1806. The half-brother of Colonel Porter, from his mother's first marriage, was Confederate General John Breckinridge Grayson, who before the war was a U.S. Army officer during the Seminole and Mexican American War. Colonel Porter graduated from Harvard University, studied in Germany at Heidelberg and Berlin, and received a degree from Harvard Law School. He was a member of the NYS Assembly before enlisting in the Union Army, where he was killed in the 1864 Battle of Cold Harbor.

Grandson, Peter A. Porter, was born on October 10, 1853. He graduated from Yale in 1874, and traveled extensively before returning to Niagara Falls. From 1880 to 1895, he owned the *Niagara Falls Gazette*, he operated the Cataract House for many years, was president of Cataract Bank and a director of the Niagara River Hydraulic Tunnel, Power and Sewer Company - the predecessor of the Niagara Falls Power Company. In 1885, his family sold Niagara Falls and much surrounding land to New York State, creating the first State Park in the U.S. Before Niagara Falls was chartered as a city in 1892, he was village president in 1878, a member of the New York State Assembly and U.S. House of Representatives. Upon retirement he was active with the Buffalo Historical Society and founded the Niagara Frontier Historical Society.

CAPTAIN SAMUEL PRATT & FAMILY

One of Buffalo's earliest residents; with the family starting
Pratt & Letchworth and M&T Bank

The family of Captain Samuel Pratt can be traced back to accompanying William the Conqueror at the Battle of Hastings in 1066. John Pratt was the first member of the family in America and in 1639 was one of the original settlers of Hartford, Connecticut. Samuel was born in East Hartford and at an early age his parents moved to Westminster, Vermont. He enlisted in the Continental Army on July 10, 1775, shortly after the outbreak of the American Revolution, serving two enlistments and participating in the Battle of Germantown and defense of Fort Mifflin.

In 1801 Captain Pratt hoped to journey from Montreal to the West to purchase furs, but he was taken sick and the expedition was rescheduled for the following year. The next year they journeyed down the St. Lawrence to Niagara and stopped at Buffalo Creek on the way to Detroit. Pratt returned to Buffalo in 1803, and being impressed by the location of the village, was determined to establish himself in the fur trade in that locality. He returned with his family in 1804, arriving in the first two-wheel coach brought to Buffalo. When he relocated to Buffalo, he and his family stayed at Crows Tavern before building a temporary log home on the Terrace. He established his first store on the north side of Exchange Street, where he actively traded with both whites and Indians.

The family selected their homestead on the high bank or terrace, upon a lot extending from the top of the bank to the Little Buffalo Creek (no longer in existence, as it was buried). This was designated as Inner Lot #1 and was located at the corner of Main and Exchange Streets. He built a two-and-a half story frame house which was the first frame home built in Buffalo. The home was called The Mansion and it later became the site of The Mansion House. His store was located next to it on the south side of Exchange Street. In 1805, his parents, Aaron and Mary Clark Pratt, relocated to Buffalo but they died shortly afterward in 1807 and 1809, respectively.

Pratt began making improvements at what is now the corner of Washington and Seneca Streets but realized that was not part of outer lots # 99-103, that he also purchased. He then built a large barn for his business at the corner of Seneca and Ellicott Streets, which is now the location near the center of the Bison's Baseball Stadium.

Samuel Pratt also purchased approximately 100 acres on both sides of the Buffalo River. He operated a ferry prior to building a toll bridge across the river, about a mile from its mouth. The road leading from Buffalo to the bridge later became Ohio Street. It was across this bridge that the Pratt family and other Buffalo residents fled to Hamburg when the British burned Buffalo on December 30, 1813. In 1831, Bella D. Coe deeded the Pratt family and Joseph Clary 228 acres south of the Buffalo River, with that land later becoming a portion of Tifft Farms.

Captain Samuel Pratt and his wife Esther Wells Pratt had eight children. He died in 1812, a victim of the respiratory epidemic during the fall 1812/winter 1813 and is one of twenty-five Revolutionary War veterans buried at Forest Lawn Cemetery. Two of his sons, Samuel Pratt Jr. and Hiram, continued his business legacy in Buffalo. His wife Esther and some of their children returned to the old family Vermont homestead, after Buffalo was burned during the War of 1812, but she returned and died here in 1830.

Samuel Junior, the eldest son, did not accompany his parents when they originally relocated to Buffalo, moving here with his wife Sophia Fletcher Pratt in August 1807. His wife was the daughter of General Samuel Fletcher, one of Vermont's most distinguished early residents. Fletcher was a veteran of the French & Indian War and American Revolution, rising from Orderly Sergeant to Major General, and serving at the Battle of Bunker Hill. Samuel Pratt Junior was involved in commerce in Townsend, Vermont and joined his father's store when he moved to Buffalo. He resigned in 1810 when he was appointed Sheriff of Niagara County and upon the outbreak of the War of 1812, he joined the army and served as Adjutant to General Porter. He assisted in defense of Buffalo after it was burned during the war, extinguishing fires for several days, with one of his associates being killed by Indians that were still pillaging in the area. After the war he formed the partnership Pratt & Leech, with his brother-in-law Elijah Leech. Samuel Pratt Sr. died in 1822, with his widow Sophia outliving him until 1862.

Born in 1800, Hiram Pratt was the youngest son of Captain Samuel Pratt. During his childhood he was close with Dr. Cyrenius Chapin and when Buffalo was burned during the War of 1812, Hiram guided Dr. Chapin's daughters to safety at the Chapin farm in Hamburg. Chapin hoped Hiram would become a doctor, but he was interested in business and in 1818 he was running Chapin's store with Orlando Allen. Allen married Hiram's sister Marilla, with Allen being elected mayor of Buffalo in 1848 and he was a member of the NYS Assembly for three terms.

Hiram started a warehouse and freight forwarding with Asa Meech, Farmers Fire Insurance & Loan Company and was one of the founders of the Bank of Buffalo in 1830. Hiram Pratt was the last mayor of Buffalo selected by the Common Council, serving in 1835 and 1839. During his first term he purchased land for a city wholesale market, which later became the Elk Street Market. He personally owned land in the Black Rock area, where in 1835 he built a mansion at the southeast corner of Niagara and Porter, on Prospect Hill. Hiram also donated two five-acre squares, across from Prospect Hill, that became Prospect Park and Columbus Park. Most of his money was lost as a result of the Benjamin Rathbun forgeries and the Panic of 1837. He died at age 39 in 1840, leaving a widow Maria Fowle Pratt and three daughters Louise Ann Hopkins, Maria Esther Ritch and Mary Burt Parsons.

Samuel Fletcher Pratt was the oldest son of Samuel Pratt Jr. and Sophia Fletcher. He was born in Townsend, Vermont on May 28, 1807 and moved to Buffalo shortly after he was born. At age 12 he went to work as a clerk at a store in Canada, returning three years later when his father died. In 1822, he obtained employment at the hardware store of George and Thaddeus Weed, which in 1828, became the George Weed & Company partnership of Pratt, George Weed and Lucius Storrs. In 1829, George Weed died, with his brother Thaddeus continuing the business as Weed & Pratt. Pratt bought out Weeds interests in 1836, and his brother Pascal Paoli Pratt joined the business renaming it S.F. Pratt & Company. When Pascal was admitted as a partner in 1842, it became Pratt & Company which began as a retail store but developed into a wholesale enterprise. They established themselves as importers and dealers in a variety of hardware, with accounts in several states, extending beyond the Mississippi River. Their offices and warehouse were located at 28-32 Terrace Street. Upon Samuel Fletcher Pratt's death in 1872 and Pascal resigning to become president of M&T Bank in 1886, Pratt & Company was succeeded by Beals & Brown, led by Edward P. Beals (who was a partner of Pratt & Company since 1846) and his son, Pascal Pratt Beals. When Brown died in 1893, Edward and Pascal Pratt Beals, along with W.R. Gass established Beals & Company.

Pratt & Letchworth was formed in 1848 by Samuel Fletcher Pratt, Pascal Paoli Pratt and William Letchworth. The company began as a manufacturer and importer of saddlery, coach and trunk hardware, with offices adjacent to Pratt & Company Hardware. They progressed into the manufacture of malleable steel and iron casting and material for locomotive and car builders. They built a plant on Tonawanda Street in the Black Rock area of Buffalo, that eventually employed approximately 1,800 workers, and a plant in Brantford, Ontario that had about 1,000 workers.

Figure 121 Pratt & Letchworth plant on Tonawanda Street in Black Rock

In 1848, Samuel Fletcher Pratt was one of the leaders in organizing the Buffalo Gas Light Company (also known as Buffalo Illuminating Gas Company), where he was president from 1848 until his death in 1872. It was the first gas manufacturing facility in the U.S. When their offices and plant at 257 West Genesee Street were built, it was only yards from the Erie Canal. To connect to the Erie Canal, at the rear of the plant the company dug a slip making it easier to deliver raw material required to manufacture the gas. The slip was named the Wilkeson Slip, in honor of Judge Samuel Wilkeson. Within the complex they burned coal, which created illuminating natural gas, used for the lighting of streets, homes, offices and industrial businesses. Several gas companies merged into the Buffalo Gas Company and the building later housed

Iroquois Gas Company, which became National Fuel Gas. The complex is listed on the National Register of Historic Places but everything except the front façade was demolished in 2000. That Romanesque façade was designed by John H. Selkirk, who is considered Buffalo's first architect. The façade was incorporated into the Blue Cross & Blue Shield, HealthNow New York Inc. corporate headquarters which opened in 2007.

In 1851, Samuel F. Pratt was one of the founders of Buffalo Female Academy, now Buffalo Seminary. He was the first president of the school and served on the board of trustees until his death. Pratt was also one of the pall bearers when Abraham Lincoln was lying in state at St. James Hall. Pratt joined the First Presbyterian Church when he was eighteen years old and continued singing in the choir until a few years before his death on April 27, 1872. In his will be bequeathed $10,000 to the Buffalo General Hospital, Buffalo Orphan Asylum and the YMCA building fund. He also left $5,000 to the Home for the Friendless and $30,000 to establish a professorship at Hamilton College in Clinton, NY.

Figure 122 Samuel F. Pratt House at 137 Swan Street

After Samuel Fletcher Pratt's death, his widow Mary Jane Strong Pratt purchased 388 Delaware Avenue, having previously lived at 137 Swan Street. She purchased the Delaware Avenue mansion from Stephen V.R. Watson and lived in the home with three of her grandchildren. In 1887, she sold the house to The Buffalo Club which still remains at this address.

The second son of Samuel Pratt Jr., Lucius Hubbard Pratt, was born in 1809. Lucius was involved in shipping on the Great Lakes and had a warehouse on the Buffalo River at the Pratt Slip. He lived at 159 Swan Street, in a house built in 1835 on the original land deeded to his grandfather Captain Samuel Pratt. After his death in 1876, that house was sold to Benjamin Fitch, who donated it to Maria Love to create the Fitch Creche, which is considered the first day care center in the country. His sons Lucius Henry, Samuel C. and Edward B. formed a wholesale and retail hardware business called Pratt Brothers, which continued into the 1900s.

Pascal Paoli Pratt was the third son of Samuel Pratt Jr. He was born in 1819 and educated in village schools in Buffalo, followed by Hamilton Academy and Amherst Academy. At 16 years of age he started working at his brother's hardware store, becoming a partner six years later when the company became S.F. Pratt & Company. In 1846, it was renamed Pratt & Company, a wholesale hardware business whose trade extended to various sections of the country and beyond the Mississippi River. In 1848, with his brother Samuel Fletcher Pratt and William Letchworth, he established Pratt & Letchworth, a manufacturing saddle and carriage hardware manufacturer that grew to become one of the principal iron and steel companies of WNY.

On August 29, 1856 Pascal Paoli Pratt and Bronson Case Rumsey founded Manufacturers & Traders Bank, to provide a bank capable of making long term loans to factories and manufacturing plants for the purchase of manufacturing equipment (existing banks were not making loans to the factories and warehouses). In 1857, he purchased the Buffalo Iron & Nail Company and the same year established the Fletcher Furnace Company in Black Rock and Tonawanda Furnace Company, operating these companies until the 1880s.

Pascal Paoli Pratt was a proponent of encouraging businesses to relocate to Buffalo. He drew attention that Buffalo was favorably located for manufacturing businesses, was a transportation center, had cheap fuel, low cost of living, a good school system and good labor force. He had faith in the future of the city and in addition to investing his own capital, encouraged others to make capital investments. He also had the reputation of being a good employer. His employees were well paid, justly treated and contented in their employment. His businesses were instrumental in building up Black Rock and Northern Buffalo as a manufacturing center. In this vicinity, Pratt & Company operated Buffalo Iron & Nail Works, located on Forest and Niagara about one half mile from their Pratt & Letchworth factory on Tonawanda Street.

In addition to starting M&T Bank, when it was incorporated Pascal was made one of the directors and was elected president of the bank in 1885. He held this position until he retired in 1901, at which time his son-in-law Robert L. Fryer succeeded him. He was also one of the founders of the Bank of Buffalo, a director of the Bank of Attica and trustee of Fidelity Trust & Guaranty Company. Commercially, he was a director of the Buffalo Street Railroad Company, Buffalo Gas Company and WNY and Pennsylvania Railroad.

In 1869, Pascal Pratt was chosen as a member of the Parks Commission of Buffalo and was elected its first president, serving until 1879. While in this position he was instrumental in working with Frederick Law Olmsted in creating the Buffalo Parks system. In 1883, he was appointed Commissioner to appraise the land taken by the Niagara Falls Reservation to create Niagara Falls State Park, recognized as the oldest state park in the U.S.

Pascal married Phebe Lorenz on August 1, 1845. She was the daughter of prominent Pittsburgh iron and glass manufacturer Frederick Lorenz. Pascal and Phebe had seven children including Katharine Pratt Horton, who was considered Buffalo's most prominent society hostess. With her husband, businessman John Miller Horton, for over a decade they traveled Europe, being received at numerous royal courts. After the death of her husband, she purchased the Birge Mansion at 477 Delaware Avenue (in the Midway rowhouses), and transformed it into a society center reminiscent of a French style salon, with sumptuous furnishings and art of the Louis XIV era. Upon her death the home, its furnishings and an endowment fund were willed to the Katharine Pratt Horton Buffalo Chapter of the National Society of the Daughters of the American Revolution.

In regard to social institutions, Pascal was the first president of the Buffalo YMCA and was the largest contributor to its original home at 19 Mohawk Street. For twenty years he was the president of the Buffalo Seminary and in 1862 was one of the founding members of the Buffalo Fine Arts Academy. He was a member of many other societies, clubs and a strong supporter of patriotic organizations. His house at 736 Main was demolished shortly after his death in 1905 to make way for the Potter Building.

Relatives of the Buffalo Pratt family were dispersed across the country. John Pratt, the patriarch of the Buffalo Pratt Family resided in Massachusetts, before he and his brother William moved west to be early settlers of the Connecticut Colony in 1639. William was the third great grandfather of Parley P. Pratt, who in 1835 was an original member of the Quorum of the Twelve Apostles in the Mormon Church of the Latter-Day Saints. Parley Pratt practiced plural marriage and was the father of 30 children. His brother Orson Pratt Jr. was also a member of the original Quorum of Twelve Apostles and was the church spokesman for the legitimacy of polygamy. It was estimated that Parley Pratt had between 30,000 and 50,000 living descendants in 2011. Mitt Romney is the great-great grandson of Parley Pratt.

According to representatives of Pratt & Lambert Company, they could not find any direct link of their founders to the Samuel Pratt Family of Buffalo. Alfred W. Pratt started a varnish factory in Long Island City in 1849 and after admitting Henry S. Lambert as a partner in 1875, incorporated Pratt & Lambert in 1885, with his brother Charles M. Pratt. Alfred Pratt was born in Massachusetts, where the Buffalo Pratt Family originated, so some relationship is plausible. They established the Buffalo factory and offices because it was mid-way between their operations in Chicago and Long Island. However, the Pratt & Letchworth and Pratt & Lambert factories became neighbors in the Black Rock area of Buffalo.

Figure 123 Pascal Paoli Pratt was one of the founding members of the Buffalo Fine Arts Academy, which became the Albright Knox Art Gallery

ASA RANSOM

Innkeeper and founder of Clarence

A sa Ransom was born in Massachusetts to Elias and Sarah Ransom. In 1773, his father passed away, leaving Asa's mother a 29-year-old widow of six children. A year later she married Ichabod Hopkins and bore eight more children. This marriage documents the relationship between the Ransom and Hopkins families in WNY.

Ransom apprenticed as a gold and silversmith and after completing his training, Asa moved to Geneva, New York in 1788. There he built a combination house and silversmith shop where he traded with the Indians (Haudenosaunee) who lived in the nearby village of Kanadasaga. Asa was well liked by the Indians and earned a decent living. He returned to Sheffield, Massachusetts where on October 12, 1794 he married Keziah Keyes. The couple returned to Geneva and on December 20, 1795 their daughter Portia was born.

After Fort Niagara was transferred from British to American jurisdiction in 1796, Asa Ransom decided to move further west and was one of Buffalo's first settlers, arriving in 1797 with his wife and daughter. They built a log cabin near Main and Terrace which was one of the first four houses built in the settlement at the mouth of Buffalo Creek. Ransom sold silver bracelets, jewelry, ornaments and brooches, becoming friends and trusted by the Seneca. On February 27, 1798, their second daughter Sophia was born. She was the first white child born in Western New York, outside of Fort Niagara or other military outposts.

In 1799, The Holland Land Company offered lots ten miles apart to any proper man who would build and operate a tavern upon it. Asa Ransom took up Joseph Ellicott's offer and purchased 150 acres at $2.00 per acre. He built a log home, tavern (the first hotel in Erie County outside of Buffalo Creek), and grist mill (opened in 1805), located near the corner of Main Street and Ransom Road. With this purchase, Clarence became first settlement in Erie County made "white Man's fashion", or by obtaining legal title to the land before settling upon it.

During the summer of 1800 the Ransom's hosted about 150 families traveling to Buffalo, Presque Isle (Erie), Pennsylvania, New Connecticut, Ohio or other points west. One night over 40 people stayed at the tavern. The first tax roll of lands west of the Genesee River was completed in 1800 and Ransom paid 61 cents in tax, on property and his personal estate valued at $410.

An 1804 Holland Land Company map showed the Ransom house to be on the west bank of Ransom Creek on Buffalo Road. The town was called Pine Grove, Ransomville and Ransom's Grove before it became known as the Hollow, later Clarence Hollow. Joseph Ellicott moved his Holland Land Company office to Clarence before permanently locating it in Batavia in 1801. At the Clarence home Harry Bolton Ransom was born in 1799, the first white male child born in Erie County. He was followed in 1801 by Asa Ransom Jr.

Figure 124 Historic plaque commemorating Asa Ransom's tavern in Clarence

In addition to the grist mill that was opened in 1805, with a loan obtained from Joseph Ellicott, Ransom opened a distillery in 1807. This operation converting grain to spirits was also made possible with a $134 loan from the Holland Land Company. The building that is now called the Asa Ransom House, dates back to 1853 and is about a block away from where Ransom's original home and tavern stood. Ruins of a mill and railroad trestle stand behind the current restaurant and bed and breakfast.

In December 1801, Asa Ransom was appointed the first white official in what is now Erie County. Governor George Clinton named him justice of the peace and his secretary DeWitt Clinton personally transmitted the paperwork. When the town of Willink was carved out of the town of Batavia, Ransom was named town assessor in 1804 and 1805. The 1807 annual Willink town meeting was moved from Peter Vandeventer's tavern to Ransom's tavern, with Ransom being elected town supervisor, replacing Vandeventer. In 1808, the 33rd session of the New York Legislature was held at Ransom's tavern.

Ransom remained active in community affairs and was a Colonel during the war of 1812. He died in 1837, leaving a large family, consisting of his children and relatives. His brothers Elias and Amasa also moved to the WNY area. Elias's home was built in 1800 about seven miles east of Buffalo. He built a frame house which was the first frame house west of Batavia. He also built the first frame barn and set out the first orchard in the Holland Land Company area. His brother Amasa lived in the city of Buffalo on Seneca Street east of Ellicott Street.

Several other early settlers and families, including the Hopkins, were influential in the Williamsville/Snyder/Amherst area and Williamsville played an important role during the War of 1812.

In 1799, Benjamin Ellicott, a surveyor and brother of Joseph Ellicott, and John Thompson were sold 300 acres of land which became the village of Williamsville. As a favor they were sold this land at $2.00 an acre. The land included the falls, now known as Glen Falls, which were called Ga-sko-sa-da-ne-o or "many falls" by the Seneca. The original name of the creek was Eleven Mile Creek, renamed Ellicott Creek in honor of Joseph Ellicott. Thompson built a mill near the falls and a house, known for years as the Evans House. The Evans House was demolished in 1955 and stood at the corner of Main and Oakgrove, in front of the current location of Ed Young's Hardware. In 1805, Jonas Williams bought the land and Thompson's abandoned mill, becoming the father of Williamsville, originally called William's Mills. In 1811, Williams also purchased and rebuilt the mill on Spring Street, known as the Williamsville Water Mill. This historic restored red building now houses Sweet Jenny's Ice Cream. Jonas Williams was also related to the Ellicott family, as his sister Sarah married Andrew Ellicott. Williams married Elizabeth Wells of Canandaigua, who was a niece of Captain Samuel Pratt. The political leaders along Buffalo Road were Jonas Williams toward the east and Timothy S. Hopkins to the west.

Timothy S. Hopkins was a half-brother of Asa and Elias Ransom. He moved to Clarence in 1800, settling near Asa Ransom's property. He and his partner Otis Ingalls cleared land east of Clarence and grew the first wheat on Holland Purchase land. They had to travel 40 miles to Chippewa, Canada, a four-day trip with a team of oxen pulling their wagon and crossing the Niagara River at Black Rock by ferry, to have the wheat ground. This journey did not change until Asa Ransom opened his grist mill. Hopkins moved near the farm of Elias Ransom, in what is now the Snyder area. There he assisted Elias in building his frame house and barn, along with planting the orchards. In 1808, the first town meeting of Clarence was held at Elias Ransom's tavern, two miles west of the current village of Williamsville. When this meeting was held, the town of Clarence was almost all of Northern Erie County and Jonas Williams was elected supervisor of Clarence at the meeting.

Hopkins was active as a citizen soldier or militiaman since 1803, when he was assigned the rank of captain. In 1811, he held the rank of Brigadier General in the New York State Militia. His original log home was replaced by a stone home in the Snyder area, near the current location of Amherst High School. There he and his southern-born wife Nancy Kerr raised nine children and lived for 50 years. On April 28, 1804, their marriage was the first recorded marriage in Erie County, and it took place in the Evans House. Their son Timothy Augustus Hopkins followed his father in political activity and built the first bridge over the Tonawanda Creek portion of the Erie Canal. He constructed drainage ditches in Northern Amherst, reclaiming the land in that area and Hopkins Road is named after him. Another son, Nelson Kerr Hopkins was an attorney and president of the Buffalo Common Council. Timothy married Louise A. Pratt, organized the first paid Fire Department and served as its commissioner for ten years. Nelson owned and sub-divided much of the land in the Hopkins Street area, which is named after him.

With the waterpower in the Williamsville area other mills were opened, in addition to Jonas Williams sawmill, gristmill, tannery and other enterprises at Glen Falls. In 1806, William Maltby, who previously ran an inn near Glen Falls, built a sawmill and gristmill north the Williams property on Ellicott Creek, in Skinnerville in what is now near Millersport and North Forest Road. John Long opened a sawmill on Buffalo Road (Main Street) near Union Road. Jacob Getz operated a sawmill on North Forest Road where it crossed Ellicott Creek. The Fogelsonger family had a cider mill and gristmill in what is now the Park Club Lane area.

Members of the Evans Family moved into the Williamsville area on other land owned by Benjamin Ellicott. David Evans' mother was an Ellicott and three Ellicott sisters married men from the Evans family. Since Joseph and Benjamin Ellicott did not have any children, they left their estates to their sisters and their children. The Evans House and Evans Street were named after the family.

During the winter of 1812, General Smyth moved his forces down Buffalo Road to quarters along Ellicott Creek, which they maintained until the of spring 1813. Jonas Williams was in Albany when the troops occupied his land and cut down timber to build their barracks. He had to issue an appeal to the federal government for compensation. When Buffalo was burned on December 30, 1813, many residents took refuge in Williamsville. In 1814, the military hospital was moved to Williamsville, in the former barracks built by General Smyth, with over 1,000 soldiers treated at the hospital. Due to the number of soldiers that died, a cemetery was built south of the hospital on Ellicott Creek. The cause of death for most of the soldiers was dysentery and diarrhea, not wounds received during battle. Over 200 regular army, militia and

British prisoners of war were buried at this cemetery, which is on Aero Drive behind the Buffalo Airport. The hospital was overcrowded, and the wounded were placed in area homes. American Colonel Winfield Scott and captured British Commanding General Phineas Riall made temporary quarters in the Evans House. Scott moved to complete his convalescence at the Batavia home of James Brisbane and Riall was sent east to be included in prisoner exchanges and paroled to England. Over 5,000 troops were based in Williams Mills and their

Figure 125 War of 1812 Cemetery where soldiers that died at Williamsville Hospital were buried

barracks were along Ellicott Creek,

near what is now Garrison Road. The drill ground was in the current location of St. Peter & St. Paul's Church.

When Buffalo and Black Rock were burned in December 1813, it was the troops of General Hopkins that were routed, but Hopkins was not with the troops as he was in Clarence. American Troops were sent

Figure 126 Eagle House on Main Street in Williamsville in 1860
Photo: Buffalo Niagara Heritage Village

from Williams Mills to defend Buffalo, but while moving west they encountered the panicked soldiers and civilians fleeing eastward on Buffalo Road. According to soldier Samuel Kittinger, of the family that later started Kittinger Furniture, they were unsuccessful in trying to stop the fleeing militia that were routed at Black Rock and Buffalo, so they joined the retreat back to Williams Mills and points east. General Amos Hall assembled a force of 200-300 men to cover the fleeing inhabitants and check the enemy advance. There was a real fear that Williams Mills would be attacked because the British were given orders to attack settlements where an arsenal was located, and one existed east of Ellicott Creek. There were reports of a skirmish at a military outpost called Bartish Hill, located on current day Chestnut Ridge Road west of the 990, but the battle theater shifted back to Canadian side of the Niagara River.

In 1802, Amherst was part of the town of Batavia in Genesee County, in 1804 it became part of the town of Erie in Genesee County, in 1808 it became part of the town of Clarence in Niagara County, in 1810 it became part of the town of Buffalo and in 1818 the New York State Legislature created the town of Amherst. Timothy S. Hopkins was elected the first Supervisor of the town of Amherst in 1819, serving several terms, and was a Justice of the Peace for 32 years. Later supervisors were his son Timothy A. Hopkins and Oziel Smith, builder and original owner of the Eagle House. Other families that were involved in the early history of Amherst were Hersey, Young, Frick, Grove, Snyder, Wehrle, Eggert, Dodge and Kittinger. Timothy A. Hopkins purchased the mill properties at Williamsville Glen Falls, including the Eagle House, in 1844. He was trained as a lawyer, served as a justice of the peace, Erie County Sheriff, NYS assemblyman, was interested in local history and wrote the first history of Amherst.

BENJAMIN RATHBUN

The builder of Buffalo who was jailed for forgery

B enjamin Rathbun was born on December 1, 1790 near Westford, Connecticut to Moses and Patience James Rathbun. His father was an ambitious store clerk and his grandfather was a Baptist minister in Windham County. His great-great grandmother was the daughter of the first Baptist minister in Connecticut and he was a descendent of the last man burned at the stake in England for religious dissent. Although the Rathbun family was not wealthy, Moses insisted that all his six children dress well, an appearance that made them look affluent and a practice Benjamin followed throughout his life.

Benjamin's uncle was John Rathbun, who owned a successful wholesale grocery that sold to retailers across the country. Many of his accounts were part of the extended Rathbun family and like most successful men of his time, Benjamin's career was started on the foundation of family support. After visiting his uncle in NYC, he was given a clerk's job at a family owned store in Oxford, NY in 1808. He worked for two years with his cousins in the branch store the family opened in the town of Lisle on the Tioughnioga River.

In 1809, he rejoined his family who had moved to Monticello, NY in Otsego County. There he worked at the store his father opened, and on December 15, 1811, he married Alice Loomis. In the early 1800s, there was a chaotic currency situation in America and small banks issued paper currency. Moses and Benjamin opened a credit exchange office, where paper bank issues were exchanged for bills, and notes were discounted, sort of like a bank. The Rathbuns expanded their operations by issuing notes that served as currency and as a basis of credit to buy and sell property.

The Rathbuns opened the second tavern in Monticello in 1815, which soon became the preferred hotel, bar and meeting place in the area. Benjamin built the tavern, which gave him experience as a builder and architect. He ran the tavern, which gave him experience as an innkeeper and he gained experience working with the stagecoach lines. In 1817, the Rathbuns filed bankruptcy, as they overextended their credit. To escape the wrath of their neighbors and avoid going to jail for unpaid debts, the Rathbuns left town. There were also rumors of forgery in the amount of $12,000, but they were never prosecuted.

Moses moved with the rest of the Rathbun family to Batavia, NY. Benjamin continued to Buffalo, where he saw opportunity, but moved on to Ohio where he settled in what is now Toledo. That settlement failed to complete their deferred payment schedule to the U.S. government, so Benjamin lost the money he invested. He moved to Sandusky, Ohio and without any prospects, he decided to rejoin his parents. The danger of prosecution in New York had either passed or relatives that remained in Otsego County had fixed the problem.

In Batavia, Rathbun unsuccessfully solicited James Brisbane and David E. Evans for financial assistance. He bypassed Buffalo and moved to Manchester (Niagara

Falls) where he saw the potential for the tourist trade and the need for a quality tavern where tourists could stay. He was not successful in getting merchant Samuel DeVeaux to assist him and Augustus Porter, of the freight forwarding company of Porter, Barton & Company, told him that he was backing Parkhurst Whitney in expanding his tavern. Then he saw an ad in the *Niagara Journal* that Kibbe's Tavern aka Norton's Tavern was for sale or lease in Buffalo.

In 1819, Benjamin Rathbun started his career in Buffalo by leasing the Eagle Tavern. It was located on Main Street at Court Street, perfectly situated on the roads to Williamsville, Batavia and Black Rock. At first it was called Rathbun's Tavern, until he gave it the more formal name of The Eagle Tavern. Within a couple years, the Eagle Tavern surpassed Joseph Langdon's Stage House as the best hotel and preferred location for events and meetings in the settlement. To assist him and his wife Alice in running the business, Benjamin hired his brother Lyman Rathbun as the bookkeeper and Henry Hawkins, a freed slave, as the maître d' of the hotel. The Eagle Tavern became the mix of a country inn, old stage house and luxurious metropolitan style hotel - the finest stagecoach stop and gathering place west of NYC.

Rathbun did not own the Eagle Tavern property but he expanded upon what he leased. After Norton sold the Eagle Tavern to NYC investors in 1822 for $10,000, Rathbun negotiated a long-term lease. With an expansion to the back, he doubled the

Figure 127 American Hotel and Eagle Tavern

capacity of the tavern. Another wing was added to the rear. He obtained permission to use the area to the south, and erected sheds and barns to accommodate arrivals by stagecoach or horseback. A Stage Office was added and Bela D. Cole, who ran the stagecoach lines, had his barns adjacent to the Eagle Tavern yards.

When William Kibbe did not accept Rathbun's proposal to finance a building constructed by Rathbun, Kibbe decided to sell the one-half acre lot north of the Tavern. Rathbun did not have the finances to purchase it but he was able to bring the right people together. Attorneys, Philander Bennett and Henry White, were joined by physicians, Dr. Benjamin C. Congdon and Dr. Henry R. Stagg, to purchase the lot. Congdon was a former partner of Dr. Cyrenius Chapin and Stagg married the daughter of Mayor Samuel Wilkeson. The building became known as the Eagle Building.

In the late 1820s, Buffalo lacked money for enterprises. Barter no longer sufficed for larger projects and wealth amassed in land and buildings was not capital until it could be translated into currency. The currency was not reliable, interest rates were high, and exchanges or discount brokers demanded a substantial share of the principal for discounting notes. That all began to change in 1829 with the funding of projects for the Buffalo Harbor, Jubilee Spring and High School Association. On September 15, 1829, the Bank of the United States announced they would be opening a branch in Buffalo. Judge William B. Rochester was selected to head the branch with a local board of Senator Albert H. Tracy, Charles Townsend, Sheldon Thompson, David E. Evans, Augustus Porter, William Peacock, James Wadsworth, Joseph Stocking and Lyman A. Spaulding. Benjamin Rathbun was given the contract to build the bank.

This contract provided him with a reputation as a builder and an architect. Rathbun purchased a large tract of land between Main Street and Delaware Avenue, near the developing northern edge of the city. He broke this into smaller lots, where he constructed homes that were sold to Buffalo's growing population. He was hired to build a new jail. Rathbun even sold the Eagle Tavern to Isaac R. Harrington and moved his store, offices and a dry goods store he added, to a four-story building at 230 Main Street. On September 6, 1831, Rathbun opened the Bank of Buffalo with Hiram Pratt, David E. Evans, Pierre A. Batker, Israel T. Hatch, Guy E. Goodrich and Stephen G. Austin, and built the bank's office on Main Street near St. Peter's Church.

Land speculation and easy credit followed in the early 1830s. The Commercial Bank of Buffalo opened in 1834 and became one of the chief sources of speculative funds, lending generously to Rathbun. Other banks opened, and due to a shortage of small bills, for the convenience of his employees and customers, Rathbun issued scrip in $1, $2, $3 and $5 denominations. This was accepted as valid currency, a testimony to the confidence the public had in Rathbun.

Rathbun became more involved with Peter and Augustus Porter when they proposed building a railroad to Niagara Falls. He invested in the project and was given the contract to build the railway, employing between 2,000 to 2,500 workers. Rathbun then began purchasing the Porter's land in Niagara Falls and purchased other farmlands. He owned land from Fort Schlosser to the whirlpool, near the current site of the Queenston Bridge. He purchased the Niagara Eagle Tavern from Samuel DeVeaux, resulting in Parkhurst Whitney moving his operations to the Cataract House. A canal was even planned to carry boats around the cataracts. On May 1, 1836, the contracts were signed and Rathbun owned most of Niagara Falls.

Prices began rising sharply in 1833. Paper currency poured into the market, some just backed by promissory notes. Wages rose but interest rates rose to a whopping 5% per month or 60% per year. However, speculation was so profitable that borrowers were willing to pay these rates. All classes of workers became involved in the speculation, and with the profits wanted fine homes, clothes, carriages and other luxuries. Many people doubled or quadrupled their net worth. This provided work for Rathbun's clerks, supervisors and laborers, with about one third of Buffalo inhabitants dependent upon Rathbun for their livelihood.

During the 1830s, he built many of the buildings in Buffalo. To support and supply his building projects he operated stone quarries, brick plants, machine shops, grocery stores, dry goods stores, stagecoaches, house drawn omnibuses and even a private bank that issued bank notes over his signature. The payroll to his workers was $10,000 a week and he paid $300,000 a year to wholesalers in NYC to supply his stores.

During 1835 and 1836, he built 99 buildings. His projects included The American Hotel (sold to Alanson "Lance" Palmer), United States Hotel on Terrace (for Dr. Josiah Trowbridge), the four-story Webster Block around Main and Perry, the Darrow Block on Washington below Clinton, Henry Sizer house, the jail and the Unitarian Church. The former Unitarian Church still stands at 110 Franklin Street, being an office of the Abstract Title Company in the Tictor Title Building for many years. Rathbun was also expanding the Niagara Eagle Tavern, building an even larger hotel at Niagara Falls, and starting construction on his greatest project in Buffalo, the

Figure 128 Unitarian Church, the only remaining Rathbun building

Buffalo Exchange, a combination office, hotel and auditorium. The exchange was to cost $500,000 and occupy the entire 245-foot block along Main Street between North and South Division, with a dome 60 feet in diameter and 34 feet high, and the building 222 feet high.

Rathbun had to look out of the area to obtain additional financing. He got creative and helped resurrect the Gransville Bank in Gransville, Ohio. Another private bank was located in Patterson, New Jersey, the Patterson Bank. At both banks Rathbun became owner of much of the stock, set up an acquaintance to run it, received loans, used the value of his investments to obtain other loans and circulated notes from the Bank of Gransville. He also started the Commercial Bank of Fort Erie in Canada. In addition, Rathbun had a NYC agent working on obtaining $500,000 in financing, with a bond signed by Rathbun and other wealthy individuals from Buffalo. It was believed that all Rathbun's financial problems would be resolved when the lots he owned in Niagara Falls were sold. On August 2, 1836, the Niagara Falls lots went on sale and in the first few hours over $30,000 in lots were sold. Buyers arrived with cash in hand and bid on the best lots. Brisk sales were anticipated for the entire week. On August 3, 1836, Rathbun was jailed for forging the names of prominent local men as guarantors on a series of his promissory notes.

His brother Lyman masterminded the forgery scheme, where the names of prominent Buffalo residents were signed on over 1.5 million dollars of notes. His nephew Lyman Rathbun Howlett was the master forger. Benjamin did not do any of the forging, but he was aware of it and after he was charged, both his brother and nephew left town. Rathbun was incarcerated in the Buffalo jail he built, was found guilty and sentenced to five years at Auburn Prison. When he was released from prison, he opened a hotel in New York City, where most Buffalo residents preferred to stay when they were in the city.

Rathbun's arrest was disastrous for Buffalo, as his employees lost the jobs that many families relied upon. All construction jobs were halted and the inventory of his stores and his other holdings were sold at auction. The Buffalo Exchange was never built, and the new Niagara Falls Hotel remained a hole in the ground. The national economy was even affected as the Panic of 1837 swept the country.

Figure 129 Drawing of Buffalo Exchange that was not built due to Rathbun's arrest

RED JACKET – SAGOYEWATHA

Seneca chief of the Wolf Clan who was known as the Great Orator

R ed Jacket was born in 1750 in the Finger Lakes area of NYS and grew up near the mouth of Basswood Creek at Keuka Lake. During the American Revolution, the Seneca sided with the British and Red Jacket served as a messenger. He was presented with a red coat by a British Officer who was impressed with his leadership qualities. That red jacket became his trademark and his English name.

At the end of the Revolution, the 1784 Treaty of Fort Stanwix, in Rome, New York, was held as a peace treaty between the Iroquois and Americans. The treaty was required because the Native Americans were slighted in the Treaty of Paris, with England not having the authority to cede Iroquois land to America. Joseph Brant was the tribal chief at the beginning of the negotiations but had to leave on trip to England so Seneca leader Cornplanter took his place. A treaty was signed

Figure 130 Portrait of Red Jacket

ceding all Seneca claims in the Ohio territory, a strip of land along the Niagara River and all land west of the mouth of Buffalo Creek. Red Jacket was not in favor of this treaty, speaking against it at the Six Nations council at Buffalo Creek, where it was not ratified.

In 1792, Red Jacket met with President George Washington in the U.S. capital of Philadelphia to present claims and grievances of the Iroquois. Washington honored him with the solid silver peace medal, which he greatly prized and wore it whenever his portrait was painted. The medal shows George Washington shaking hands with Red Jacket and is inscribed George Washington, Red Jacket and 1792.

Cornplanter and Red Jacket were both at the Treaty of Canandaigua, when they, along with 50 other Seneca sachems and war chiefs, signed the treaty on November 11, 1794. This treaty affirmed Haudenosaunee land rights in the state of New York and confirmed boundaries established by the Phelps and Gorham Purchase of 1788. Red Jacket was against the loss of any land but felt it was better to lose a part than to be deprived of it all.

In 1797, at the Treaty of Big Tree, Cornplanter was in favor of the sale which Red Jacket considered greased by liquor and trinkets. Red Jacket's opposition was overruled and much of WNY was deeded to the whites and the Seneca were relegated to reservations.

Figure 131 Stone memorial placed at Indian Burial Ground by John Larkin in 1912

The bitter rivalry between Cornplanter and Red Jacket came to a head when Cornplanter was prompted by the religious leader Handsome Lake, and accused Red Jacket of witch-craft. Such a charge required a trial and Red Jacket decided to act in his own defense, where a conviction could result in the ultimate condemnation of death. The people were divided regarding the issue, but Red Jacket's eloquence during a three-hour speech prevailed. He was judged not guilty. This took a toll on Cornplanter as Red Jacket replaced him as chief and Cornplanter moved to the Salamanca Reservation on the western bank of the Allegheny River. The Trial of Red Jacket is depicted in the painting by John Mix Stanley, currently in the Smithsonian Institution.

During Red Jacket's time, the Buffalo Creek Reservation was all land south of Buffalo Creek, so it touched the initial city of Buffalo along the shore of the River on Exchange Street. Red Jacket owned one of the first houses at the entrance to the reservation, which extended to what is now West Seneca along current Seneca Street and as far north as William Street.

In 1801, Red Jacket defended Stiff-armed George, who attacked innkeeper John Palmer on a bench in front of his inn and ended up killing John Hewitt, who came with a number of other white men to subdue him. At this time, Buffalo had a larger Indian than white population. When George was arrested and jailed, there was almost an uprising, but a smart decision was made when George was released in the custody of Red Jacket. During the trial Red Jacket argued that many white men killed Indians and were not punished, so Stiff-armed George should also be released. George was found guilty, but Governor Clinton pardoned him, with the stipulation that he leave the state of New York.

Red Jacket became a traditionalist and argued for working with the Americans, but he always believed in retaining Indian traditions. He was successful in getting the missionaries removed from the Buffalo Creek Reservation. After his wife converted to Christianity, he refused to live with her. His son was one of the first Indian Christian marriages on the reservation. Before Red Jacket died, he requested to be buried with his people and asked that white man not be permitted to bury him. Although not a Christian, at his wife's request he agreed to be buried in the Indian

Burial Ground, in a Christian ceremony, at Buffum Street and Fields Avenue off Seneca Street in South Buffalo.

In the Buffalo Creek Treaty of 1842, the Buffalo Creek Reservation and the cemetery were eliminated. Settlers wanted to develop that area and people were talking about removing the remains, especially those of Red Jacket and Mary Jemison from the Indian Burial Ground. John D. Larkin of the Larkin Company purchased the cemetery grounds to save it from development, and donated the land to the city of Buffalo to be utilized as a park. During her youth, Larkin's wife taught at the Seneca Mission House located on Indian Church Road. She was born Hannah Frances Hubbard and was the elder sister of Elbert Hubbard, founder of the Roycroft movement. Mary Jemison was later interred at Letchworth State Park in Glen Iris, where she had lived most of her life before moving to the Buffalo Creek Reservation.

In December 1863, Chief Strong gave a lecture to the Historical Society to rescue Red Jacket's remains from the Indian Burial Ground and bury them in Forest Lawn Cemetery. William C. Bryant from the Society received permission in 1876 from the Council of the Seneca Nation to approve the project. In 1879, Red Jacket's remains were exhumed along with other bodies identified as Young King, Destroy Town, Captain Pollard, his wife, his granddaughter, Tall Peter and Little Billy. Nine other unknown warriors were excavated, with the remains entrusted to the Buffalo Historical Society.

On October 8, 1884, the bodies were buried at Forest Lawn Cemetery and the nine warriors were buried as the unknown braves. All expenses and travel by Native American dignitaries were covered by the Historical Society. That evening 3,000 people gathered at the Music Hall to hear additional speeches, including one by Native American General Ely Parker. Parker was also later buried at Forest Lawn, next to the final resting place of Red Jacket. In 1891, after funds were raised, the bronze statue of Red Jacket was placed at the buried site.

Figure 132 Red Jacket statue and Seneca Burial plot at Forest Lawn Cemetery

GENERAL BENNETT RILEY

*Bennett Riley served as commander of the Poinsett Barracks from 1842
to 1845 and vowed to return to Buffalo when he retired from the military*

B orn in St. Mary's, Maryland in 1787, Bennett Riley apprenticed in a cobbler shop
and became a foreman in a shoe factory. Riley joined the military during the War
of 1812 and saw action at the Battle of Sackets Harbor, NY, a battle fought to retain
control of the shipyards on Lake Ontario. He was promoted in rank to major and led
the first military escort along the Santa Fe Trail in 1829. Riley married Arabella Israel
of Philadelphia in 1834, and in 1837 was with the 4th Infantry at Fort Gibson on the
Arkansas River. He then served until the conclusion of the Second Seminole War in
Florida and was transferred to Buffalo.

In 1842, Riley was promoted to Colonel and became the fourth and final
commandant of the Poinsett Barracks. His time in Buffalo was among the happiest
during his military career. Five officers under his command married women from
Buffalo and while he was here his officers were welcomed, entertained and honored
by the Society of Buffalo. His 2nd Regiment of Infantry left Buffalo in mid-1845
when they were ordered to the Mexican Border. After the Mexican War, he served at
Fort Hamilton in Brooklyn, NY in 1848.

Figure 133 Commandants quarters at Poinsett Barracks, later the Wilcox Mansion

Riley commanded the Military Department in Upper California during 1849 and 1850, serving as the provisional Governor of California. In this assignment he commanded eight companies of infantry, two artillery and two dragoons between San Diego and San Francisco. This was a difficult role because he had to transition the California Territory from Mexican to American laws, along with attempting to bring law and order to the Gold Rush camps. After he organized the first free elections and guided California toward statehood, he turned the reins of government over to the elected officials. Riley was offered a post on the Rio Grande but due to his health and since he was eligible for retirement, he moved to Buffalo.

When he arrived back in Buffalo in 1850, Riley and his family were met at the Exchange Street train station by a crowd of officials, with a band playing during a military parade and following reception. He settled at 1238 Main Street at Barker Street, a few blocks from the former Poinsett Barracks, in a home he referred to as "Soldiers Retreat." In 1897, that home became the location of St. Joseph's Collegiate Institute until being moved to Kenmore Avenue. It then became Bishop Fallon High School in 1950 and is now Delta Sonic. The original St. Joes/Bishop Fallon school building is still standing behind the Delta Sonic gas pumps and is used as a training facility.

During his retirement Riley enjoyed purchasing second-hand furniture for his home. He purchased so much, that when Riley was away, Mrs. Arabella Riley would send furniture downtown to be sold at auction. One time, Riley returned from being out of town and went to the auction. There he purchased furniture his wife had sent there, which he previously owned.

Riley died of cancer on June 9, 1853 and was given a full military funeral and escorted to Forest Lawn by the 65th Regiment commanded by Major Bidwell. When Riley Street was built in 1859, it was named after him. Camp Center in Kansas Territory was renamed Fort Riley in his honor in June 1852 and Riley County, Kansas is named after General Bennett Riley.

AARON RUMSEY & FAMILY

Tanning factories, railroads, banks and Buffalo's largest property owners

Aaron Rumsey was born in Hubbardstown, Vermont in 1797. His brother Calvin moved to Warsaw, New York and opened a tannery, with Aaron walking all the way from Vermont to join his brother in the business. He married Sophia Phelps from Warsaw in 1819, with their sons Bronson Case Rumsey being born in Warsaw in 1823 and Dexter Phelps Rumsey in Westfield in 1827.

Aaron opened several tanneries in East Aurora, Westfield, Holland and the largest being on Exchange Street in Buffalo. He moved to Buffalo in 1832 and in 1838 partnered with George Howard. Howard left in 1842, forming a partnership with John Bush and opening their own tanneries. Aaron's sons had been working with their father, and in 1847 he took them on as partners, renaming the business Aaron Rumsey & Sons. In 1856, Aaron began investing in properties around the city and purchased woodlands around Delaware Park. Aaron's home, where Bronson and Dexter were raised, was at the corner of Delaware Avenue and North Street.

Rumsey Park was the area along Delaware Avenue from Tracy to West Tupper Street, extending back to Carolina Street. Bronson Rumsey purchased the land in 1862. Previously it was the Hodge and Baldwin lumber and brick yard, where a brook ran through the yard and was fed by a spring. Architects Henry and Edward Rose were hired to enhance the features of the land. They used the spring to create a lake

Figure 134 Aaron Rumsey home at Delaware and North
Photo: Courtesy David Rumsey

Figure 135 Rumsey Park landscape Photo: Courtesy David Rumsey

of clear water, where they placed a boat house, a Swiss chalet and a Grecian temple. The native trees were augmented by new plantings and the gardens near the house were terraced and set with flowers and fountains.

Bronson's house was at 330 Delaware Avenue at Tracy (he previously lived at 1 Park Place at Delaware from 1850 to 1862) and other family members had homes along Delaware to West Tupper. Parties were held at Bronson's mansion that rivaled the Vanderbilt and Astor society events in New York City. Numerous festivals and social gatherings were also held on the property. The entire property, except the Delaware Avenue side was surrounded by a high, tight-board fence. When the family sold the property in 1914, Rumsey Lake was filled in, the lot subdivided and Elmwood Avenue was extended across the property connecting Virginia Street to downtown.

In the late 1880s, Rumsey Park became the playground for children of several of the wealthy families that lived on Delaware Avenue and the relationships built among these children lasted throughout their lifetime. Members of the group that played hockey together included children from the following families: Rumsey, Wheeler, Goodyear, Spaulding, Wright, Laverack, Dart, Cary, Milburn and others. The homes on the Delaware Avenue side of Rumsey Park were: Bronson Rumsey at 330, Lawrence Rumsey and his wife Jennie Cary later lived at 330, Edward Movius and Mary Lovering Rumsey Movius at 334, Dr Charles Cary and Evelyn Rumsey Cary at 340, Bronson (Bert) Rumsey at 132 West Tupper and Laurence Rumsey a block away at 1 Park Place.

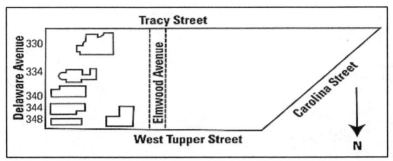

Figure 136 Map of Rumsey estate

Two other houses south of West Tupper and within the Rumsey Park area were 344 and 348 Delaware. Samuel K. Worthington, who resided at 344, was initially active in the grain and coal industries and later became Water Commissioner. He and Grover Cleveland were the only original honorary members of the Buffalo Club. Worthington was followed at 344 by Franklin D. Locke, who was one of Buffalo's leading attorneys. In 1886, Locke formed the Erie County Bar Association at his summer estate on 18 Mile Creek, and he worked with George Milburn to bring together the principals from Scranton and Buffalo to form Lackawanna Steel. Henry A. Richmond lived at 348 Delaware. He was the son of Dean Richmond, a power broker in NYS business and politics. Henry studied law, but due to his wealth, he did not have to earn a living. He became an avid clubman, art connoisseur and world traveler.

Dexter Rumsey built his home at the corner of Delaware and Summer in 1857, at the northeastern point of a tract of land his father Aaron purchased in 1856. The house at 742 Delaware was originally a two-room bungalow built by Captain Allen in the 1830s. It was expanded by the architectural gardeners, the Rose Brothers, into a farmhouse. Dexter turned it into a mansion that was the center of Buffalo society from 1857 to 1945, as the Rumsey's hospitality was internationally known. The home hosted eminent statesmen, writers, concerts, artists and cultural leaders. In 1945, it was sold to the VFW Post #2647.

In 1893, Bronson and Dexter sold Aaron Rumsey & Sons to United States Leather Company, and each brother received ten million dollars making them one of the richest families in Buffalo. They invested the money in railroads (where they partnered with the Vanderbilt family), banks (Bronson was a founder of M&T), and real estate. At one time the Rumseys owned 22 of the 43 square miles that comprised Buffalo, and it was upon their land that the Pan-American Exposition was held. That land was leased upon the stipulation that it was to be returned in its original condition. Mrs. Dexter Rumsey later donated seven acres of that land to the city of Buffalo to become part of Delaware Park.

Children of the Rumsey family married into other prominent Buffalo families. The children of Bronson were: Lawrence, Mary, Bronson II and Evelyn. After Lawrence married Jennie Cary, they moved into his father's former house at 1 Park Place; and when Bronson died in 1902, they moved into 330 Delaware. Lawrence devoted most of his time managing the family business and real estate holdings. Mary Lovering Rumsey married Edward Movius, who was an attorney and son of railroad agent Julius Movius. Bronson "Bert" Rumsey II graduated from Oxford and returned to work with his father and uncle in the leather and real estate business. He was married to Mary Coxe, Elizabeth Lockwood and Edna Lewis. Evelyn Rumsey married Dr Charles Cary. Evelyn painted the Pan-American Exposition poster "The Spirit of Niagara," decorated the Woman's Building at the Pan-Am and designed the "Give Her of the Fruit" poster for the Women's Suffrage movement.

Dexter Rumsey was married three times. He had two daughters with Mary Coburn, Cornelia and Mary Grace. There were no children from his marriage to Mary Bissell, and two children with Susan Fiske, Ruth and Dexter Jr. When Cornelia married Ansley Wilcox in 1878, Dexter purchased 675 Delaware for their home. She died in childbirth in 1880 and in 1883 Wilcox married Mary Grace, for whom Dexter purchased 641 Delaware as a wedding gift. Theodore Roosevelt was inaugurated as President at the Wilcox mansion in 1901.

Dexter's daughter Ruth married William "Wild Bill" Donovan, a decorated war hero in WWI, who during WWII ran the wartime intelligence agency Office of Strategic Services (OSS), the predecessor to the CIA. During Prohibition Donovan feuded with Buffalo Mayor Frank Schwab, a former brewmeister, about enforcing prohibition and raided the Saturn Club and Country Clubs. Ruth and her brother Dexter Jr. were upset that many of those arrested were family members and friends. This was the beginning of marital problems between Ruth and her husband. Donovan's law partner Bradley Goodyear dissolved their partnership and never spoke to him again.

Several of the Rumsey grandchildren had interesting and successful careers. Laurence and Jennie Cary Rumsey's daughter Evelyn married Dr. Walter Russell Lord, rector of Saint John's on Colonial Circle. Evelyn was an artist who established the Rumsey Award at the Art Department of UB; and she and her brother, Charles Cary Rumsey, were invited to exhibit at the 1913 Exposition of Modern Art in NYC. Charles married Mary Harriman, daughter of railroad tycoon E.H. Harriman. The artwork of Charles included the frieze on the Manhattan Bridge in NYC, The Centaur in front of the Buffalo History Museum and a replica of The Three Graces in Forest Lawn, which he designed for the Harriman estate. Laurence and Jennie's daughter Gertrude married Carlton M. Smith of Smith, Fassett & Company, a lumber company on Tonawanda Island in North Tonawanda; daughter Grace married Charles W. Goodyear Jr.; and son Laurence Jr. was a member of the Lafayette Escadrille, a squadron of American aviators who flew for France before the U.S. entered WWI. Bert Rumsey, the son of Bronson Rumsey II, spent most of his time at the Rumsey Ranch in Cody, Wyoming, where the family was close friends with Buffalo Bill before he became a world figure. After Jennie Cary Rumsey died in 1943, 330 Delaware Avenue was sold to the Children's Aid Society and commercialization began at the site of the former Rumsey Park.

JOHN NEWTON SCATCHERD

John Newton Scatcherd was a lumber baron, president of the
Ellicott Square Company and chairman of the executive committee
of the Pan-American Exposition

John Newton Scatcherd's father, James Newton Scatcherd, was born in Wyton, Ontario in 1825. John Newton's grandfather, John Scatcherd, was a member of Canadian Parliament, and along with his brothers, Thomas and Robert, was prominent in the public life of the London, Ontario area. James grew up on the family farm in London, Ontario and was taught about the lumber business during the time his father owned a sawmill.

In 1852, James moved to Buffalo to work for a Canadian lumber company, Farmer de Blaquiere & Deeds, with offices and a lumberyard on Elk Street. The nature of the lumber business at this time was lumber reached Buffalo by barges or vessels on Lake Erie and was forwarded to the East Coast on the Erie Canal. James Scatcherd bought out his partners in 1857 and operated under his name. In 1865, he added Samuel J. Belton as a partner in the firm Scatcherd & Belton, and during the Civil War, the lumber business boomed. Their company was involved in both pine and hardwoods but dropped pine to become exclusively a hardwood company in 1878. Their purchasing headquarters was moved to Indianapolis, when the supply of lumber by lake sources diminished. The headquarters was eventually moved to mills in Memphis, since they purchased most of their lumber in the Middle Western (Indiana, Kentucky and Tennessee) and later the Middle Southern States (Mississippi, Louisiana and Arkansas). Scatcherd's company specialized in oak but also sold ash, poplar and other hardwoods.

James married Annie Belton from Fairfield, Ontario, whose father was also in the lumber business. They lived at 615 Delaware Avenue and had two children, John N. Scatcherd who followed his father into the lumber business and daughter Emily, who married sportsman Seward Cary. James was Chairman of the Buffalo Board of Water Commissioners, where he discontinued political favoritism and equalized rates for all customers. He was also president of the Board of Trustees for Buffalo General Hospital, where he was responsible for getting the hospital out of debt and cutting services costs. Additionally, known for his philanthropy, James was a founder of Delaware Avenue M.E. Church.

John N. Scatcherd was born in Buffalo on September 12, 1857. He was educated in the Buffalo Public Schools, Professor Briggs Classical School and Hellmuth College in London Ontario, where he graduated in 1872. Upon returning to Buffalo he went to work for his father in the lumber industry at Scatcherd & Belton. When he became a partner in 1879, the firm became Scatcherd & Son on Peabody Street. The Scatcherd lumber company became one of the largest hardwood lumber concerns in the country. Scatcherd was also president of the Batavia-New York

Woodworking company, a manufacturer of inside finishing and high-class cabinet work, at its plant in Batavia and offices in New York City. When his father died in 1885, John and Emily took over the lumber company, with John being the managing partner.

Scatcherd was president of the Buffalo Lumber Exchange from 1886 to 1888, president of the National Wholesale Lumber Dealers Association, and for two years was president of the Buffalo Merchants Exchange where he worked to abolish railroad grade crossings. In addition to lumber, Scatcherd was president of the Bank of Buffalo from 1892 to 1896, a director of the Third National Bank, director of Buffalo Loan, Trust & Safety Deposit Company, director of the Buffalo Railway Company and its successor the International Railway Company. For several years, John N. Scatcherd and George Urban Jr. were leaders of the Republican Party in WNY.

The Ellicott Square Company built the Ellicott Square Building, which upon the completion of its construction was the largest office complex the country. It was named after Ellicott because it was built on the lot Joseph Ellicott originally purchased for his home, with the land purchased from Ellicott's relatives. John N. Scatcherd was president of the company from 1894 to 1906. It was Scatcherd who leased the basement restaurant to Ellsworth Statler when the building opened in 1896. When

Figure 137 Scatcherd & Son Lumber Yard

Figure 138 Ellicott Square Building

Statler was faced with almost certain bankruptcy after a year of operating the restaurant, Scatcherd spoke up for Statler and helped convince the creditors to give Statler more time to make the restaurant a success. That extra time resulted in the success of the restaurant and eventual formation of the Statler Hotel chain.

In 1899, Scatcherd became a member of the Board of Directors of the Pan-American Exposition and was elected Chairman of the Executive Committee. His committee was responsible for practically all activities at the event other than financial matters. He devoted almost all his time and energy to the Pan-Am during its construction and time of operation in 1901.

John Newton Scatcherd married Mary Wood in 1879 and they built a home at 703 Delaware Avenue in 1880. Their daughters, Dorothy and Emily, along with Mrs. Scatcherd's sister, Emily Wood, were killed in a tragic train accident in 1894 when their buggy was hit at a crossing of the Belt Line Railway. Mrs. Scatcherd never recovered from the tragedy, but the family remained at the Delaware Avenue home until Mary Scatcherd's death in 1914 and John's in 1917.

JACOB SCHOELLKOPF

Tanneries, flour mills, chemical plants and hydroelectric power

Jacob Schoellkopf was born on November 15, 1819 in Kirchheim Unter Teck in Germany and began learning about the tannery trade at 14 years old from his father, a large leather manufacturer. He completed an apprenticeship and became a clerk at a mercantile house in Strassberg for two years before deciding to move to the U.S. When he arrived in America in 1841, he did not speak English.

After initially living in New York City, he moved to Buffalo in 1844 and with $800 loaned to him by his father, he opened a small leather store on Mohawk Street. While operating this business, he became fluent in the English language and American business practices. He purchased a tannery in Whites Corners (Hamburg), a sheepskin tannery in Buffalo in 1846, and in 1848 a tannery in Milwaukee, Wisconsin. In the 1850s he became associated with tanneries in Chicago, Illinois, in Fort Wayne, Indiana and in North Evans, New York.

Schoellkopf made his first investment outside of the tanning business in 1857 when he erected the North Buffalo Flouring Mills, which proved so successful that in 1871 he bought Frontier Mills of Buffalo and two years later built other mills in Niagara Falls. His approach to business was to purchase or build a business, make it successful and sell it at a profit, allowing him to seek out other outlets for his increasing capital.

He remained invested in the flour milling business because of his association with George B. Matthews, who was involved in milling management since the end of the Civil War. Matthews worked at what was considered a local mill in Elmira. He wanted to progress in the industry, and it would have been logical for him to relocate to Rochester, with the three cataracts of the Genesee River became the largest milling center of the county, gaining the city the moniker The Flour City. Instead, Matthews moved to Buffalo and obtained employment with Thornton & Chester Milling Company It was Matthews that convinced Schoellkopf to purchase Frontier Mills, which later became Schoellkopf and Matthews. He also influenced Schoellkopf to build the Niagara Flouring and Central Mill in Niagara Falls. When hydroelectric power was introduced at the flour mills, they became the greatest capacity mills in the area.

When the Niagara Falls Canal Company went bankrupt in 1877, Schoellkopf purchased it for $71,000 at an auction. He improved the canal, and in 1881 Schoellkopf Power House No. 1 was completed as the first company to generate electricity from Niagara Falls in 1882. He formed the company Niagara Falls Hydraulic Power & Manufacturing Company, later shortened to The Hydraulic Power Company and built Power Stations 2, 3A and 3B. During WWI they consolidated with the Niagara Falls Power Company, headed by Edward Dean Adams, who worked with George Forbes, Westinghouse and Nikola Tesla to transmit alternating current. Jacob Schoellkopf Jr. was elected Chairman of Niagara Falls

Figure 139 Niagara Falls Hydraulic Power & Manufacturing Company

Power Company in 1918, a position he held for 18 years. The equivalent, current day value of that company would be over 1 billion dollars. The company later became part of Niagara Mohawk, which is now National Grid. In 1929, the Schoellkopf family organized the Niagara Share Company as a trust for all the stock owned by family members.

In addition to tanning, flour and electricity Schoellkopf was on the board of the German Insurance Company, started Schoellkopf Chemical & Dye Company, was president of the Board of Trade, trustee of Buffalo General Hospital and on the board, an officer or trustee of six banks: Third National Bank of Buffalo, Merchant Bank of Buffalo, The German Bank of Buffalo, Farmers & Merchants National Bank, Power City Bank and Bank of Niagara. Schoellkopf and former Buffalo Mayor Philip Becker, financed the rebuilding of the Saengerhalle, or Buffalo Music Hall, at Main and Edward Streets. The theater was renamed the Teck in tribute to the town where Schoellkopf was born in Germany.

In 1848, Jacob married Christina Duerr, who was originally from Stuttgart, Germany and emigrated to America a year before Jacob in 1840. They had six sons and one daughter that survived to adulthood and four children that died in infancy. Their children were: Henry (1848), Louis (1855), Arthur (1856), Jacob Frederick (1858), Alfred (1860), Carl Phillip Hugo (1862) and Helen (1870). They were all born in Buffalo and grew up at 157 Ellicott Street during the 1850s, 486 Franklin Street during the late 1860s and 1870s and moving to 553 Delaware in 1882.

Henry attended local Buffalo schools and began the family tradition of study in German. In 1870, he started working with his father in the tanning business. When their father became involved with the power company in 1877, Henry and his brother

Louis renamed the Mississippi Street sheepskin tannery J.F. Schoellkopf's Sons. When Henry died in 1880, brother Alfred joined Louis in the company. Alfred later built a home at 537 Delaware, next to his father's mansion.

Arthur Schoellkopf worked at the flour mills in Buffalo and Niagara Falls, becoming an officer and general manager of Niagara Falls Hydraulic Power and Manufacturing in 1878. With his father and Charles Brush, they started the Brush Electric Light Company of Niagara Falls and of Buffalo, which built an electric generator operated by mechanical power from hydroelectric canal water to illuminate Niagara Falls at night by 16 carbon arc lights. Arthur was elected mayor of Niagara Falls in 1896, built a stone house at Main Street and Pine Avenue, and owned Niagara View Farms in the Town of Niagara where he bred race horses. He only served one term as mayor due to his business interests. In addition to the power company, he was president of Power City Bank, Gluck Realty Company, Cliff Paper Company, Park Theater Company, constructed the first horse-drawn streetcar system in Niagara Falls and served on the board of directors of other banks and companies. His son Paul Arthur Schoellkopf graduated from Cornell University in 1906 and succeeded his father in his many Niagara Falls interests.

Jacob F. Schoellkopf II completed seven years of chemistry study in Munich and Stuttgart, graduating from Stuttgart Polytechnic College in 1880. His knowledge of chemistry convinced him that extracting of dyes from coal tar would be a very profitable business in the U.S. He and his father founded the Schoellkopf Aniline and Chemical works on six acres of land on what was then named Abbott Road (now South Park), near the iron bridge on the downtown side of the Buffalo River. The company became Schoellkopf, Hartford, Hanna & Company, with 350 employees working in 30 buildings and expanding to a site encompassing 36 acres. In later years, the company was acquired by Allied Corp. which was sold to Buffalo Color Corp. Jacob remained engaged in the family's other businesses and also started the

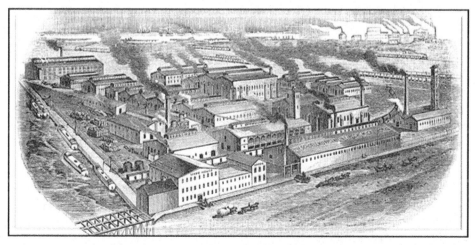

Figure 140 Schoellkopf, Hartford, Hanna & Company chemical plant

brokerage firm Schoellkopf, Hutton and Pomeroy. He lived in his father's former home at 486 Franklin Street until he moved to 499 Delaware in the Midway Row Houses, also owning an estate on Lake Shore Road where he died in 1942. His son Jacob F. Schoellkopf III graduated from Cornell and received a doctorate in chemistry from the University of Strasbourg. During WWI, Jacobs II and III further expanded the family chemical company because the U.S. had previously been dependent upon imports from Germany and now the Schoellkopf plant became the largest of its kind on the continent. Jacob III also managed all his father's other business interests.

C.P. Hugo Schoellkopf was the youngest son in the Schoellkopf family. At sixteen he entered the Oberrealschule in Stuttgart, followed by study at the Stuttgart Polytechnic Collage (where his brother Jacob was a student) and specialized in chemistry at Polytechnic Collage at Berlin. When he returned to Buffalo, in 1885 he entered the aniline end of the family business. He was later involved in other aspects of the Schoellkopf enterprises and other chemical companies. After his death, his son Alfred H. carried on his interests. When Hugo's first wife Annette died at a young age, his scandalous second marriage to flapper Irene brought notoriety to the family. Originally with Hugo's consent and later in an affair that resulted in their divorce, Irene became involved with Barrie Carman. Carman was a dancing playboy escort of The Roaring Twenties and he accompanied Irene to the NYC clubs and cabarets, with her then still husband Hugo picking up the bills. At a New Year's Eve Party in 1923, Irene was robbed of $300,000 in jewelry during a party at Carman's home. Carman was accused of complicity in the crimes but never charged because even Hugo Schoellkopf believed he was innocent. Mrs. Schoellkopf and Carmen married in 1927, only to be divorced four month later from an argument over a payment of a $100,000 nuptial gift Irene was to make to her new husband.

The only Schoellkopf daughter Helen married Hans Schmidt, who was born in Hanover, Germany in 1865. Hans came to America at seventeen and became a salesman for J. F. Schoellkopf & Company. He was made a partner in 1891, married the daughter of his boss in 1893 and was elected president of the company in 1901. Hans became involved in other Schoellkopf family businesses and was interested in music, being president of the Buffalo Philharmonic Orchestra. After Jacob Schoellkopf I died in 1899, Helen and her family lived at 533 Delaware with her mother Christina until she passed away in 1903. In 1918, Helen, Hans and their three children moved to an estate in Derby on Lake Erie. The home was 17,000 square feet, with 14 bedrooms on 15 acres along the lake. It was sold to the Diocese of Buffalo in 1947 and became St. Columban retreat home. In 2017 the diocese sold it to Suncliff on the Lake.

Later Schoellkopf generations remained active in the electric power generation and the chemical dye industry. They have been diplomats, Congressmen, bank presidents and investment brokers. Heirs served as directors in Buffalo companies including: Bell Aircraft, Dunlop Tire & Rubber, Marine Midland Bank, American Steamship and Trico Products.

JOHN C. AND WILLIAM F. SHEEHAN

Politicians, lawyers and Tammany Hall

William Sheehan Sr. and his wife Hanora Crowley Sheehan were both from County Cork in Ireland. They emigrated to America and settled in Buffalo where they resided at 422 Elk Street. Their son John was born on August 5, 1848 and William was born November 6, 1859.

Sheehan Sr. was a prosperous railroad contractor and engineer but lost a considerable amount of money during the Civil War, being forced to obtain work as a day laborer. To assist in contributing to the family finances, he put his sons John and William to work on the Buffalo River, ferrying longshoremen to their places of employment at the elevators and docks along the waterfront. A marble block fell on John, necessitating the amputation of his leg. He could no longer perform manual labor, so he attended Buffalo Commercial College and obtained a position as a telegraph operator and later a clerk on the railroad. John

Figure 141 William "Blue-Eyed Billy" Sheehan portrait

became involved with the younger element of the Democratic Party and was elected city assessor in 1874. While assessor he continued his study of law at the office of Thayer & Benedict, and was admitted to the bar in 1875.

John Sheehan became the political boss of the Democratic First Ward. This was at the time when the standard late 19th century Irish American machine politicians were considered more adept at ballot-stuffing than government. At age 29 in 1877, he was elected Comptroller for the City of Buffalo. Grover Cleveland was asked to run for mayor of Buffalo as a reform candidate in the election of 1881. Cleveland considered Sheehan a devious and corrupt Democratic boss and felt he could not fight corruption in government with Sheehan on the ticket. He agreed to run for mayor only if Sheehan was not running for office. Sheehan withdrew and attempted to derail the election of Cleveland, but Cleveland realized the importance of the Irish vote and vigorously campaigned at the taverns of South Buffalo, winning the mayor's office. If Sheehan had been successful in stopping his election, Cleveland's political future possibly may not have progressed to the office of the presidency.

After the new controller Timothy Mahoney, a friend of John Sheehan, took office he found a shortage of $5,900 in the city funds. Efforts to cover up the suspected embezzlement and attempts to repay it became complicated, so in 1885 John Sheehan moved to New York City. In NYC he became involved with Tammany Hall, as it was the primary engine for the political advancement of the Irish in the city. He was appointed secretary of the aqueduct commission, and in 1892 he was selected as police commissioner despite the fact that he was an outsider and many were aware of his financial scandal in Buffalo from articles published in the *New York Times*. In 1895, after only ten years in NYC politics, John assumed the powerful position of leader of Tammany Hall, a seat previously held by Boss William Tweed. With the assistance of his brother William Sheehan Jr., he continued to have influence over New York State politics until his death on February 9, 1916.

William "Blue-Eyed Billy" Sheehan followed his brother into the legal profession. He attended St. Joseph's Collegiate Institute and studied law as a clerk in the Tabor & Sheehan office of his brother at 83 Franklin Street. William was elected to the New York State Assembly at age twenty-six in 1885, where he served as Minority Leader from 1886 to 1890 and Speaker of the New York State Assembly in 1891. While in the Assembly he secured the appointment of his brother to the New York Aqueduct Board and his brother's law firm partner, Charles F. Tabor, as first Deputy New York Attorney General. He also continually secured funds for the Buffalo Harbor and patronage jobs for his First Ward constituents. In 1892, at age 33, William Sheehan was elected as the youngest lieutenant governor in the history of New York State, serving with Governor Roswell P. Flower. Also, in 1892 he patched up his political differences with former Buffalonian Grover Cleveland as he served as a national manager of Cleveland's 1892 presidential campaign. However, he did not befriend the Roosevelt Family, as Sheehan was the mastermind of the presidential nomination of his law partner, Alton B. Parker, who was the Democratic candidate that lost the 1904 election to republican Theodore Roosevelt.

When William S. Sheehan's term as Lieutenant Governor expired, he moved to NYC and started a prestigious law firm with Alton B. Parker in 1895. He remained active in the Democratic Party; and when a Senate seat became available, he was considered the favorite to get the appointment. At this time the State Senator was not elected, the senator was appointed by the State Legislature. Sheehan served the Democratic Party for decades, had just assisted in obtaining a democratic majority in the Legislature and was the choice of Tammany Hall boss Charles F. Murphy. All looked well until Sheehan was opposed by a newly elected state legislator named Franklin Delano Roosevelt. He objected to Sheehan as he was the choice of corrupt Tammany Hall and according to Conrad Black, one of Roosevelt's biographers, Roosevelt would have viewed Sheehan as "a smooth but corrupt political roué." Sheehan resorted to threats and political rallies to silence Roosevelt and the rest of his opposition, but Roosevelt was not intimidated, the opposition held together, and Murphy offered another candidate for the Senate seat.

William Sheehan returned to his law career and amassed a multi-million-dollar fortune from his law practice built on the political connections he made while in office. He died on March 14, 1918 and was buried in the Holy Cross Cemetery in Lackawanna, a few miles from his childhood home.

The Sheehan Brothers became wealthy political bosses and crossed paths with two future presidents. They almost succeeded in stopping one of them from beginning his political career.

WILLIAM SHELTON

Rector of St. Paul's Episcopal Church for over 50 years

William Shelton was born in Fairfield, Connecticut September 11, 1798. He was the son of Reverend Philo Shelton, the first clergyman ordained by a bishop of the Protestant Episcopal church in the U.S. William graduated from the NYC General Theological Seminary, was ordained a deacon in 1823 and a priest in 1826. Shelton served as minister at Plattsburg, NY on Lake Champlain in 1823 and after a year, moved to Fairfield, where he remained until he accepted the rectorship of St. Paul's Church in Buffalo in 1829. After traveling to Buffalo by wagon and Erie Canal barge, Shelton gave his first sermon in St. Paul's on September 13, 1829, two days after his 31st birthday.

Figure 142 Portrait of Reverend William Shelton
Photo: Courtesy St. Paul's Episcopal Cathedral

Reverend Davenport Phelps held the first Episcopal Church services in Buffalo on July 2, 1802. He was a missionary and returned to give another service on January 8, 1803 but there were no further services in Buffalo until 1816. That year Reverend Samuel Johnston began ministering in Batavia and during the winter of 1816 conducted a series of meetings in Buffalo. On February 10, 1817 a meeting was held in Elias Ransom's tavern on the northwest corner of Main and Huron and St. Paul's Episcopal Church was organized. The congregation of twenty families who were worshipping as members of the First Presbyterian Church held meeting worships at: the Ransom Tavern, the Eagle Tavern on Main and Court, the Court House on Batavia Road and Washington Street and the schoolhouse on Niagara Street.

The members of the church included many leading citizens, and led by Erastus Granger, asked Joseph Ellicott for a piece of land suitable for building a church. Ellicott responded with a gift of land at Church and Pearl Streets. This land was part of the site where Ellicott had planned to build his house and Church Street was initially named Stadnitski after Peter Stadnitski, a Dutch banker who was one of the Holland Land Company agents. Funds were raised, the cornerstone was placed on June 24, 1819 and on February 25, 1820 Bishop Henry Hobart of NYC consecrated the first permanent house of worship in Buffalo.

Reverend William A. Clark resigned as pastor in 1820, but with the opening of the Erie Canal in 1825, the congregation grew. They retired the debt from the building of the first church and began increasing the capacity of the church with the addition of side galleries. Bishop Hobart named Reverend Deodatus Babcock as rector of the church, and he served until 1824 when he became rector at Ballston Springs and Saratoga Springs in Saratoga, NY. Reverend J.L. Yeonnet of Troy, NY accepted the rectorship of the church but died en route to Buffalo. In March 1825, Reverend Addison Searle accepted the position of rector and he served until the end of 1828 when he left to accept the posting of Chaplin in the Navy Yard at Brooklyn, NY. The position of rector was offered to Reverend Kearney, who accepted but resigned in June. Reverend Shelton had previously turned down the offer to relocate from his parish in Fairfield, Connecticut, but in June 1829 he accepted to position as Rector of St. Paul's.

In 1829, Reverend William Shelton was the perfect person to guide the Episcopal Church during this period of growth. St. Paul's was outgrown by 1835 and a new congregation of Trinity Episcopal Church was formed. By 1845 the church again needed more space and St. John's Episcopal Church was formed. Members of St. Paul's concluded that their downtown church needed to be replaced with a new cathedral. In 1848, they began working with architect Richard Upjohn who had recently completed Trinity Church in NYC and was considered one of the greatest American Gothic Church designers.

The cornerstone was placed by Bishop DeLancy on June 12, 1850, and the new church was dedicated on October 2, 1851. The old church was sold for $800 to St. Peter's German Evangelical Church on Genesee and Hickory. They moved it to their site and used the building until 1877. While the new cathedral was being built, Rector Shelton was given a paid leave of absence. The congregation leased space for services at Clinton's Hall, at the corner of Washington and Clinton Streets, but since Reverend Shelton was on paid leave, the congregation attended either Trinity or St. John's Episcopal Church.

Architect Richard Upjohn wanted to have the church built out of limestone. However, that proved to be too expensive, so it was built out of Medina sandstone, which became part of the cathedral's signature appearance. The initial $50,000 projected cost of construction escalated to $160,000 by the time the church was completed. Although the cathedral was dedicated in 1851, construction continued until 1873.

Figure 143 The Churches in 1880s. St. Paul's to the left, St. Joseph's in the center rear and the old 1st Presbyterian to the right

After Rector Shelton arrived in Buffalo in 1835, he was elected the first president of the Young Men's Association which later became the Buffalo Public Library. He received his doctorate degree from Hobart College, and on April 7, 1845 married Mrs. Lucretia (Stanley) Grosvenor. While serving in the original church through March 17, 1850, Shelton baptized 950 people and performed 273 weddings. He conducted the first graveside service at Forest Lawn Cemetery during the burial of John Lay on July 12, 1850, the first internment at the cemetery. In March of 1874, Shelton gave the funeral sermon at the service for President Millard Fillmore. Reverend Shelton retired as Rector in 1881 and died on October 11, 1883. After his death in 1897, the square next to St. Paul's Cathedral was named Shelton Square in his honor.

In 1888, a gas explosion burned the interior of St. Paul's Cathedral, with only the towers and walls left standing. The church was rebuilt by architect Robert W. Gibson, who made minor changes to the exterior but made the interior more substantial, spacious and ornamental. It reopened in 1890.

St. Paul's Cathedral was listed on the National Register of Historic Places in 1973, and in 1987 it was named a National Historic Landmark, the highest designation a building, place or site can achieve in the U.S.

JAMES D. SHEPPARD

The owner of the first music store in Buffalo and it is still in business

James D. Sheppard moved to Buffalo in 1827 from Frome, England, where he was a church organist and choir member. At age 29, he opened a music store in the old Court House, where the Buffalo & Erie County Library is now located. He brought the first piano to Buffalo, with the piano crossing the ocean from England in a sailing vessel, towed by mules along the Erie Canal on a barge and carried by six men from the docks at the foot of Main Street to his store.

The Seneca Indians had never seen or heard a piano. They were intrigued by the instrument and referred to it as "hearing the big music box sing." The Indians would gather on the steps of the Court House to listen to the piano and enjoyed singing songs along with the music.

In an advertisement in 1827, Sheppard referred to his store as a Piano Forte Warehouse – Music and Fancy Store, stating he kept a large assortment of music publications and musical instruments including a number of finely tuned pianos, flutes, clarinets, bassoons, French horns, bugle horns, drums, trumpets, guitars, violins, violas, violincellos and flageolets. Sheppard also tuned pianos and repaired instruments. Since the population of Buffalo in 1827 was approximately 8,000 people, there was not a big market for musical instruments, so the store also sold games, toys,

Figure 144 Old Court House where Sheppard's first music store was located

Figure 145 Sheppard's home at 175 West Chippewa, the current site of Hutch Tech High School

medicine, drugs and perfumery. The first person to purchase a piano at the store was Bela D. Coe, founder of the Buffalo & Albany Stagecoach company.

Sheppard was also the organist at St. Paul's Church, where the first organ in Buffalo was installed in 1829. He remained organist at the church for more than 25 years. He held choir practice at his music store for area churches and gave music lessons. Starting in 1831 he presented a series of concerts, serving as the band leader and beginning in 1838 The Handel and Haydn Society was based at the music store, where it remained for the next 100 years.

In 1854, fellow Englishman Hugh Cottier moved to Buffalo, becoming Sheppard's student, employee and eventually his business partner. Robert Denton joined the company in 1863, and upon Sheppard's death the business name was changed to Cottier & Denton. When William Daniels became the third partner in 1887, the store became Denton, Cottier & Daniels, a name still in existence over 130 years later.

The original Lafayette Square store moved to 269 and 271 Main Street. This was a five-story building where they sold pianos, sheet music, a large variety of musical instruments, had a repair department and recital halls. They also had a storefront at 32 Court Street to display their merchandise and, where they were active for over 100 years. In 1976, a suburban store was opened in the Northtown Plaza and in 1999 they moved to their present complex at 460 Dodge Road in Getzville.

James D. Sheppard and his family lived at a home he built in 1844 at 175 Chippewa Street near Elmwood. The music business served him well. When he died at age 83, he left an estate of $100,000. He created a good business model, as the company he created has been in operation for almost 200 years.

FRANKLIN SIDWAY

The Sidway Block and the Sidway Building

James Sidway was born in Dudley Woodside, England on May 8, 1759 and came to America as a drummer boy in the British Army. He served in the 62nd Regiment of Foot under General John Burgoyne which was defeated by General Horatio Gates at the Battle of Saratoga in 1777. Following the surrender of the British Army, James and other British soldiers were offered enlistment in the American Army, which Sidway accepted. After the Revolutionary War he remained in America and married Rebecca Milk, settling in Goshen, New York.

Jonathan Sidway was born on April 1, 1784 in Goshen, about 50 miles northwest of NYC. He was educated in Goshen and worked as a farmer until he moved to Buffalo in 1812, where he was engaged in the shipping business and became an early pioneer in Great Lakes commerce. On January 1, 1826 he married Parnell St. John, a daughter of Margaret St. John who owned the only home not destroyed during the burning of Buffalo by the British during the War of 1812. Johnathan and Parnell Sidway had nine children, four of whom lived to adulthood, Katherine (who married Asaph S. Bemis), Jonathan (who married Caroline B. Taunt), Franklin and James Henry Sidway. James was a fireman who died at 25 years of age battling the fire at the American Hotel on January 25, 1865.

One of Jonathan Sidway's investments was The Sidway Block at 178-194 Main Street, built in 1832. It was across the street from the Spaulding Exchange and later Memorial Auditorium. This four-story brick multi use building stood until 1967 when it was torn down to become the site of the parking garage for the Marine Midland Tower.

In 1834, Benjamin Rathbun began building a mansion for Mayor Pierre Augustus Barker on land Barker purchased from Mayor Ebenezer Walden, which included almost the entire block bordered by Hudson, Plymouth, Pennsylvania and West. Barker was married to Annache G. Livingstone, helped write the Buffalo city charter in 1832 and was the sixth mayor of Buffalo in 1837-8. The grounds of 290 Hudson Street were like a country estate, surrounded by trees in a pastoral setting, with most of the area around it not settled until after the Civil War. After Barker's term as mayor, he moved to Mississippi, and in 1843 the estate was leased by the Sidway Family, who purchased it in 1845.

When Jonathan Sidway died on July 21, 1847, his widow Parnell St. John remained in the Sidway Mansion at 290 Hudson Street. Her brother, Le Grand St. John, an engineer, inventor and artist, moved into the home to assist in raising her children and managing the estate. During the 1850s the mansion again became a social center for parties and was admired for its landscaping, construction, furniture and paintings. Thomas LeClear is believed to have painted the portraits of Jonathan and Parnell Sidway, which were displayed in the house. In 1865, Franklin Sidway commissioned LeClear to paint "Interior with Portraits", a portrait of his deceased siblings Parnell and James Sidway, which hung at the mansion for years. It is now owned by and displayed in the Smithsonian Institute in Washington DC.

Franklin Sidway was born in Buffalo on July 23, 1834. After being educated at private schools, the Canandaigua Academy, George W. Francis's School in Yonkers and other institutions, he toured Europe in 1853. Upon returning to Buffalo he organized Sidway, Skinner & Moore, general ship chandlers and grocers, which was active until the beginning of the Civil War. He married Caroline Spaulding, the daughter of Elbridge G. Spaulding, in 1866. After the marriage, Franklin began working at Farmers & Mechanics National Bank, eventually becoming Vice-President and remaining with the bank until it was liquidated in 1898. During his lifetime he managed the Sidway Block and in 1907, built the Sidway Building at 775 Main which was sold in 2006 for over seven million dollars.

After the death of Elbridge Spaulding, Franklin and Charlotte Spaulding Sidway were deeded the 350-acre River Lawn estate. They built a sprawling Georgian mansion that overlooked the Niagara River. The Spaulding-Sidway Boathouse was built in 1870 by Elbridge Spaulding in the late Victorian Stick Style on the River Lawn estate. It is architecturally and historically significant as an existing late 19th century recreational building. The boathouse was listed on the National Register of Historic Places in 1998 and was moved upriver before the River Lawn estate was deeded to New York State for the creation of Beaver Island State Park.

Figure 146 *Sidway mansion that was located on the present grounds of Beaver Island State Park Photo: Courtesy Grand Island Historical Society*

ELBRIDGE GERRY SPAULDING

Elbridge Spaulding was a Buffalo congressman who is credited with being the "Father of the Greenback" as he wrote the law that allowed the government to print money and call it legal tender

The ancestors of the Spaulding family were puritans who arrived about ten years after the Mayflower, with Edward Spaulding coming to America from Lincolnshire, England in 1630. During the American Revolution, at the Battle of Bunker Hill, there were nine members of the Spaulding family in the American ranks, including Elbridge's grandfather Captain Levi Spaulding. Levi served throughout the war, was under Washington's direct command and was present at the final surrender at Yorktown. Elbridge's father Edward was too young to serve at Bunker Hill, but later in the war he enlisted as a private.

Elbridge was the youngest of nine children and was born at Summer Hill, New York on February 24, 1809. He attended Auburn Academy, began his study of law at 20 years of age with Fitch & Dibble in Batavia, continued his law education with Harvey Putnam in Attica and was admitted to the bar in 1834. Spaulding moved to Buffalo and went to work for Potter and Babcock, considered the foremost law firm in Buffalo, as Potter was the first District Attorney in Buffalo and was the prosecuting attorney in the trial of the Thayer Brothers.

In 1837, Spaulding married Jane Antoinette Rich, who he met while studying law in Attica. Her father Gaius B. Rich was the founder of the Bank of Attica in 1836, and in 1842 Spaulding convinced Rich to move himself and the bank to Buffalo.

Figure 147 The Spaulding Exchange, built 1845

Spaulding was a substantial stockholder in the bank and its president Gaius B. Rich was succeeded by his son Andrew J. Rich in 1855, who was followed by his son G. Barrett Rich in 1880. The bank operated as the Bank of Attica until 1890 when the name was changed to Buffalo Commercial Bank. It is one of the oldest surviving or continuous banks in Buffalo as it was absorbed by Marine National Bank in 1902 and later became part of Marine Midland Bank. Rich also started Western Savings Bank in 1851. That bank later became Buffalo Savings Bank and Goldome, being liquidated in 1991.

Spaulding was also associated with the Farmers and Mechanics Bank. It was founded in Batavia in 1840 and moved to Buffalo in 1852. When it moved, Spaulding acquired most of the stock and became president of the bank, a position he held until shortly before his death. The bank became known as the Spaulding Bank because of the dominance of Spaulding family influence at the institution. The board of directors never exceeded six and most were associated with the Spaulding family. In 1852, Henry M. Kinne and Samuel F. Pratt, who each married sisters of Spaulding's wives Nancy and Delia Strong, became directors. Franklin Sidway joined the bank when he married Charlotte Spaulding. Sons Edward and Samuel joined the bank when they reached maturity. Also associated with the bank was Henry McMahon Watson, who had a family connection but was not a relative. In 1882, the board of directors consisted of the three Spauldings, Sidway and Watson. The bank was successful but was liquidated a year after Elbridge Spaulding's death presumably because his sons and son-in-law were not interested in carrying on the business.

The Spaulding Exchange Building at 162 Main Street was built in 1845 and acquired shortly afterward by Elbridge Spaulding. After moving to Buffalo, both the Bank of Attica and Farmers & Mechanics Bank were initially located in the Spaulding Exchange. In 1851, the building was destroyed by a fire but rebuilt to the original plans with improvements within six months. It was a five-story building, with shops and stores on the first floor, Farmers & Mechanics Bank on the second floor and lawyers and business offices on the upper floors. The Spaulding Exchange was considered one of the finest office buildings until it was torn down to provide space for Memorial Auditorium.

Spaulding was president of the Buffalo Gas Light Company for 25 years, a company he founded in 1848 with his brother-in-law Samuel F. Pratt. It was the first manufactured gas plant in the country. In 1870, the American International Bridge Company, founded by Elbridge Spaulding and E. Carlton Sprague, merged with the Canadian Colonial International Bridge Company to form the International Bridge Company, which built the first bridge across the Niagara River. He was also one of the founders of the University of Buffalo, serving as a member of its council until his death in 1897. Spaulding was also involved with the financing and management of the street railways of Buffalo. His pride of his Revolutionary War ancestry was instrumental in Spaulding founding the Buffalo Chapter of the American Revolution.

When he was mayor of Buffalo in 1847 and 1848, the federal government ceased providing funds to improve the Buffalo Harbor. Due to the importance of the harbor

Figure 148 Spaulding-Sidway Boathouse on Grand Island
Photo: Courtesy Grand Island Historical Society

to Buffalo commerce, Spaulding enacted a city tax to enlarge the harbor and increase docking. He supported the continuance of the free school system in Buffalo, along with the importance of fire protection and clean water. Spaulding promoted lighting the streets by suggesting a "lamp district" that would extend through the important streets and be extended annually. He started the first general sewage system and got a law passed to add new sewage sections every year and that no street could be paved until a sewage system was added. He resigned from the Mayor's office when he was elected to the New York State Assembly in 1848.

Between 1854 and 1856 Spaulding was instrumental in forming the Republican Party in New York and he was a member of the Congressional Executive Committee which conducted the campaign for the 1860 presidential election of Republican Abraham Lincoln. As a member of the House of Representatives (1849-1851 and 1859-1863), he spoke out against slavery and he was chairman of the Ways and Means sub-committee entrusted with preparing new laws to meet the needs of the government. Since he was a banker and former New York State Treasurer, he wrote the Greenback or Legal Tender Act and the National Currency Bank Bill. Previously all paper money was printed by banks, backed by gold or silver, and there was no central bank. These bills suspended the printing of money by banks and established a national currency. This provided the funds necessary for the U.S. Government to finance and be successful in winning the Civil War.

Spaulding purchased the former Hollister Mansion at 775 Main Street in 1850. This home was built in 1836 by William Hollister, who purchased the lot from

Deacon Jabez Goodell. He moved into the home prior to the 1842 death of his first wife, Antoinette Rich Spaulding. In 1843, Spaulding married Nancy Selden Strong of Windsor, Connecticut. They had three children, Charlotte, Edward Rich and Samuel Strong. After Nancy passed away in 1852, Spaulding married her sister Delia, but they did not have any children.

In addition to his Buffalo mansion, in 1870 he built an even larger summer retreat on Grand Island called River Lawn. It was a 350-acre estate adjacent to the home of Lewis Allen, who built the first estate on the island. Grand Island became a mecca for the socially prominent of Buffalo to build retreats, with the Falconwood Club building their clubhouse next to the Spaulding house. The Spaulding-Sidway Boathouse, which is listed on the National Register of Historic Places, was moved up-river by Spaulding's grandson Franklin St. John Sidway in 1935 and the River Lawn estate was donated by Spaulding's heirs to become the basis for Beaver Island State Park.

Samuel Strong Spaulding was the son of Elbridge Spaulding and he followed his father in the banking business and Buffalo Street Railway, becoming president of the East Side Street Railway. He married Annie Watson, daughter of Stephen V.R. Watson, who was also associated banking and the railway. They resided in the former Mark Twain home at 472 Delaware Avenue. Later they later lived at the former Sherman S. Rogers mansion at 698 Delaware and built a summer home in Cooperstown. The former Twain house was damaged in a 1963 fire and after it was demolished, the Cloister Restaurant was built upon the foundation of the home and carriage house.

Edward Spaulding worked with his father and brother Samuel at Farmers and Mechanics Bank. After the bank was liquidated, Edward moved to Santa Barbara, California, where he died in 1908. Charlotte married Franklin Sidway, who managed his businesses, along with Sidway and Spaulding family enterprises. They inherited the River Lawn property on Grand Island.

When Spaulding died in 1897 at age 88, his will stipulated that the 775 Main Street property be demolished. Two buildings were built on the property by heirs of Elbridge Spaulding. The Spaulding Building was constructed by Edward Spaulding in 1906 at 763 Main Street. It is a three-story building which was purchased in 1989 by Foit-Albert Associates, who renovated the building to include 7,000 square feet of commercial space and 20 upper floor apartments. They sold it in 2015 to Nick Sinatra & Company Real Estate for 2.75 million dollars. The Sidway Building at 775-783 was built by Charlotte and Franklin Sidway in 1907 as a four-story commercial building. Two floors were added in 1913 and the Sidway Building now houses luxury loft apartments.

Spaulding was buried in the family plot at Forest Lawn Cemetery. In addition to the grave of Elbridge G. Spaulding, his parents, his three wives, two of his children and other relatives, there is a Bunker Hill Cenotaph, memorializing the nine Spaulding veterans of the Battle of Bunker Hill.

EBEN CARLTON SPRAGUE

*Lawyer and Chancellor of The University of Buffalo and son
Carlton associated with Buffalo Pitts Company*

The first member of the Sprague family in America was Francis Sprague who arrived on the ship *Anne* in July 1623. In 1669, his grandson Samuel Sprague married Ruth Alden, the granddaughter of John Alden, a signatory of the Mayflower Compact. Noah Paul Sprague, the great-great-grandson of Samuel was born in 1798.

Noah Paul Sprague lived in Bath, New Hampshire, where he married Abiah Carlton, granddaughter of Peter Carlton, a member of the convention to rewrite the Federal Constitution in 1791 and a Representative in Congress. On November 28, 1822, Eben Carlton Sprague was born to Noah and Abiah in Bath, NH, and in 1825 they moved to Buffalo.

E. Carlton Sprague attended the Buffalo Public Schools and prepared for college by attending Phillips Exeter Academy. He graduated from Harvard College in 1843, returning to Buffalo where he read law at the offices of Fillmore, Hall and Haven. After being admitted to the bar in 1846, he was a member of several leading law firms, including a partnership with Millard Powers Fillmore, President Fillmore's son. His law career continued for 50 years, and his clients included major companies such as the Great Western Railway Company, New York, Lake Erie & Western Railway Company, Erie County Savings Bank and the International Bridge Company. He was a member of many professional, educational, social, benevolent and cultural organizations, serving as the 3rd Chancellor of the University of Buffalo from 1885 until his death in 1895.

In June 1849, he married Elizabeth Hubbard Williams, daughter of John R. Williams. They lived at 235 Delaware Avenue at the corner of West Chippewa, currently the location of Starbucks. The Spragues had four children, Henry Ware, Carlton and two daughters who married and moved to NYC. Henry Ware Sprague followed his father into the legal profession. He attended Buffalo Public Schools, Professor Brigg's Classical School and also studied at Leipzig University in Germany. After studying law at his father's firm, he became a junior partner in law firms with his father and formed his own firm after E. Carlton Sprague's death. In 1888, he married Mary Noyes, daughter of John Sedgwick Noyes, a primary developer of the Buffalo lumber forwarding trade.

Carlton Sprague followed his father by attending Buffalo Public Schools, Phillips Exeter Academy and graduating from Harvard College in 1881, where he was editor of the *Harvard Lampoon* and president of the *Harvard Advocate*. Returning to Buffalo, he formed the Saturn Club in 1885, with the charter members being college graduates from the wealthy families of Buffalo. They wanted a less formal setting than their father's traditional clubs. The other thirteen founding members included Ansley Wilcox, John. B. Olmsted, William F. Kip and Francis Almy. Carlton served as the first Dean (officers titles were based on the members college experience – common of the University Clubs of this time period), of the Saturn Club, which obtained its name because the initial meetings were held at a vacant Sprague property on Saturdays, which was called Saturn's Day. The annual meeting was to be called Saturnalia, the ancient Roman festival to honor the god Saturn, but they decided to change that name when the club members discovered the festival connotated an orgy. The club opened in 1890 and continues today at 977 Delaware Avenue.

After studying law with his father, Carlton decided to work for the Buffalo Pitts Company, a leading manufacturer of threshers, steam tractor engines and other farm implements. In 1883, Carlton married Alice L. Brayley, daughter of James and Mary A. (Pitts) Brayley. Mary was the daughter of John A. Pitts, one of the founders of the company. Sprague became vice-president in 1883, president in 1891 and later served as chairman of the board.

The Buffalo Pitts Company began when twin brothers Hiram and John Pitts received the patent for the Pitts Thresher in 1837. Hiram relocated his businesses to Chicago, where his company Hiram Pitts Sons' Company was referred to as Chicago Pitts. John moved to Buffalo and constructed a large factory operated by his son-in-law James Brayley at Carolina and 4th Streets, on the Erie Canal.

In 1910, the Buffalo Pitts Company and Charles Morgan Olmsted started a syndicate to manufacture airplanes, the third company incorporated in the U.S. to make aircraft. This was an advanced style plane, with the wings covered by thin gauge chrome-vanadium steel or aluminum sheet metal rather than canvas. The design was a pusher plane with the propellers behind the wings, similar to the later designs of Dick Rutan. Unfortunately, the airplane portion of the company was discontinued

Figure 149 Buffalo Pitts Company along Erie Canal

Figure 150 Drawing of Sprague home on Lake Erie

due to lack of financing, but a prototype was found when their factory was being demolished in the 1950s. That prototype was salvaged and is now in storage at a Smithsonian satellite museum.

The Buffalo Pitts Company had a large display of farm and other products at the Pan-American Exposition because Sprague was a member of the Building Committee with J.N. Scatcherd, Colonel W. Symons, George K. Birge and Harry Hamlin. Carlton was also president of the Buffalo Fine Arts Academy.

In 1888, Carlton and Alice Sprague built a Shingle Style Estate designed by architect Edward Austin Kent at 4325 Lake Shore Road in Hamburg. The 11,731 square foot, nine-bedroom estate on 4.6 acres was their summer home. The home was built at a cost of $3,500 and last sold in 2018 for $550,000. Carlton later moved to New York City, where he was a director for Western Union Telegraph Company. He died in 1916.

MARGARET ST. JOHN

Margaret Kinsman Marsh St. John convinced the British to not destroy her home when Buffalo was burned on December 30, 1813, during the War of 1812

Margaret was born in Wilton, Connecticut on July 15, 1768, the daughter of Presbyterian clergyman Cyrus Marsh. In 1788, she married Gamaliel St. John and they moved to Danbury, Connecticut where five of their children were born. The lure of opportunities in the west drew the St. John family to Westmoreland, NY where Gamaliel built seven miles of the road between the Cayuga and Owasco Lakes and where three more children were born to the family.

In 1807, the St. Johns moved to Williamsville and settled on a farm owned by Andrew Ellicott, the nephew of Joseph Ellicott. Gamaliel viewed the lands in WNY and decided upon moving to the Village of Buffalo, and in 1810 they purchased Lot #53 from Mrs. Chapman. The lot included the frame of a front building and a completed small back building. Gamaliel and his sons Elijah and Cyrus cut the logs and moved them to the Williamsville saw mill for cutting into lumber and made the shingles during the winter of 1809/10, along with cutting the blocks for the basement from Granger's quarry near Scajaquada Creek. The families eleventh child was born in the back building while the front house at 460 Main Street was being completed.

On June 6, 1813, Gamaliel St. John and his son Elijah drowned in the Niagara River while ferrying supplies in their boat to resupply the American troops occupying Fort Erie. During the previous December, their son Cyrus died of distemper that affected the military camp in Buffalo. An attack by the British was feared by the people of the village of Buffalo, which consisted of about 100 buildings. When the alarm was sounded on December 30, 1813 that the British were beginning their attack, many of the residents began to flee the village. Asaph Bemis, the husband of the St. John's second oldest daughter Aurelia, gathered six of the younger St. John children and his wife into a wagon and attempted to flee down Main Street to Williamsville. That road was blocked by the attacking British and their Indian allies, so he circled back and fled over Buffalo Creek toward Hamburg. He hoped to return to pick up Margaret and her older daughters Maria and Sarah but was unable to make it back to the village.

Margaret and her daughters watched the British and their Mohawk allies burn down the homes and businesses of Buffalo. In desperation, Margaret begged the British commander General Phineas Raill to spare her home and the lives of herself and her daughters, so Raill assigned his dwarf interpreter to guard their home. Even with a guard posted in front of their home, Mrs. St. John and her daughters had to ward off threats during the burning of December 30 and 31. During the evening, Sarah St. John would sneak out of the home to forage for food, catching chickens and pigs, along with gathering vegetables and collecting water from the well.

On January 1, 1814 the Mohawk returned to burn all buildings that were not destroyed. They burned the tavern the St. John family built next to their home. That

Figure 151 Drawing of the only house in Buffalo not burned down during the War of 1812

morning several Indians broke into the St. John home, and the people who had taken refuge in the house fled in panic. Sarah was chased by an Indian who had a raised tomahawk in his hand. Out of fear, Sarah stopped, turned toward her assailant with raised hands and started laughing. The Indian was stunned, shook Sarah's hand, painted her face and motioned her back to her house. A British officer stopped her and asked why her face was painted like an Indian. He told her to wash off the war paint, but she refused fearing the Indian may return and become upset if she removed the paint. Extraordinary courage for a 16-year-old girl.

The St. John home was the only residential building not burned during the British attack on Buffalo. The only other buildings left standing were the stone walls of the jail, David Rees' stone blacksmith shop and part of a Captain Pratt's recently built barn, where the timbers were still too green to be burned by the fires. When the residents of Buffalo began to return to the city, several of them just put roofs over their cellars and lived underground to survive the winter. Many were given food and shelter in the only remaining house of Margaret St. John.

During the War of 1812, Margaret St. John lost her husband, two oldest sons, their tavern and most of their possessions. She was left to raise her family with her youngest son, only three and a half years old. They persevered, regained their position in the village, were respected by all for the bravery shown during the burning of Buffalo and acknowledged for the assistance they provided to the people of the village.

Several of St. John children and descendants played significant roles in the development of Buffalo. Maria St. John married Abram J. Fisk, and their daughter Calista Maria Fisk married prominent businessman Orson Phelps. Her monument, created in Rome by famous sculptor Nicola Canatamessa-Papotti, is one of the finest in Forest Lawn Cemetery. Sarah St. John was the second wife of Mayor Samuel Wilkeson, the builder of Buffalo harbor. She lived in the Wilkeson Mansion on Niagara Square, now the site of City Hall. Sarah's grandson by marriage, Tellico Johnson, was the developer of Orton and St. Johns Places. Sarah was known for her charitable contributions in assisting the poor and was given the honor of turning over the first shovelful of soil to commence the construction of the Erie Canal in Buffalo on August 9, 1823. Parnell St. John married Jonathan Sidway. After Jonathan's death in 1847, she remained at the Sidway mansion on Hudson Street, and her bachelor brother Le Grand St. John moved in to help maintain the home and assist in raising her children. Le Grand was an engineer, inventor and artist. He received a NYS patent for a steam heater in 1851 and U.S. patent for an improved boat propeller in 1858. His drawing of the Burning of Buffalo during the War of 1812, to which he was an eyewitness, are in the collection of the Buffalo Historical Society.

After her children left home, Margaret St. John lived in a home on Seneca Street. She died in 1847, and the home at 460 Main Street that survived the burning of Buffalo was demolished in 1871.

Figure 152 St. John family monument in Forest Lawn Cemetery

JOHN STEDMAN

Ran portage route between Lewiston and Fort Schlosser during
time of English control of WNY

The British became involved with the Niagara Frontier after winning the French
& Indian War. When they acquired Fort Niagara, this established a foothold in
the WNY area for British control.

The first recorded conflict between white men and Indians in Erie County was in
October of 1763, when British soldiers under Major Wilkes attacked a band of Seneca
Indians near the present location of Black Rock. About 50 soldiers came ashore, but
were repulsed by the Indians, after the British suffered ten killed and many wounded.
In Niagara County, a larger battle occurred at Devil's Hole on September 14, 1763.

The Seneca Indians had been employed by the French to carry shipments of goods
and merchandise up the slope of the Niagara River valley at Lewiston and around the
Falls to the upper Niagara River. When the British took over control of the portage
in 1763, they made further improvements and employed even fewer Indians. The
Seneca complained to the British government that they had lost their jobs. A
combination of the labor situation and the Pontiac War led to the Devils Hole
Massacre on September 14, 1763 about two miles south of Lewiston.

After the French & Indian War, James Sterling and John Duncan, established the
business of transporting cargo along the portage trail from their Upper Landing above
Niagara Falls to the Lower Landing at Lewiston and on to Fort Niagara. The British
were not satisfied with the percentage of profits they were receiving from the Sterling-
Duncan portage business. To take over the business and give the British more of the
profits, they gave this business to John Stedman, who arrived in the Niagara area in
1762. John Stedman took possession of French trader Joncaire's former land and storehouse (Little Fort Niagara) above the Falls and the portage facilities in Lewiston.

Stedman rebuilt the sawmill abandoned by Joncaire, providing the only mill for lumber in the region. To protect his interests, he permitted a British garrison to be posted near his Upper Niagara property. This

Figure 153 Old Stone Chimney was part of Joncaire's Little Fort Niagara
and Stedman's house at Fort Schlosser

evolved into Fort Schlosser, which included a stockade with four bastions, mess hall and barracks. He also constructed a fortified blockhouse at the Lower Landing in Lewiston and established the shipyard on Navy Island, about four miles upstream from Fort Schlosser. Stedman profited off everything he did, selling the lumber from his mill to the British for construction, providing a tavern where the soldiers could quench their thirst, and running a store where the soldiers could purchase their supplies.

Stedman's style of doing business antagonized the Seneca. He would not allow them to camp on his land and was reluctant to sell them rum or supplies at his store. The grading of the portage trail made it passable for wagons, which put a number of Seneca out of work. When the Seneca agreed to participate in Pontiac's Rebellion to remove the British and white settlers from the Great Lakes area, it was only a matter of time until there was Indian retaliation to Stedman's and the British policies in the Niagara Frontier.

On September 14, 1763, Stedman was leading a wagon train of supplies, destined for the British troops in Detroit, from Lewiston to Fort Schlosser. One hundred Seneca warriors, led by Seneca War Chief Farmer's Brother, laid in wait near the crest of the Lewiston Escarpment at the area known as Devil's Hole. The Seneca backed the wagon train against the 80-foot drop of the Niagara Gorge with the teamsters, horses, mules and wagons plunging to their death on the rocks below. Stedman escaped the carnage but retreated by side trails to Fort Schlosser rather than alerting the troops stationed at Fort Grey closer at Lewiston. Lieutenant George Campbell heard the gunfire at Fort Grey on the Lower Landing and rushed 80 members of the 80th Regiment of Light Armed Foot trained in guerrilla tactics for Indian fighting to the rescue. Farmer's Brother positioned his best marksmen on the higher ground at Devil's Hole, trapping the British with their backs against the gorge, killing all members of the regiment.

After he was removed from his portage position, Stedman unsuccessfully tried to sue the British government for his losses incurred at the Devil's Hole Massacre. He was relieved of his portage-master duties but regained the position when his successor was drafted to British service during the American Revolution. Returning to England as a very rich man, he even filed a land claim against the American government, arguing the Seneca gave him title to all the land from Devil's Hole to Fort Schlosser.

In April 1764, Sir William Johnson concluded a treaty with the Seneca, with the Indians conveying to England a tract around Niagara Falls 14 miles in length and 4 miles in width for the purpose of portage around the Falls. This was in retribution for Devils Hole Massacre. That summer General John Bradstreet, with 1,200 British and American soldiers came to Fort Niagara, accompanied by Iroquois warriors. They held a council with friendly Indians at the fort, but the local Seneca did not attend. Bradstreet ordered their immediate attendance under penalty of the destruction of their settlements. The Seneca then complied and adhered to the terms of the treaty.

Bradstreet's forces visited the Seneca village at Buffalo Creek across from Fort Erie. A Lieutenant colonel in that force was Israel Putnam, a member of Roger's

Rangers in the French & Indian War and later an American Commander in the Revolution. At the Battle of Bunker Hill, Putnam is one of the officers credited with coining the slogan "Don't fire until you see the whites of their eyes."

Fort Erie, across the Niagara River, was originally built in 1764, and during the American Revolution it was a trading post for the Native Americans, although Fort Niagara was the main British post. The original Fort Erie was built right on the shoreline and was destroyed by flood waters in 1779. The second fort stood from 1779 to 1803. Just before the war of 1812 it was rebuilt higher up the land on a 35-foot bluff so it would not be destroyed by flood waters.

In 1775, Joseph Brant, the war chief of the Mohawks and a Loyalist, settled his tribe along Ridge Road (Route 104). He moved his tribe to Brantford Ontario after the Revolution. Loyalists from the Eastern states came to Lewiston to cross into Canada. In 1791, the Lieutenant Governor John Simcoe of Upper Canada created a ferry service between Lewiston and Queenstown. The traffic was so great that at times wagons were lined up for three miles to cross the river.

During the American Revolution the battles between the loyalists and patriots took place in central New York. The American forces victory over British General John Burgoyne at the second Battle of Saratoga on October 7, 1777, was considered the turning point of the Revolution. General Sullivan's Scorched Earth policy against the Seneca did not reach as far as WNY, but many Seneca retreated to the area. With the British possession of Fort Niagara and the fact that the area was not yet settled, there were not any battles in WNY. The British did not surrender Fort Niagara until 1796, with the U.S. flag first flying over the Fort on August 11, 1796. When Fort Niagara was transferred to the U.S., the British built Fort George across the Niagara River at Niagara-on-the-Lake, Ontario.

Lewiston was the American forces staging area for the Battle of Queenston Heights, the first major battle of the War of 1812. Cannons installed on Barton Hill were aimed at the village of Queenston, across the Niagara gorge from Lewiston. In the early morning hours, the American forces crossed the river and fought their way up the incline at Queenston Heights. The British lost their commanding officer, General Brock, who was considered the best British commanding officer in Canada. The Americans lost the battle because local militia refused to cross the river, claiming their job was to defend the United States, not invade Canada. The monument to General Brock can be seen across the river from Lewiston.

On December 18, 1813, a force of 560 British regulars, commanded by Colonel John Murray, crossed the Niagara River about three miles above Fort Niagara. After capturing the American pickets at Youngstown, the British made a surprise night-time attack on Fort Niagara highlighted by a silent bayonet assault. During the Battle of Fort Niagara, the Americans casualties were 65 killed, 16 wounded, 344 captured and only 20 escaping. Control of Fort Niagara facilitated the British destruction of Lewiston, Manchester (Niagara Falls), Black Rock and Buffalo. The British held Fort Niagara for the remainder of the war, ceding it back to the U.S. in 1815.

OLIVER GREY STEELE

The first Superintendent of Schools in Buffalo

Originally from Connecticut, Steele was born in 1805 and moved to Buffalo in 1827. He was a successful businessman, opening a book bindery upstairs at 206 Main Street in 1828. Steele was also President of Buffalo Waterworks and for 30 years was secretary and manager at Buffalo Gaslight Company.

Education was important in Buffalo with the first school started by Joseph R. Palmer, brother of tavern owner John Palmer. He petitioned Joseph Ellicott of the Holland Land Company to supply a lot for the school. That was approved by the Holland Land Company with the stipulation that the school be built by the villagers at their own expense. The committee was led by Samuel Pratt, Joseph Landon and Joshua Gillett. Prior to this building, classes were held in 1806 and 1807 by teacher Hiram Hanchett in the Middaugh house.

The building of the first schoolhouse started in 1806, but records show it was not completed until 1808, when Samuel Pratt donated 2,000 shingles in November 1808. It was constructed by donation of labor and materials from the settlers at the southwest corner of South Cayuga (now Pearl), and Swan Streets, across from the later home of George Coit. The lot where the school was built was known as the Forbes Lot. Contributors were Captain Samuel Pratt, Cyrenius Chapin, Gamaliel St. John, Joseph Landon and Zenas Barker, with other subscribers Sylvanus Maybe, Joseph Wells, Thomas Fourth, John Johnston, Nathaniel W. Sever, Isaac H. Bennet, Levi Strong, William Hull, Richard Mann, Asahel Adkins, Samuel Andrews, Garret Freeland and Bill Sherman. Most of the children in the village attended this school as there was no other educational facility in Buffalo. The first teacher was Samuel Whiting, a Presbyterian minister, followed by Amos Callender. Some parents desired other instruction for their children and Gamaliel St. John introduced Asaph Hall, who opened a grammar school in the courthouse.

There was another school district created north of Court Street, called District #2. It was formed during a meeting at the home of William Hodge. The school opened in 1807 with the first teacher being a Scottish man named Sturgeon. It served the children living in the 12 homes between North Street and Granger Creek.

During the War of 1812, the schoolhouse in Buffalo was burned down. After the War of 1812, a new school was opened and supported by

Figure 154 Cold Springs School at Main and Ferry where Millard Fillmore taught, built 1820

a school tax levied in the village. Amos Callender was again the teacher, along with a Mr. Pease, Reverend Deodatus Babcock, Wyatt Camp and others. This school did not have a permanent location.

In 1822, a permanent school was established in a house on the west side of Main Street between Mohawk and Genesee Streets. It was at this location that Millard Fillmore first taught before taking on the responsibility of the Cold Springs school. By 1836 few people took interest in the public-school system, the trustees were busy with other employment and only children from the poorest families attended the schools. The children from more affluent families attended private schools which were opened by individual teachers in Buffalo, Springville, Clarence, Aurora and Williamsville.

Due to the loss of funding during the Panic of 1837, many of the private schools in Buffalo closed and the public-school system was the only alternative for education in Buffalo. A committee was formed to appraise the condition of the schools and the Common Council passed a law for the entire school system to be reorganized. R.W. Haskins was appointed city superintendent of common schools, but he resigned after a year because he did not have the power to make changes to improve the system. N.P. Sprague was offered the position but turned it down due to the lack of power expressed by Haskins. Without his knowledge, Oliver Steele was appointed superintendent at a City Council meeting in 1838, and he was induced to accept the position by Judge Hall, who promised to amend the laws so the superintendent could make any required changes.

Oliver G. Steele and Nathan K. Hall championed a tax-supported, tuition-free public-school system. After Steele surveyed the existing schools and the established districts, such a system was formed in Buffalo, the first in New York State. NYC had an earlier free education system, but the costs were supplemented by private donations and other sources.

In 1838 Steele became the first superintendent of Buffalo Schools, and he has the distinction of being appointed the first person in the U.S. to be called a superintendent of schools. Steele was Superintendent of Buffalo Schools in 1838, 1839, 1845 and 1851. He was also Alderman for the Fourth Ward in 1842 and 1847 and unsuccessful candidate for Mayor in 1844. Steele was one of the original members of the Buffalo Historical Society. At its formation, Charles D. Norton was appointed Treasurer, but he resigned in September 1862 and was replaced by Oliver G. Steele. In 1874 Steele was appointed president of the Society, and several of his speeches presented to the Society are included in the Publications of the Buffalo Historical Society.

When Steele was superintendent, twelve new elementary schools were built, bringing the total number of schools to 15 elementary buildings. During his tenure, a building to house Central School, the first high school, was purchased. For his accomplishments he is considered "Father of Public Schools in Buffalo."

CHARLES F. STERNBERG

The builder of 414 Delaware Avenue

In 1869, Charles F. Sternberg built a 20,000 square foot mansion for his bride Mary Blackmar. The home was designed by architect George M. Allison, who designed several costly Delaware Avenue homes during the 1860s and 1870s, but this is the only home that remains. The Second Empire style mansion had 18' ceilings, over 200 windows and several 12' windows that filled the house with natural light. Construction cost for the house was $200,000, or more than three and a half million current dollars.

Sternberg was the son of socialite Pearl Sternberg and was the operator of an Ohio Street grain elevator, but he died while the house was being completed. He was only 31, so his legacy to Buffalo is this mansion at the corner of Delaware Avenue and Edward Street, a home with a very interesting history.

After Sternberg passed away, the house was purchased by lumberman William H. Gratwick. He only lived there for a short time as in the early 1880s he moved into the mansion designed by H.H. Richardson at 776 Delaware. Gratwick was followed by railroad contractor and Civil War veteran, John Condit Smith, who was a staff officer of General Sherman during his notorious march through the South.

Figure 155 Mansion on Delaware at Delaware and Edward Photo: Courtesy Mansion on Delaware

Smith passed away, and the home was purchased by Samuel Curtis Trubee in 1883. He converted the house into a family hotel and built an addition for the Pan-American Exposition. The Trubee Hotel was one of the most expensive hotels for the Pan-Am, charging three dollars a night. It was rumored that after WWI these rooms were used for purposes which were the farthest thing from a family hotel.

In 1947, the building was purchased by restaurateur Hugo DiGiulio, who operated other top-quality restaurants such as DiGiulio's Club 31 on Johnson Park. The restaurant opened as Victor Hugo Wine Cellar and became one of Buffalo's most elegant dinner clubs. Luxury apartments were maintained in the building and rented to celebrities who were performing in Buffalo.

The restaurant closed in 1977, and it remained vacant until 2001 when after a 2.7 million-dollar conversion by Dennis Murphy, it reopened as The Mansion on Delaware. It is now considered one of the most prestigious small hotels in the country, catering top quality wedding receptions and special events.

Between the Buffalo Club at 388 Delaware and the current Mansion on Delaware, there were two other homes; 396 and 410 Delaware. 396 Delaware was built by brewmaster Abel T. Blackmar. Upon his death it was sold to Edward L. Stevenson, who from 1823 to 1842 operated the stagecoach lines servicing Buffalo and later made a fortune in real estate investments. In 1891, 396 Delaware was purchased by retired banker James M. Ganson. His wife continued to live at the mansion until her death in 1918 when she willed the property to Trinity Church across the street. The church sold the house to the Buffalo Club.

410 Delaware was built by James G. Forsythe, an executive at Sidney Shepard & Company, who lived there with his nephew James Foster, also employed at Sidney Shepard. When Forsythe died in 1903, he willed $200,000 to each the Buffalo Parks Department and Fine Arts Academy. A rooming house called The Edward was later at 410 Delaware until The Buffalo Club purchased and razed it to retain the integrity of the neighborhood. This resulted in the current day parking lot between the Buffalo Club and the Mansion on Delaware.

NIKOLA TESLA

*Visionary inventor who championed AC current, developed the AC motor
and harnessed the transmission of hydroelectric power from Niagara Falls*

Nikola Tesla was an ethnic Serb born on July 10, 1856 in Smiljan, part of the Austrian Empire, later part of Yugoslavia and is now in Croatia. His father (Milutin Tesla) and his mother's (Djuka Mundic Tesla) father were both Eastern Orthodox priests, with Nikola destined to follow in their footsteps. However, Nikola had a natural mechanical aptitude and eidetic memory, including an ability to visualize concepts in 3D and do integral calculus in his head. During high school in Karlovac, Tesla completed his studies a year early in 1873, and it was here that his physics teacher introduced him to electricity, which Tesla considered a mysterious phenomenon about which he wanted to know more.

*Figure 156 Portrait of
Nikola Tesla*

Tesla returned home after finishing school and contracted cholera. He was near death several times and was bedridden for nine months. His father had planned for Nikola to enter the priesthood but promised him that if he recovered from his illness, he would send him to school for engineering. After Tesla recovered, at his father's request he went to the mountains in 1874 to regain his strength and evade conscription into the Austro-Hungarian Army. In 1875, he entered the Austrian Polytechnic in Graz, Austria, and during his first year he received the highest grades allowed. The institute wrote letters to Tesla's father warning that Nikola would kill himself from overwork if he kept up the pace of studying 20 hours a day, seven days a week. His father was concerned for Nikola's health, so he did not praise him for his accomplishments. Rather than getting Tesla to reduce his workload, this lack of praise led Nikola to become severely depressed and disillusioned, neglect his studies and resort to excessive card playing. At the end of the second year, Tesla lost his scholarship, gambling away his allowance and tuition money. Tesla left the university and did not graduate.

In 1881, Tesla moved to Budapest, Hungary and obtained a job at the Budapest Telephone Exchange working for telephone pioneer Tivadar Puskas. After a year, Puskas obtained Tesla a job working for Consolidated Edison in Paris in 1882. Here Tesla gained experience in electrical engineering, improved the company dynamos and was sent to troubleshoot engineering problems at other facilities in France and Germany. When his manager in Paris, Charles Batchelor, was transferred to the Edison Machine Works in NYC, he asked that Tesla be hired to work with him. In June 1884, Tesla emigrated to the U.S. and was given a job troubleshooting installations and improving generators. Tesla only remained in the employment of Edison for about six months. He left the company claiming Edison had promised him a bonus of $50,000 if he successfully redesigned several generators. After he succeeded in his design the bonus was not paid, with Edison teasing that Tesla did not understand American humor.

After leaving Edison's employment, Nikola Tesla started Tesla Electric Light & Manufacturing with two New Jersey engineers, Robert Lane and Benjamin Vail. He was successful in the project and through attorney Lemuel W. Serrell learned how to obtain patents. His first U.S. patent was assigned to the company for stock and when the company closed, Tesla was relegated to digging ditches for $2.00 a day to survive. In 1887, Tesla worked with Western Union superintendent Alfred S. Brown and NY attorney Charles Peck to form Tesla Electric Company. Tesla patented his revolutionary alternating current (AC) rotating magnetic field induction motor, published papers, gave lectures and became fairly well known.

George Westinghouse, the inventor of air brakes for the railroad industry, read Tesla's papers and became interested in electricity. For the licensing of Tesla's alternating current induction motor and related polyphase AC patents, Westinghouse offered Tesla $60,000, with 90% of that being in Westinghouse stock, and a royalty of $2.50 per installed kilowatt. Financier J.P. Morgan, working with Edison, tried to bring all U.S. hydroelectric power under his control. Morgan attempted to manipulate the stock market with the intent of starving out Westinghouse and buying Tesla's patents. George Westinghouse approached Tesla requesting a change of the initial contract that gave Tesla generous royalties. Tesla tore up his contract with Westinghouse because George had believed in him when no one else did. That action saved the Westinghouse company.

In 1894, the Niagara Falls Power Company (which evolved from Schoellkopf's company) began placing contracts for the Edward Dean Adams power station #1. On April 15, 1895, the first Niagara Generator which bore Tesla's name and patent numbers was successfully tested. On either August 25 or 26, 1895 Powerhouse #1 began producing power, but Tesla did not attend the opening. He did not come to Niagara Falls until November 1896.

At midnight on November 16, 1896, a switch in the Niagara Falls Powerhouse completed a circuit that powered the Buffalo Streetcars located 22 miles away. It signaled Tesla's triumph over Thomas Edison in what was called the War of the Currents, when in the late 1880s Tesla's Alternating Current (AC) challenged Edison's Direct Current (DC).

On January 12, 1897, there was a banquet to fete an extraordinary event – the transmission of electricity from Niagara Falls to Buffalo. Only two months earlier Nikola Tesla had figured out how to use alternating current to transmit hydroelectric power from Niagara Falls to Buffalo. The event was attended by 400 people including members of Buffalo's upper class, investors from New York City and engineers from around the world.

The exclusive, opulent and celebratory event, called the "Power Banquet" was held at The Ellicott Club, located in the newly opened Ellicott Square Building.

Guests were served a 10-course meal, which included oysters, deviled lobster and a dessert called electric sorbet.

Other businesses in Buffalo that were early subscribers to Tesla's inventions licensed to Westinghouse included the AM&A's department store on Main Street, which electrified the building with a generator in 1886. George Urban opened the first flour mill entirely powered by electricity in 1903. One negative use of Tesla's alternating current was its application in the electric chair, invented by Buffalo dentist Alfred P. Southwick in 1881. Thomas Edison championed the use of AC in the electric chair to prove that it was not safe, so his DC current would receive a larger portion of the growing electric market.

In 1893, Westinghouse and Tesla won the contract to supply AC power over Edison's DC power at the Columbian Exposition or Chicago World's Fair. Tesla anticipated using Edison's GE light bulbs, but Edison refused to grant permission to incorporate his bulbs into the Chicago Fair system; so, Westinghouse developed a more efficient double stopper light bulb, producing 250,000 plug-in bulbs for the fair. After Tesla won the rights for the 1901 Pan-American Exposition in Buffalo and supplied the power by transmitting it from electricity generated at Niagara Falls, AC achieved victory in the AC/DC war and dominated the electricity market. Interestingly, Tesla did not attend the Pan-American Exposition, but Edison was there to film it.

At the corner of the Twin City Memorial Highway and Robinson Street in North Tonawanda, there is an old building that played an important part in the history of electricity. This building was the transfer station for sending electricity from Niagara Falls to Buffalo, following a design by Tesla. It was through this building that the first electricity to power the Buffalo streetcars was sent in 1896 and transferred the electricity to the Pan-American Exposition in 1901. The existence of this power station resulted in North Tonawanda receiving electric power in 1896 and assisting the city in becoming a manufacturing center.

The importance of this building in the history of electricity is signified by a photo of the building displayed at the Edison-Ford Museum in Fort Myers, Florida. National Grid once applied for a permit to destroy the building. Thankfully that was denied, and the building is still used by National Grid. The building has been given designation as a historical landmark, so it will be preserved. Someday the building may be a Tesla Museum, displaying its importance to the history of electricity, along with bringing attention to Tesla's many inventions.

Figure 157 Electric distribution building in North Tonawanda through which alternating current was first distributed to Buffalo

SHELDON THOMPSON

First mayor of Buffalo elected by the people of the city

Sheldon Thompson was born in Derby, Connecticut on July 2, 1785. The Thompson family can be traced back in America to Anthony Thompson, who arrived in 1638 and was one of the founders of New Haven, Connecticut. His grandfather was an officer during the French & Indian War, fought at the Battle of Bunker Hill and was killed at the retreat from New York City in 1776 during the Revolutionary War. His father Jabez Thompson was a sailor who was lost at sea in 1794 and Sheldon himself first went to sea at age ten on his brother William's ship. Sheldon became a captain of his own ship while in his early twenties, trading in the West Indies for the New Haven company of Gillet & Townsend. In 1810, he moved to Lewiston to work for the company of Townsend, Bronson & Company, owned by Jacob Townsend who he worked for in New Haven. Townsend and Alvin Bronson built ships in Lewiston, had stores in Lewiston and Oswego, sold salt from the Onondaga salt mines and had a shipping business on Lake Ontario. In 1811, he married Catherine Barton, the daughter of Benjamin Barton who was a partner of Peter and Augustus Porter in the freight forwarder company of Porter, Barton & Company.

After the War of 1812, he moved to Black Rock into a home at Niagara and Ferry Streets. He worked in freight forwarding with Townsend, Barton & Company, formed Sill, Thompson & Company and traded with his father-in-law Benjamin Barton. Thompson also began building ships in Black Rock, was the construction contractor of the harbor and worked with General Peter B. Porter to locate the terminus of the Erie Canal at Black Rock. Regardless of which village won the rights for the Erie Canal terminus, Thompson wanted to position himself to benefit by obtaining the very lucrative freight forwarding business.

Figure 158 Sheldon Thompson mansion at Broadway and Washington Streets
Photo: Buffalo History Museum

When the decision was made to make Buffalo the terminus, Thompson sent his younger brother to Batavia to purchase land from the Holland Land Company on the Buffalo waterfront. He moved his base of operations to Buffalo and established the freight forwarding company of Sheldon Thompson & Company, built the third steamboat to operate on Lake Erie and owned one of the first canal boat lines, the Troy & Erie

Figure 159 Mansion on Porter Hill owned by Hiram Pratt, Bela Coe and Porter Thompson

Company. S. Thompson & Company merged with Townsend & Coit, to form Coit, Kimberly & Company in 1836, one of the premier freight companies in Buffalo. One of Thompson's other investments was a white lead company.

On March 8, 1840, the first general election for Mayor of Buffalo was held. Previously the mayor was selected by the Common Council. Sheldon Thompson won the election over George P. Baker by a vote of 1,135 to 1,125, a difference of only ten votes. After serving a one-year term, he returned to his businesses and in 1845 retired to his mansion at Broadway and Washington Streets near the location of the current downtown library. Thompson died on March 13, 1851 at age 65.

His son Augustus Porter Thompson, known as Porter, was born in Black Rock on February 14, 1825 and was educated at academies in Lewiston and Canandaigua, along with Buffalo private schools. He clerked for his father Sheldon at his waterfront offices and worked at the Thompson & Company lead works on Georgia Street. Porter left his father's employment to assist in founding a blast furnace, which became known as Buffalo Union Iron Works. He returned to his father's company and later purchased an interest in S.G. Cornell & Sons, eventually becoming president of Cornell Lead Works on Delaware Avenue at Virginia. Porter remained with Cornell until 1887 when the company was transferred to The National Lead Company and he became a director and manager of the Buffalo branch.

Porter Thompson was married to Matilda Cass Jones of Detroit on June 9, 1853 and they had eleven children. In 1855, he purchased the Mansion on Prospect Hill from the widow of Bela D. Coe. He lived at this home for 44 years, passing away at age 87 in 1911. The family donated the home to the National League for Women's Service, who with the War Camp Community Service established a service club at the home. The clubs sold the property to the city of Buffalo, and when the house was demolished, Thompson's granddaughter Geraldine Thompson Case and her husband Edward Case had the mansion's sandstone blocks set aside for future use. In 1925, they used the blocks to build a home at 92 Cleveland Avenue in Buffalo's Upper West Side. School #3, now called D'Youville Porter Campus School, was built on the site of the Mansion on Prospect Hill.

GEORGE WASHINGTON TIFFT

Businessman, industrialist and real estate developer

George Washington Tifft was born on January 31, 1805 in Nassau, Rensselaer County in Eastern New York. He was the youngest of twelve children and began his business career when he purchased five acres of land in Orleans County, northeast of Buffalo near Lake Ontario. After realizing he could hire men to cut down trees and make a profit off their labors, he purchased larger tracts of land and engaged more woodchoppers.

In 1841, Tifft moved to Michigan where he became involved in purchasing grain that he shipped to the east. These business activities introduced him to shippers from the Buffalo area; and in 1842, Tifft moved to Buffalo. He went into business with Dean Richmond, who had relocated to Buffalo from Batavia, and formed a partnership with Henry H. Sizer. In 1844, he was involved with the milling, produce, commission and transportation industries but concentrated on the milling business where he owned several mills and an elevator. He also helped establish the International Bank of Buffalo, and was elected its first president in 1854.

Figure 160 Tifft House at 465 Main Street, later the location of Hengerer's Department Store and now Lafayette Court

The Financial Crisis of 1857 affected all businesses, but Tifft prevailed and became involved in additional activities. He invested $100,000 in the Buffalo Steam Engine Company and purchased coal interests in Mercer County, Pennsylvania. Tifft built two additional blast furnaces in Mercer and experimented with the idea of smelting iron ore with coal, an idea that was successful but he failed to patent. To transport the iron ore from Lake Superior to Mercer, Pennsylvania, Tifft purchased a fleet of lake vessels. In addition to shipping, Tifft was president of New York, Lake Erie and Western Railroad and the Buffalo, New York and Erie Railroad.

Tifft began investing in real estate, building seventy-four dwellings in 1863. Part of this construction were the Tifft Row Houses on Allen Street, which are still standing and include Gabriel's Gate Restaurant. In 1865, he built the Tifft House at 465 Main Street at the former location of the Phoenix Hotel. The Phoenix House was built on the site of the house where Mrs. Lovejoy was killed during the burning of Buffalo in 1813. Raphael Cook built the Phoenix House in 1816 and Millard Fillmore stayed there when he first moved to Buffalo in 1821. After serving as a hotel during the Pan-American Exposition, Hengerer's Department Store was built at the address in 1903. The building is currently known as Lafayette Court, a nine-story office building.

Tifft Farms was a 600-acre tract of land south of the Buffalo River along the shore of Lake Erie that Tifft purchased in 1847, with the land previously owned by Bela D. Coe, Joseph Clary and the Pratt Family. The farm included 17 barns for dairy cows and was managed by George's nephew Wilson Tifft. They sold milk commercially to grocers and the hospitality industry. Stockyards were also built on the property and were managed by Leonard L. Crocker, who was later an early superintendent of the New York Central Stockyards, opened by Tifft's early partner, Dean Richmond.

In the 1870s Tifft began selling off parcels of land from Tifft Farms, with the Lehigh Valley Railroad purchasing 519 acres with the intention of developing the property into a rail and shipping lines center. From 1881 to 1915 Lehigh owned railroads and great lakes shipping companies. It prospered until the Interstate Commerce Commission declared it a monopoly, resulting in the Lehigh Valley Railroad having to divest their interests. The City of Buffalo took over Tifft Farms in 1971 and grants from the NYS Department of Conservation, along with the efforts of concerned citizens, resulted in preserving the property. In 1982, the Buffalo Museum of Science became manager of the property and it is now Tifft Nature Preserve.

In 1827, George Tifft married Lucy Enos, and they had seven children. In his later years he managed the George W. Tifft Sons and Company, the successor to Buffalo Steam Engine Works, which employed over 400 workers. He supported the Civil War by donating funds to provide substitutes for the army and providing for soldier's families, along with supporting other charities, churches and institutions. Tifft died on June 24, 1882 at the age of 77, always considering that he was blessed to have made his fortune and was in the position to help others.

BISHOP JOHN TIMON

The first Bishop of the Catholic Diocese of Buffalo

John Timon was born in Conewago, Pennsylvania on February 12, 1797 of immigrant parents from County Cavan, with Timon often saying he was conceived in Ireland but born in America. When John was three years of age, his family relocated to Baltimore, Maryland where his father James was a successful merchant. Timon enrolled in St. Mary's College in 1811 and upon graduation worked at the family business. Due to the recession that preceded the Financial Crisis of 1819, business decreased and the Timon family moved to Louisville, Kentucky in 1818 and St. Louis, Missouri the following year. In St. Louis, because of the unfavorable business climate and death of a woman to which he was engaged, Timon decided to enter the seminary and become a priest.

Timon was ordained a priest in September 1826 and was assigned to the St. Louis Diocese. There he served as a parish priest, spiritual director, missionary, and taught English and natural sciences at the seminary and college. Timon was credited with making more converts and bringing back more lapsed Catholics to the faith than all other priests combined in the St. Louis diocese. For his skills he was named head of the Catholic church in the Republic of Texas, also working as a missionary in states along the Mississippi River. His name was submitted as Bishop for various communities, but Timon continually turned them down because he wanted to continue his missionary work. That changed when he was offered the position as the first bishop of Buffalo.

Figure 161 Original location of Sisters of Charity Hospital

In 1847, John Timon became Bishop of the newly created Western New York diocese centered in Buffalo which included twenty counties with 4,600 parishioners. When Timon arrived in Buffalo there were four schools, sixteen priests and sixteen churches - some of them mere huts and shanties. He visited the entire diocese, holding services in barns, halls, homes or courthouses. In Buffalo, there was an ethnic division between the French, German and Irish Catholics, and since the city was predominantly Protestant, most institutions were run by Protestants. In addition, Archbishop John Hughes of New York and many other American Catholic bishops, believed in separate Catholic and Protestant social facilities and institutions which was against the fabric of Timon's thoughts.

The Irish began arriving in Buffalo when the Erie Canal was being built, but the majority arrived during the Irish Potato Famine in the 1840s. They settled in the First Ward area near the harbor, grain mills, railroad yards and factories where they worked. The Irish were isolated in this area as it was enclosed by the lake on the west, Buffalo River on the south, railroad tracks on the east and the downtown central business area to the north. They were the poorest people in Buffalo and lived in the poorest areas, evidenced by over 90% of the deaths during the 1849 cholera epidemic being Irish. The Irish population was large but due to their socioeconomic status, they were almost invisible. Timon changed that. He became the spokesman for the Irish, speaking up for the unskilled workers during their strikes on the docks and at the factories.

When Timon arrived in Buffalo, the Bishop's residence was at St. Louis Church on Main and Edward Streets. Founded in 1829, this was the first Catholic church built in Buffalo. It was constructed by the French with the land donated by Louis Stephen LeCouteulx de Caumont, one of Buffalo's earliest settlers. By 1847, St. Louis was a German and French church, since the Irish did not feel welcome, they built St. Patrick's on Broadway and Ellicott in 1837. The French eventually felt no longer welcome at St. Louis and they built St. Peter's in 1850, on the current site of the Lafayette Hotel. Timon affiliated with the impoverished Irish and moved out of St. Louis to an apartment next to St. Patrick's so he could be closer to the First Ward. The feud between the bishop and parish continued, with Timon later refusing to permit diocese priests to say Mass at St. Louis and taking legal action against the church trustees.

Timon believed that the only way to integrate Catholics into American Society was to Americanize the Catholic Church. To accomplish this he opened hospitals, schools and social institutions that were available to people of all religious affiliation. The best example of this ideology was inviting the Sisters of Charity to open a hospital in Buffalo. This hospital and other institutions made the Roman Catholics part of WNY society.

Bishop Timon was an intellectual and spoke several languages, which he felt was necessary so he could converse with the immigrants arriving in Buffalo. Speaking several languages was also beneficial because when he made a trip to Europe to raise funds for a cathedral in Buffalo, he was able to speak to the Pope and European monarchs in their native language. He even learned Spanish in a few weeks before making a trip to Mexico. This helped him raise the funds in Europe and Mexico to build St. Joseph's Cathedral at 50 Franklin Street. The Irish laborers did not have the money to donate to the church. So, after they finished their work, they would arrive at the cathedral construction site to donate their labor.

When Bishop Timon arrived in Buffalo there were only 16 priests serving the diocese. To expand the church, during his twenty years as head of the Buffalo diocese, he invited other religious orders to the WNY area, including the Daughters (Sisters) of Charity, School Sisters of Notre Dame, Ladies of the Sacred Heart, Franciscans, Jesuits, Sisters of Saint Mary of Namur, Oblates of Mary Immaculate, Sisters of St. Joseph, Vincentians, Sisters of the Good Shepherd, Grey Nuns of the Sacred Heart, Sisters of Mercy, Sisters of St. Francis, Passionists and Christian Brothers.

In addition to St. Joseph's Cathedral and Sisters Hospital, Bishop Timon helped establish Nardin Academy, St. Mary's School for the Deaf, Niagara Seminary (University), St. Joseph's Collegiate Institute, St. Bonaventure University, House of the Good Shepherd, (home for unmarried women), Providence Lunatic Asylum, St. Vincent's Infant Asylum and several orphanages and schools.

When Bishop Timon died at age 70 in 1867, an estimated 100,000 people came to view his body before he was entombed in a crypt at St. Joseph's Cathedral. He was successful in making the Catholic Church part of the fabric of Western New York.

Figure 162 Providence Asylum - one of the social organizations established by Bishop Timon

MARK TWAIN

"America's greatest humorist and one of her greatest writers."

S amuel Langhorne Clemens was born in Florida, Missouri on November 30, 1835, and when he was five, his family moved to Hannibal, Missouri, on the Mississippi River. He grew up with the sights and sounds of the river and with Missouri being a slave state, spent much of his youth playing in the slave quarters, enjoying hearing tall tales and listening to spirituals. When he was eleven his father died and Clemens went to work at a newspaper as a printer's assistant, leaving formal schooling after completing the fifth grade. He also trained as a Mississippi River boat pilot, which is where Clemens obtained his pen name of Mark Twain. The saying Mark Twain was the leadman's call when the river depth reached two fathoms, which is considered the safe water level for a steamboat.

Figure 163 Photo of Mark Twain in 1869, during the time he lived in Buffalo

In 1861, Twain's brother Orion Clemens became secretary to James W. Nye, the governor of Nevada Territory. He moved to Virginia City, where he was unsuccessful as a miner but obtained a job writing for the *Territorial Enterprise*. This is where he first used the pen name of Mark Twain, and while in Nevada, he began writing humorous travel articles.

He moved to San Francisco and in 1865 published his first successful humorous work, "The Celebrated Jumping Frog of Calaveras County." When this story was printed in the NYC weekly *The Saturday Press,* it brought him national attention. While in California, he began giving lectures based off his trip to Hawaii. In 1867, Twain joined a junket to Europe and the Holy Land financed by a San Francisco newspaper. His travel dispatches brought him additional fame and fortune, with the travel letters later compiled as *The Innocents Abroad*, published in 1869.

One of the fellow passengers on this overseas junket was Charles Langdon. Twain saw a miniature daguerreotype of Langdon's sister Olivia. During the trip Twain continually asked Langdon if he could see the photograph, proclaiming he was going to marry her. After the trip, when Twain was in NYC, he visited the Langdon home in Elmira to see Charles and meet Olivia. Over the next two years he courted Olivia, often visiting the Elmira home. After an initial rejection, Olivia agreed to marry him.

Olivia's father Jervis Langdon was a wealthy coal merchant and a leading citizen of Elmira, NY. At first, he did not approve of his daughter's marriage to Twain, but in 1869 he gave Twain $20,000 to purchase a one-third interest in the *Buffalo Express*, the forerunner to the *Courier-Express*. Twain moved into Mrs. Randall's boarding house at 39 East Swan Street and began working at the newspaper, located at 14 East Swan Street.

In August 1869, during his first three months at the newspaper, he wrote 20 articles, along with handling the editorial and layout responsibilities. Twain put in 14-hour days, working with the writers, writing feature articles and a gossip column called "People and Things." His co-editors at the paper were Josephus Larned, who wrote the book *A History of Buffalo: Delineating the Evolution of the City* in 1911, and David Grey, after whom Twain named the central character in *A Murder, a Mystery and a Marriage*. A collection of writings by Twain during this time period was published as *Mark Twain at The Buffalo Express: Articles and Sketches by America's Favorite Humorist*.

Both Larned and Grey were active with the Young Men's Association, the predecessor to the Buffalo and Erie County Public Library, with Larned being named director in 1877. In 1885, Twain donated the second half of his manuscript for *Adventures of Huckleberry Finn*, thinking the first half had been lost by the printer. The

first half was actually sent to James Fraser Gluck, the lawyer for the Buffalo Library, who took the manuscript home with the intention of having it bound. Gluck died in 1897 and the manuscript was in his belongings, ending up stored in a steamer trunk. That missing manuscript was discovered in the trunk in Los Angeles in 1991. The two parts of the manuscript were reunited in 1992 and are showcased in the Buffalo and Erie County Library Mark Twain Room, with other Twain writings and memorabilia.

Since Twain was concerned about the expense of getting married, he embarked on a lecture tour in October 1869, that would last until their wedding. While Twain was on tour, Jervis Langdon

Figure 164 Twain mansion at 472 Delaware Avenue
Photo: Buffalo History Museum

purchased the mansion at 472 Delaware Avenue for his daughter and her new husband. Olivia and her mother shopped in NYC to furnish and decorate the house. It was completed in time for their wedding on February 2, 1870 in Elmira.

Twain was not aware of the wedding gift. When the newlyweds got off the private train that brought them and the wedding party to Buffalo, they were met by a sleigh, with a driver who Twain had given instructions to find suitable housing for him and his bride. They drove through bad parts of town and Twain began to get worried. The driver stopped at the brightly lit mansion at 472 Delaware and Jervis Langdon, who had rushed to the house before their driver arrived, met them at the door. He handed the astonished Twain the deed to the home.

The happiness in the new home would not last long. In August of 1870 Jervis Langdon died of cancer. Olivia's friend Emma Nye came to stay at the Twain home to console Olivia after her father's death. Nye became ill and Olivia tried to nurse her back to health, but Nye died at their Delaware Avenue home. The Twain's first child Langdon Clemens was born prematurely in Buffalo in November 1870 and Olivia contracted typhoid fever. Due to all their hardships, on March 2, 1871 Twain put his interests in the *Buffalo Express* up for sale and they moved to Elmira.

Mark and Olivia moved to Hartford, Connecticut later in 1871. Unfortunately, their son died in 1872, but with Twain's income from his books and lectures, along with Olivia's inheritance, they lived a lavish lifestyle. In 1874, they built the Mark Twain house designed by Edward Tuckerman Potter in the American High Gothic style. The Twains lived in this home until 1891 and owned it until 1903. In Hartford, his neighbors and friends included abolitionist writer Harriet Beecher Stowe, abolitionist statesman Frederick Douglass and author William Dean Howells. He was also close with Nickola Tesla and Helen Keller, with presidents, artists, industrialists and European royalty considering him a friend.

In addition, for 20 years the Twains made Elmira their summer home and in an octagonal study built behind the Langdon vacation home at Quarry Farm, he wrote most of his famous works, including The *Adventures of Tom Sawyer* and *The Adventures of Huckleberry Finn*. Their three daughters Olivia Susan, Clara and Jean were born in the Langdon Mansion.

Due to bad investments, Twain filed bankruptcy in 1894, losing the bulk of his book profits and a substantial part of his wife's inheritance. However, with the advice and assistance of Henry Huttleston Rogers of Standard Oil, he repaid all his debtors in full. His success as an author and lecturer resulted in him leaving an estate in 1910 of $471,000 or about thirteen million current dollars.

Mark Twain only lived in Buffalo for two years and during that time he suffered several setbacks. However, his time here influenced his career and he returned to Buffalo many times for lectures. The Mark Twain historic sites and museums are at his birthplace in Florida, Missouri, boyhood home in Hannibal, Missouri, Mark Twain Home in Hartford, Connecticut, study in Elmira and the Mark Twain Room in the downtown Buffalo and Erie County Public Library.

GEORGE URBAN

The flour business and early proponent of the utilization of hydroelectric power

In 1835, George Urban Sr. and his parents, Philip Jacob Urban and Katherine Gass Urban, were among the first German settlers in Buffalo. They arrived from Alsace in France but occupied by a German speaking population that aligned with Germany. Mrs. Urban's father George Gass had previously arrived in Buffalo in 1828. The family purchased land in northeastern Buffalo, along what is now East Ferry, from Fillmore to Moselle and south to Glenwood.

After attending Buffalo schools, George Urban Sr. took a position with the general merchandise business of Manly Colton at Main and Genesee Streets, remaining with that firm until 1846. That year he purchased property at Genesee and Oak Streets, opening a wholesale flour business.

George Urban Jr. was born in 1850 and educated in Buffalo Public Schools. At 16 years of age he entered his father's wholesale flour business and was made a partner in Urban & Company in 1870. Due to the success of the wholesale business, they opened their own mill in 1882 at Genesee and Oak, across the street from the wholesale business. It was the first flour mill in Buffalo to use steel rollers, instead of millstones, to grind the flour. It had a capacity of producing 275 barrels of flour a day and wheat storage capacity of 12,000 bushels. When Urban Sr. retired in 1885 a partnership was formed consisting of George Urban Jr., his brother William Charles Urban and Edwin G.S. Miller, later president of Gerhard Lang Brewery. After George Urban Sr. died in 1887, the company name was changed to Urban Milling Company, and they marketed Liberty Flour.

In addition to the flour business, Urban Jr. was involved in other business ventures, especially hydroelectric energy. His interest in electricity resulted from Urban visiting Edison, where he purchased an electric generator for this flour mill. It was one of the first generators that Edison made. With William and Charles R. Huntley, Urban formed the Brush Electric Light Company, which in 1880 was Buffalo's first municipal lighting plant. Urban was also an officer of Cataract Power & Conduit, Thompson-Houston Electric Light Company and Buffalo & Niagara Falls Electric Light & Power Company. These firms merged into the Buffalo General Electric Company that distributed the power generated at Niagara Falls to Buffalo and for which Urban was Vice President. He was also an officer or director of several banks and financial institutions, Buffalo Elevator Company and the Ellicott Square Company. Additionally, Urban was involved in land development with the Bellevue Land & Development Company and Depew Land Company, from which George Urban Boulevard was named.

Figure 165 George Urban Jr. Estate at 280 Pine Ridge in Cheektowaga

In 1875, George Urban Jr. married Ada E. Winspear and built his mansion at 280 Pine Ridge Road on an estate that included the present location of Villa Maria College. The estate was once a large working farm with a horse racing track, poultry houses for raising chickens, grape vineyards and extensive gardens that featured 150 varieties of roses. Since he was a friend of Thomas Edison, he had the home wired for electric usage before electricity was available. He also had a large pipe installed under the house because he heard indoor plumbing was going to be developed.

Although a Republican and associated with Presidents Benjamin Harrison and William McKinley, he was a personal friend of Democrat Grover Cleveland, and Cleveland's presidential campaign was announced at Urban's Pine Ridge estate. The house has already been designated with local landmark status and the owners are working to have it named a national historic landmark. Tours of the home are periodically offered, and it is available for wedding receptions and other functions.

In 1903, George Urban opened a new plant on Kehr Street on the East Side of Buffalo on land the company purchased at a Sheriff's sale in 1870. The state-of-the-art plant was the first mill in Buffalo to be entirely powered by electric power. It was built on the New York Central Beltline, with private railroad tracks connecting the mill to the Beltline. Flour production capacity was 1,200 barrels per day and the grain elevator could store 60,000 bushels of wheat. The mill and elevator were five stories high, with each floor devoted to a particular stage of the flour milling process.

By 1930, Buffalo was the flour milling capital of the U.S., surpassing production in Minneapolis. The daily capacity of Buffalo mills in 1930 was 40,000 barrels, which increased to 51,000 barrels in 1948. Buffalo mills were known for the quality flour produced as they could choose the best U.S. and Canadian wheat that passed through the Buffalo port. Over 42% of Buffalo flour was exported to Western Europe.

When George Urban Jr. died in 1928 at the age of 78, his son George P. Urban became president of George Urban Milling, with his two sons joining the business. The company survived the Depression by expanding their product line to include Urban's Pie Flour and Up-and-Up, a self-rising cake flour. They also began shipments to New England, New Jersey and Pennsylvania. In 1940, the company employed three eight-hour shifts of 120 employees; and by 1946, the daily output was 1,500 barrels a day. The company was rebuilt during the 1950s and was successful during the early 1960s, but in 1965 Urban family involvement decreased and the outside board of directors sold the company to Seaboard Allied Milling in 1965, who subsequently sold the company to Cargill in 1983.

Cargill closed the company in March 1994 claiming that the plant had become obsolete and with its location on the belt line, rather than the water, it was more expensive to operate. The 45 remaining employees were left to find work with the four remaining Buffalo mills; ConAgra, General Mills Flour, Archer Daniels Midland and International Multifoods. By 2001 the milling industry was reduced to only two mills, General Mills and Archer Daniels Midland.

Figure 166 Current photo of the Urban Estate
Photo: Courtesy the George Urban Mansion

EBENEZER WALDEN

The first lawyer in Buffalo and a successful real estate investor

Ebenezer Walden was born in Massachusetts in 1777 and graduated from Williams College in 1799. After studying law and being admitted to the New York State bar he decided to relocate to Buffalo. In 1806, Walden arrived in Buffalo by walking the 40 miles from Batavia. Upon his arrival he presented a letter of introduction from D.B. Brown to Erastus Granger, who was then the postmaster of Buffalo.

Walden rented space on Willik Avenue (Main Street), between Crow (Exchange), and Seneca Street, nailing a sign to the door, Ebenezer Walden: Attorney and Counsellor-at-Law. For the next two years he was the only lawyer in town and for most of that time, the only lawyer west of Batavia. However, there were not enough people in the area to support a full-time attorney, so to make ends meet, Walden worked as a clerk in stores and did other odd jobs.

By 1808, there were eight attorneys in the Niagara County bar association; and in 1810, Walden purchased a lot at the northeast corner of Main and Eagle Streets for his residence. In 1812, he married Suzanna Marvin and he was elected to the NYS Legislature, representing the area that now includes Erie, Niagara, Chautauqua and Cattaraugus Counties. During the burning of Buffalo in 1813, Walden was one of the few that stayed behind to save as many lives as possible. He was temporarily captured but escaped when he was left alone by the British.

After Buffalo was burned, Walden practiced law in Williamsville with his future law partner Herman B. Potter until he was able to return to the city. He was on the committee to assess the damage to the city and served as a director of a brickmaking company. To replace his home that was destroyed, Walden built the first brick house in Buffalo, which for a time was used as General Winfield Scott's headquarters.

Walden was one of the original four trustees of the Village of Buffalo in 1816, was a member of the Buffalo Harbor Company formed in 1819 for Buffalo to be named the western terminus of the Erie Canal, was the first judge of Erie County when it was formed in 1821 and in 1831 was one of eighteen citizens on the committee to form the charter for the city of Buffalo. When Walden was selected as mayor of Buffalo in 1838, many of the private schools in Buffalo had closed after the financial crash of 1837. His administration reorganized the school system and appointed the first superintendent of schools, Oliver G. Steele. The new system featured larger schools and free instruction to all children living in the city.

Dating back to before the War of 1812, Walden began purchasing real estate in the city and surrounding area. He owned a large farm in the current area of Walden and Fillmore Avenues. Although he never lived there, it was called Walden Farms, and when a road was laid out going through the land in 1873, it was named Walden Avenue. Walden owned another parcel of land known as Walden Hill or lot #52, which he purchased from the Holland Land Company on March 1, 1809 for $232.50.

Figure 167 Ebenezer Walden mansion at Main and Edward

He lived upon this lot at the corner of Main and Edward, with orchards and gardens extending to Franklin Street. This site of his home later became the location of the Teck Theatre. In 1830, Lewis F. Allen purchased five acres of the lot at the southwest corner of Delaware and North from Judge Ebenezer Walden for the North Street Cemetery, which is now the site of Hotel Lenox. Franklin Street from Edward to Allen Street was developed from Walden's property. In 1835, he sold a portion of lot #52 to Alanson Palmer who sold it to Benjamin Rathbun. Rathbun may have begun building on the property, but when he filed bankruptcy in 1836, the property reverted back to Walden. In 1839, Walden leased the lot bounded by Allen, Franklin, Delaware and North Streets to the government for the Poinsett Barracks. The officer's quarters on that land became the Wilcox Mansion where Theodore Roosevelt was inaugurated. In 1846, the government terminated their lease to the property, and on September 22, 1847 Walden sold the portion of lot #52 that included the officer's quarters to Judge Joseph Masten.

In 1837, Walden purchased a 272-acre farm along Lake Erie where, after he retired, he built a mansion called Lake View at 5926 Old Lakeshore Road. Most of the present hamlet of Lake View was part of this farm. His son James lived at the property before Ebenezer retired and James became the first postmaster of Lake View. Ebenezer Walden resided in Lake View until his death in 1857 at age 80. His daughter Catherine built the Lake View Hotel in 1880 for traveling salesmen,

Figure 168 Walden retired to his Lake View home that stood on the east side of Old Lake Shore Road, north of Lake View Road; his daughter Catherine later lived at this house with her husband, General Albert Myer, the founder of the Army Signal Corps and the National Weather Service

providing a place to stay and rent a horse and buggy when they were selling in the Hamburg area. This became the popular mid-1900s Lakeview Smorgasbord Restaurant.

Catherine was the wife of General Albert Myer, a physician and founder of the Army Signal Corps and the National Weather Service, started by the Signal Corps when recording and reporting meteorological data and storm information. In addition, Myer patented a cipher disk that enabled secret signals to be sent. Myer founded the Signal Corps before the Civil War and headed the reorganized Signal Corps from 1867 until his death in 1880 at Pierce's Palace Hotel on Niagara and Prospect Streets in Buffalo.

STEPHEN V.R. WATSON

*Property developer, businessman, leading member of society and
original owner of the Buffalo Club building*

Stephen Van Rensselaer Watson was born in Rensselaerville, New York on June 18, 1817 and moved to Buffalo in 1844. Upon moving to Buffalo, he purchased large tracts of land on the East Side and Fruit Belt area, where he laid out lots and sold primarily to German immigrants. In 1862, he owned one of the largest grain elevators on the Buffalo waterfront and was involved in Great Lakes shipping. The Watson Elevator was on Kelly Island where the City Ship Canal joined the Buffalo River.

During the 1860s Watson became associated with the Buffalo Railway Company, at that time a horse drawn railway. He was president of that company that ran the first track in the city and evolved into the International Railway Company. Watson was also one of the original directors of M&T Bank, was Vice President of Erie County Savings Bank, served as Buffalo's representative in the NYS Legislature in 1860 and was a benefactor of the Buffalo Public Library.

In 1870, he built a mansion at 388 Delaware at Trinity Street, one of the city's most elegant homes. He lived there with his wife Charlotte and three daughters Annie, Jennie and Gertrude. Their daughter Annie married Samuel S. Spaulding, Jennie was the wife of Peter Norton and Gertrude never married. Gertrude was an accomplished pianist who performed recitals in Buffalo and Pittsford, Massachusetts. There her philanthropy established Camp Onota, originally a low-cost vacation resort for the working-class women of New York City and later a boy's camp where Leonard Bernstein had his first conducting assignment.

*Figure 169 Watson mansion became the Buffalo Club
at 388 Delaware Avenue*

The ballroom third floor of the 388 Delaware mansion was developed into a 300-capacity theater where the Watsons hosted three theater parties a year. For Christmas 1872, they presented the play *Look Before You Leap* by the theater group known as the Buffalo Amateurs. Maria Love read the prologue, written by E. Carlton Sprague. The cast included Tom Viele, Trumbull Cary, Charles Cary, Jennie Cary and Annie Watson. The Watsons spared no expense, with the entire mansion decorated for the Christmas holiday.

After Watson died in 1880, the mansion was sold to the widow of Samuel Fletcher Pratt. She lived there with three of her grandchildren until 1887 when she sold it to the Buffalo Club. 388 Delaware became the third home of The Buffalo Club, founded on January 2, 1867. Millard Fillmore was the first president of the club and Stephen V.R. Watson was among the 93 founding members. Grover Cleveland was a member of the Buffalo Club when it purchased the former Watson mansion.

The Buffalo Club was one of the most elite of the private clubs of the late 19th and early 20th century. During this time period, the graduates of Ivy League and other prestigious colleges joined exclusive private clubs when they returned to Buffalo or moved into the city. Here they dined with their upper-class colleagues, lobbied for employment, made contacts for promotions, established friendships to obtain alliances and befriended influential older members who could assist them in reaching the top of their professions. Club affiliation was the final stage of the socialization process, with status and prestige enhanced by membership to the proper clubs.

After the assassination attempt of President McKinley at the Pan-American Exposition and when McKinley was fighting for his life at the Milburn Mansion, several members of the Presidential Cabinet were living at The Buffalo Club. The director's room became the quasi-cabinet room and a direct telegraph line was connected to the White House. The Buffalo Club was the headquarters for VP Theodore Roosevelt and the Cabinet, and during this time the club functioned as the center of the U.S. government.

As a tribute to the philanthropy of Stephen V.R. Watson, seventeen years after his death, when the Buffalo Public Library was being built at Lafayette Square in 1887, his widow Charlotte Watson was given the honor of turning over the first spade of soil. The former home of Mr. Watson continues to be The Buffalo Club, the prestigious private club which remains as one of the vestiges of old Buffalo.

Figure 170 Original Buffalo Public Library on Lafayette Square

PARKHURST AND SOLON WHITNEY

Niagara Falls pioneers and developers of the Cataract House

The Whitney family was descended from John Whitney, an 11th-century Englishman who took his name from the Parish of Whitney in Herefordshire, England. One of the family relatives in America was Eli Whitney, the inventor of the cotton gin.

Parkhurst was born in 1784, and five years later his father Jonathan Whitney relocated the family from Massachusetts to Ontario County in Western New York. In 1810, Parkhurst moved to a farm about four miles above Niagara Falls with his wife Celinda Cowen, who he married in 1805. In addition to working the farm, Parkhurst rented a sawmill from Augustus Porter. Whitney was also a surveyor and made the first survey of Goat Island along with other surveying projects for the Holland Land Company and New York State.

When the War of 1812 was declared, Whitney began his long military career as a Captain with the New York State Militia. He served under General Winfield Scott at the Battle of Lewiston Heights, where he was taken prisoner and later paroled. Parkhurst remained with the militia and was promoted by Governor DeWitt Clinton to brigadier general of the 5th Brigade in 1820 and major general of the 24th Division in 1826.

After the village of Manchester (the original name of Niagara Falls), was burned by the British, in 1814 Parkhurst Whitney leased the Eagle House from Josiah Fairbanks. It was a log tavern located on Old Main Street near Falls Street. In 1817, he purchased the entire block where the Eagle House was located from Augustus

Figure 171 Cataract House along the Niagara Rapids near the bridge to Goat Island

Porter and Peter Barton. Several mills and factories were built along the Niagara River across from Goat Island to take advantage of the waterpower supplied by the rapids. One of these mills built in 1816 was converted in 1825 to the Cataract House by David Chapman to provide for the increasing tourist trade being attracted to Niagara Falls. In 1831, Whitney purchased the Cataract House to accommodate the overflow business from his nearby Eagle House. Four years later, a four-story addition was added along with a wing on the riverside of the building. He worked to promote the city as a pleasure resort.

General Whitney's daughters were believed to be the first settlers to explore the three islands off Goat Island. There were not any bridges to Goat Island, so they crossed the rapids of the Niagara River on an ice jam. In 1817, Parkhurst approached Peter and Augustus Porter, the owners of Goat Island, about naming the islands, Three Sisters Islands, after his daughters. In 1834, the first island was still called Deer Island but eventually the names were changed to Asenath, Angeline and Celinda Eliza, with the fourth small island named Solon, after Parkhurst's son.

Parkhurst was a participant in one of the most bizarre and disturbing promotions in the history of Niagara Falls. In 1827, William Forsyth of the Pavilion Hotel purchased a condemned lake schooner called *The Michigan* and along with John Brown of the Ontario Hotel and Whitney from the Eagle Hotel, they announced that a boatload of wild animals would be floated down the rapids and go over Niagara Falls. The ship was made to look like a pirate ship, with human dummies tied about the deck. The hotel owners expected the animals would survive and the ship would succeed in going over the Horseshoe Falls. Visitors were permitted to view the animals onboard the ship and it was put in the water at Navy Island on September 8, 1827, with a crowd of around 10,000 people assembled to view the spectacle. Two bears escaped and swam to Goat Island, but unfortunately only one goose survived the trip over the Falls. The mighty Niagara has claimed many other lives. It is estimated that over 5,000 bodies have been found at the foot of the Falls, most of them suicides and only about 25% of the daredevils that have attempted the stunt of going over the Falls have survived.

When the Eagle House was sold to Benjamin Rathbun in 1836, Whitney concentrated his business on the Cataract House and his son Solon joined in the management of the hotel. The Cataract Hotel became the most elegant and popular on the American Side of the Falls, and so, Whitney assisted in establishing Niagara Falls as the "Honeymoon Capital of the World."

In 1837, Solon purchased lots 60 and 61 on the Mile Strip where he would later build the Whitney Mansion at 335 Buffalo Avenue. Solon married Frances Drake in 1846, whose father owned the United States Hotel and Congress Hall in Saratoga Springs. The Whitney Mansion was delayed by the depression of 1837, along with Solon's military service and was not completed until 1851.

In 1846, Parkhurst turned the Cataract Hotel over to his son Solon Whitney and his son-in-law Dexter R. Jerauld and Joseph F. Trott, for whom Trott Vocational School was named after his involvement with the Niagara Falls Board of Education.

The hotel was further improved and enlarged, with running water piped down from tanks on the upper floors of the property. It was during the 1850s and 1860s that the Cataract Hotel became one of the important stops on the Underground Railroad. Most of the hotel staff were free blacks; and after hiding escaped slaves in the basement, they assisted them to freedom in crossing the Niagara River by ferry or in horse drawn vehicles across the Suspension Bridge.

Parkhurst and his wife Celinda celebrated their 50th Wedding Anniversary at the hotel in 1855, an uncommon event as people did not live that long in the mid-1800s. Whitney lived between the Falls and the Suspension Bridge, a home that later became the Trott residence. When Parkhurst died in 1862, over 3,000 people came to pay their last respects.

In addition to operating the hotel, Solon Whitney was president of the Niagara Falls Gas Works, director of the Cataract Bank and president of the Village Council. He lived at the Whitney Mansion until he passed away at age 92 in 1907. Solon's life spanned almost the entire 19th century, with him observing the resort village of Niagara Falls grow from a population of less than 3,000 to an industrial city of over 30,000 people.

Solon Whitney sold The Cataract House to Peter A. Porter, and the hotel remained in the Porter family until it was sold to John McDonald in 1909. The hotel's glory days were from about 1870 to 1920, coinciding with the period when the railroad dominated transportation to Niagara Falls. The Depression and World War II reduced tourism and the hotel burned down in 1945. The Whitney Mansion became the home of the president of Carborundum Company, and it was listed on the National Register of Historic Places in 1974.

Figure 172 Solon Whitney's mansion still stands at 355 Buffalo Avenue in Niagara Falls

JAMES PLATT WHITE

Assisted in founding the University of Buffalo, Sisters Hospital,
Buffalo General Hospital and Buffalo Psychiatric Center

The White family history can be traced back to the very beginning of settlement of America. Peregrine White was the first male child born in the Plymouth Colony. His parents, William and Susanna Winslow White, were passengers on The Mayflower and Peregrine was born on November 20, 1620 on The Mayflower as it was docked in the Cape Cod harbor. Dr. White was a direct ancestor of Peregrine White, his grandfather fought in the American Revolution and father, David Pierson White, served in the War of 1812.

James Platt White was born in Austerlitz, New York, about a hundred miles north of NYC, on March 14, 1811. His family moved to East Hamburg, an area between West Seneca, Aurora, Boston and Hamburg, in 1816. He originally studied law but changed his field of education to medicine, attending lectures at Fairfield Medical College and transferring to the Jefferson Medical College, graduating in 1834. When the cholera epidemic affected WNY in 1832, as a medical student, he came to Black Rock to assist in caring for the afflicted. White began his medical practice in Buffalo in 1835 and for the next ten years was a general surgeon before specializing in gynecology.

Dr. White was one of the founders of the Buffalo Medical College, which evolved into the University of Buffalo. In 1845, Austin Flint founded the Buffalo Medical Journal, while James Platt White and Frank Hastings Hamilton organized the Buffalo Medical Association, with White later becoming president of the Buffalo Medical Association, Erie County Medical Society and New York State Medical Society. White, Flint and Hamilton were active in the Young Men's Association with Millard Fillmore, Samuel Pratt,

Figure 173 The Young Men's Association located at Main and Eagle Streets was responsible for obtaining the charter for the Buffalo Medical College

Figure 174 Buffalo Medical College building at Main and Virginia Streets

Nathan Hall (Fillmore's law partner), Elbridge Spaulding and other prominent Buffalo citizens. That organization collected artifacts, started a library and sponsored lectures. It was responsible for the eventual establishment of the Buffalo Public Library, Historical Society and Academy of Fine Arts. Hall was successful in getting a charter granted for the Buffalo Medical College in the State Assembly; and in 1846, White was appointed chair of Obstetrics and Gynecology, teaching the first classes at the school which graduated its initial class of medical students in July 1847.

The first building utilized by the Buffalo Medical School was the old post office at Seneca and Washington Streets, until the school constructed their own building at Main and Virginia in 1849/50. While studying in Europe, Dr. White observed clinical instruction in Midwifery called Demonstrative Obstetrics. On January 18, 1850 he assembled a class of 20 students for the first course of clinical obstetrics in the U.S. Each student examined the patient and the students observed the delivery, which occurred after eight hours of labor. This visual instruction was scorned in the local and national press, with a lawsuit even being filed. Despite the objections, visual or clinical obstetrics was eventually taught at medical colleges across the country. White was also instrumental in implementing other medical practices and procedures, and at the time of his death he was Dean of the Buffalo Medical College. Although he was an Episcopalian, White worked with Catholic Bishop John Timon in 1848 to establish Sisters of Charity Hospital, the maternity and foundling hospital, and Providence Retreat, an asylum for the insane. The new site of the medical school at Main and Virginia was chosen as it was adjacent to Sisters Hospital, which the medical school used to provide facilities for bedside instruction. In 1858, White and many from the same group of individuals that spearheaded the formation of the medical school were instrumental in forming Buffalo General Hospital. White was one of the chief factors in bringing the Buffalo State Hospital, which became Buffalo Psychiatric Center, to Buffalo. During the Civil War, White was Government Inspector of Military Hospitals in the West and Southwest.

In addition to his medical and community contributions, White constructed the White Building at 298 Main Street, one of the first fireproof office buildings built in Buffalo. Dr. White and his wife Mary Elizabeth Penfield did not have any children, but they adopted the son of White's sister, James Penfield White. He managed his father's estate and completed the building of the White Mansion at 173 North Street. His wife Mary Ann Dobbins White, and their children Seymour Penfield White and James Platt White, rebuilt the White Building from a seven-story to a ten-story building. The White Building or White Block later became known as Cathedral Place. 298 Main Street is now Class A office space on the lower floors and upscale apartments on floors seven to ten. The former White home is now luxury apartments named The Mansion on North, adjacent to the Ambassador Apartments.

The James Platt White Society is still active in furthering the advancement of the University of Buffalo School of Medicine. Individuals who contribute a gift of $1,000 or more are members of the society, which shares the school's vision and commitment to innovative medical practice, theoretical and clinical research, and high-quality instruction.

Figure 175 Buffalo History Museum was an organization founded by the Young Men's Association; its first president being Millard Fillmore; it was designed by George Cary and is the only remaining building from the Pan-American Exposition

ANSLEY WILCOX

Theodore Roosevelt was inaugurated president at his
641 Delaware Avenue mansion

Ansley Wilcox was a descendant of one of the founders of Hartford, Connecticut, but his father was a cotton broker and Ansley was born in Summerville, Georgia in 1856. His family was in the Atlanta area during the Civil War, where they evaded General Sherman's marauders and returned safely back in New Haven before the end of the war.

He graduated from Yale in 1874 at eighteen years of age. While studying at Oxford, he met Cornelia Rumsey, who was on holiday in England with her family. After being accepted to the bar, Ansley moved to Buffalo, where he began his legal career and married Cornelia Rumsey in 1878. As a wedding gift, Dexter Rumsey gave his daughter the mansion at 675 Delaware Avenue. Unfortunately, Cornelia died giving birth to their daughter Nina in 1880.

In 1883, Ansley married his first wife's younger sister Mary Grace Rumsey. When they married, Dexter Rumsey purchased 641 Delaware in his daughter's name as their wedding gift. This was the home that was built upon the expanded former officer's quarters of Fort Poinsett. Previous owners had built a frame rear addition, and during the time the Wilcox family lived at the home, they made numerous alterations. Wilcox hired architect George Cary to rebuild additions and remodel the interior, transforming the house into a stately mansion.

After Wilcox relocated to Buffalo, he became a partner in the law firm of Crowley, Movius and Wilcox. Edward Hallam Movius was married to Dexter Rumsey's niece Mary and lived on the Rumsey compound at 334 Delaware Avenue. Although Wilcox was primarily a corporate attorney, he devoted much of his time to advisory law. He was appointed as counsel to the commission to acquire land for the New York State Reservation at Niagara Falls by then Governor Grover Cleveland. While serving on this commission from 1882 to 1885, he met and became friends with Theodore Roosevelt. He served on the commission for civil service reform and was the attorney in Rogers v The Common Council of the City of Buffalo, which established the constitutionality of the state's civil service law that championed merit rather than political connections in determining promotions. Wilcox aided in creating the Civil Service Reform League. He also developed the plan of holding local elections in odd numbered years, with national elections being held in even number years. This was an attempt to free local government from the influence of national political policies. Academically, Wilcox was professor of medical jurisprudence at University of Buffalo from 1885 to 1906.

Wilcox was influenced by friendship and his personal views, not the allegiance to a political party. In 1884, he was a Republican but supported Democrat Grover Cleveland. He then supported Republican Theodore Roosevelt, but when Roosevelt ran as a Progressive in 1912, he supported the Republican nominee William Howard Taft. It is interesting to note he was close friends with each of these presidents.

Theodore Roosevelt stayed at the Ansley Wilcox home when visiting the Pan-American Exposition. When Roosevelt received the news of McKinley's death while in the Adirondack Mountains, he returned to Buffalo and the Wilcox mansion. The inauguration was scheduled to take place at the Milburn House, but when Roosevelt found out McKinley's body was still at the Milburn home, he moved it to the Wilcox House.

Roosevelt had arrived back in Buffalo from the Adirondacks at 1:30 in the afternoon on September 14, 1901. Wilcox met him at the train station and Roosevelt was driven rapidly up Delaware Avenue to the Wilcox home. Roosevelt traveled to Buffalo in his traveling suit, so he was attired in borrowed clothing for the inauguration. After having lunch, Roosevelt went to the Milburn mansion to pay respects to the McKinley family and returned to 641 Delaware Avenue. He was back at the Wilcox house at 3:00 and the six cabinet members that were in Buffalo arrived at the house. United States District Judge John R. Hazel was asked to administer the

Figure 176 Wilcox Mansion where, after the death of President McKinley, Theodore Roosevelt was inaugurated

oath. Most of the cabinet members and Roosevelt had tears in their eyes as Roosevelt was sworn into office in the library of the Wilcox home, with about fifty dignitaries and press in attendance. A bible was not obtained for the ceremony, with Roosevelt being the only president sworn into office without his hand being placed upon a bible or book of law. After the ceremony was completed, everyone left the library except Roosevelt and the cabinet members, who held a short meeting. Roosevelt remained at the Wilcox Mansion until September 16, when he departed with the McKinley funeral procession.

There are no photographs of the Inauguration of Theodore Roosevelt. Reportedly, there were two photographers in the dining room, one official and one not official. They were arguing over who should take the photos and the camera equipment was knocked over. Tensions were so high that Roosevelt demanded both photographers to leave the room.

Wilcox and Mary Grace raised Cornelia's daughter Nina, who became a pioneer in body psychotherapy. Their daughter Frances was born in 1884 and married Tom Cooke. Ansley Wilcox died on New Year's Day 1930 and his wife Mary Grace died in October 1933. Since Mary Grace died last, it was her will that bequeathed their property. In her will she left her estate to her daughter's family requesting that she give her husband's daughter a generous share of her effects.

After Ansley and Mary Grace died, the furniture from their home at 641 was sold at an auction in September 1935 and the house was purchased by the Lawrence family. They operated it from 1939 until 1959 as the Kathryn Lawrence Dining Room, with the Ansley Wilcox and White Rooms decorated as the home looked when Roosevelt was sworn in as president. After the restaurant closed the property was purchased by Benderson Development, and it was announced the home would be demolished with the site becoming a parking lot. Congressman Thaddeus Dulski and Leo O'Brien unsuccessfully tried to obtain funds from the U.S. Government to save the home. Liberty Bank finally purchased the building and raised money in the community until the National Parks System designated the building as a national historic landmark.

SAMUEL WILKESON

The Builder of Buffalo who championed Buffalo over Black Rock as the Western Terminus of the Erie Canal

Wilkeson was born in 1781 in Carlisle, Pennsylvania. A sailor and shipowner, he first visited Buffalo in 1812 to assist with the War of 1812 effort. Intrigued by the city, he moved his family to Buffalo in 1814, opening a general store on Main and Niagara while building a house on Main and Genesee. Wilkeson immediately became involved in the community, becoming a Justice of the Peace in 1815 and a Village Trustee in 1816-1817 and 1819-1821. Later in his life he was referred to as Judge Wilkeson.

In 1819, he formed the Buffalo Harbor Company with Ebenezer Johnson, Ebenezer Walden, Charles Townsend, George Coit and Oliver Forward. They obtained a $12,000, twelve-year loan from New York State to improve the Buffalo Harbor. This was necessary

Figure 177 Portrait of Samuel Wilkeson

because a sandbar 330 feet wide and 990 feet long, blocked the mouth of the Buffalo River. They moved the mouth of the river 1,000 feet south by building two piers, each over 1,000 feet in length and to a depth of 13 feet into Lake Erie.

When the company was at risk of defaulting, Wilkeson, Townsend and Forward each pledged $8,000 to back the loan; and when the employees of the Buffalo Harbor Company stopped working, they personally built a temporary retaining wall. Offering the workers bonuses to complete the project, they channeled the high spring waters of the river to blast away the sandbar which opened the river to navigation by lake ships. Since boats could now enter the protected Buffalo River, the city of Buffalo was awarded the designation as the Western Terminus of the Erie Canal.

Wilkeson continued his public service as Erie County Court judge in 1821, New York State Assemblyman in 1822, New York State Senator in 1824 and Mayor of Buffalo in 1836. After his term as Mayor in 1838, Wilkeson was general agent of the American Colonization Society, relocating freed slaves to Liberia.

In 1825, he built a house on Niagara Square in the location of the current City Hall. John Hicks was the builder of the central section of the house, and John Wilkeson added two wings in 1860. The home was demolished in 1915 and was replaced by Buffalo's first drive-in service gas station. Designs for City Hall were submitted in the 1920s and construction began in September 1929. City Hall was completed in 1931 and is considered an example of the Art Deco style of architecture.

Figure 178 Wilkeson Mansion on Niagara Square at the current location of Buffalo City Hall

In addition to his public service, Wilkeson and Ebenezer Johnson were given a contract by the Canal Commission to construct a dam across Tonawanda Creek, where it joined with the Erie Canal. As part of this project they built a toll bridge over the creek which led to the development of Tonawanda village. This resulted in the Builder of Buffalo and First Mayor of Buffalo also being influential for the early development of the City of Tonawanda and City of North Tonawanda. Wilkeson and Johnson were also partners in shipping and real estate enterprises.

Other enterprises in which Wilkeson participated included owning a small fleet of ships operating on Lake Erie and being involved in the iron industry. He purchased iron ore deposits and a blast furnace in Ohio which he renamed the Arcole Furnace Company. Wilkeson also opened a foundry in Buffalo where he manufactured steam engines and stoves.

Wilkeson was married to Jane Oram, with whom he had seven children. Jane's father William Oram as well as Samuels father John Wilkeson were veterans of the Revolutionary War. After Jane passed away, Samuel married Sarah St. John, the daughter of Margaret St. John who convinced the British not to burn down her home during the War of 1812. When Sarah died in 1836, she was so beloved by the people of Buffalo, the burial ban, imposed due to the cholera outbreak fears, at the old Franklin Square Cemetery was waived so she could be buried in that downtown cemetery. She was later laid to rest at Forest Lawn Cemetery.

His eldest son John was eight when the family moved to Buffalo in 1814. John managed his father's interests in Ohio and acquired extensive timber and oil interests in Pennsylvania. Returning to Buffalo after his father's death in 1848, John later opened Wilkeson Grain Elevator at the foot of Washington Street and was chairman of Western Elevator Company. During the Civil War, due to his knowledge of metallurgy, he was a consultant to improve military armaments. He also accompanied his Niagara Square neighbor, former president Millard Fillmore, on a tour of Europe.

Judge Wilkeson's grandson was Bayard Wilkeson, a Lieutenant in the Union Army at the Battle of Gettysburg. Bayard's father was Samuel Wilkeson Jr. and his mother, Catherine Cady, the sister of suffragist and women's rights activist Elizabeth Cady Stanton. Lieutenant Wilkeson was severely wounded in the leg on the first day of the Gettysburg battle. The field hospital where he was taken for his leg to be amputated was overrun by Confederate forces and all the surgeons fled. Bayard attempted to amputate his leg with his own knife but died of shock.

Samuel Wilkeson Jr. was a Civil War correspondent for The *New York Times* and was assigned to cover the Battle of Gettysburg in 1863. He wrote a touching article about the battle and his son's death which was published on the front page of the *New York Times*. Several points in his article were echoed in Lincoln's Gettysburg Address delivered four months later. Wilkeson's article is considered one of the greatest battlefield dispatches in American History and was the basis for the book *Imperfect Union* by Charles Raasch.

Eight of Judge Wilkeson's descendants fought in the Civil War and another grandson, Lieutenant John Wilkes Wilkeson was killed during the war at Seven Pines in 1862. John's younger brother, Samuel Wilkeson, was discharged as a Colonel after a distinguished career with Scott's guerrilla cavalry. After the war, Samuel married and moved to an estate in Cheektowaga. When his father John died in 1894, he moved back to Niagara Square to manage the estate. Colonel Wilkeson died in 1915 and was the last member of the Wilkeson family to live in the mansion.

Judge Wilkeson is buried with many of his relatives in the family plot at Forest Lawn Cemetery. Wilkeson Pointe on the Outer Harbor is named after the man whose efforts in creating the Buffalo Harbor resulted in the village of Buffalo Creek becoming the City of Buffalo.

Figure 179 Niagara Square during the 1800s

SOURCE NOTES

INTRODUCTION

History of Buffalo and Erie County by Perry Smith
An Authentic & Comprehensive History of Buffalo Volume 2 by William Ketchum
A History of Buffalo and Niagara Falls by John Devoy
Papers of William Hodge, Buffalo Historical Society Publications Volume 26.
Black Rock Historic Resource Survey, Clinton Brown Company. November 2010.

ROBERT BORTHWICK ADAM & J.N. ADAM

Buffalo's Delaware Avenue Mansions & Families by Edward T. Dunn
J.N. Adam and His Gifts to Buffalo, by Susan J. Eck. Wnyhistory.org

JOHN JOSEPH ALBRIGHT

The Ivy Grows Again: A history of the Albright Estate by Betsy Taylor
Albright-Knox Art Gallery website albrightknox.org

LEWIS ALLEN

Fair info from ecfair.org Erie County Fair website
History of the City of Buffalo and Erie County by Henry Perry Smith
Second Looks by Scott Eberle and Joseph A. Grande
North Tonawanda: The Lumber City edited by Donna Zeller Neal

BENJAMIN BARTON

Early Reminiscences of Western New York and the Lake Region of Country. Address given
by James L Barton to Young Men's Association of Buffalo February 16, 1848
Buffalo's Delaware Avenue Mansions and Families by Edward T. Dunn.

PHILIP BECKER

Western New York History. wnyhistory.com. Susan J Eck.
Second Looks by Scott Eberle and Joseph A. Grande.
Through the Mayors Eyes by Michael F, Rizzo.
Picture Book of Earlier Buffalo by Frank H. Severance.
Buffalo's Delaware Avenue Mansion and Families by Edward T. Dunn.

LEWIS J. BENNETT

Memorial and Family History of Erie County
The Early businesses and churches of Parkside by Steve Cichon. Buffalostories.com excerpt
from The Complete History of Parkside
Genealogical and Family History of Western New York by William Richard Cutter.
Buffaloah.com

LOUISE BLANCHARD BETHUNE

Buffalo Good Neighbors, Great Architecture by Nancy Blumenstalk Mingus.
Pioneering Woman of American Architecture by Kelly Hayes McAlonie
Louise Blanchard Bethune: Buffalo Feminist and Americas First Woman Architect. Austin M.
Fox. Buffalo Spree Summer 1986.

WILLIAM A. BIRD

History of the City of Buffalo and Erie County by Henry Perry Smith.
Black Rock Historic Resource Survey. Clinton Brown Company November 2010
Discovering Buffalo, One street at a time. William Bird. By Angela Keppel.

WILLIAM WELLS BROWN

Second Looks by Scott Eberle and Joseph A. Grande
High Hopes: The Rise and Decline of Buffalo New York by Mark Goldman.
William Wells Brown - 1814 – 1884. African American History of Western New York.
Math.buffalo.edu
William Wells Brown. Albrightknox.org
Anti-Slavery Activist and Writer. William Wells Brown, Buffalo, NY.
historicalmarkerproject.com

TRUMBULL CARY

Buffalo's Delaware Avenue Mansions & Families by Edward T. Dunn
Holland Land Company in Western New York by Robert Silsby, bechsed.nylearns.org

CYRENIUS CHAPIN

History of the City of Buffalo & Erie County by Henry Perry Smith
Authentic and Comprehensive History of Buffalo by William Ketchum
Buffalo Cemeteries by William Hodge, presented to the Buffalo Historical Society on February 4, 1879.
Second Looks by Grande
Niagara 1812 Legacy Council. The Devil for us all – Dr. Cyrenius Chapin.
discover1812.blogspot.com
Memorial and Family History of Erie County.
Through the Mayor's Eyes by Michael F Rizzo.

DR. DANIEL CHAPIN

A visit to Flint Hill on Halloween, Buffalorising.com. by Tara Mancini October 31, 2016
Brochure by the Friends of Historic Flint Hill reprinted in Buffaloah.com

NED CHRISTY

History of Buffalo Music & Entertainment by Rick Falkowski.
America's Crossroads: Buffalo Canal Street/Dante Place by Michael N. Vogel, Edward J. Patton and Paul F. Redding.

GROVER CLEVELAND

Western New York History: As We Were. By Susan J. Eck
AN Authentic & Comprehensive History of Buffalo by William Ketchum.
Info on Halpin from President Cleveland's Problem Child by Angela Serratore.
Smithsonian.com September 26, 2013.
A gay first lady? Yes, we've already had one, and here are her lover letters. By Gilliam Brockell, Washington Post, June 20, 2019.

George William Clinton

A history of the City of Buffalo, Its Men & Institutions.
Memorial and Family History of Erie County.
Through the Mayor's Eyes. Michael F. Rizzo.
Buffalo Museum of Science. About us. Sciencebuff.org

Bela D. Coe

Western New York History. The Mansion on Prospect Hill 1835-1921. Susan J. Eck.
wnyhistory.org
The Rise and Fall of a Frontier Entrepreneur – Benjamin Rathbun, Master Builder and
Architect by Roger Whitman.

George Coit

George Coit. Discovering Buffalo, One Street at a Time. Angela Keppel.
History of the City of Buffalo and Erie County by Henry Perry Smith.
Coit House Mystique, Christopher N. Brown, Allentown Association Inc. & Kleinhans
Community Association. June 4, 2007

S. Douglas Cornell

Second Looks by Scott Eberle and Joseph A. Grande.
Buffalo's Delaware Avenue Mansions & Families by Edward T. Dunn.

Joseph Dart

Monuments of a Vanished Prosperity: Buffalo's Grain Elevators and the Rise and Fall of the
Great Transnational System of Grain Transportation. By Francis R. Kowsky. In Reconsidering
Concrete Atlantis: Buffalo Grain Elevators. Buffalo, NY 2007

Joseph Ellicott

Biographical and Historical Accounts of the Fox, Ellicott and Evans Families by Charles W.
Evans.
New York Heritage: Holland Land Company Maps, Historical Context. nyheritage.org

William Caryl Ely

Memorial and Family History of Erie County.
Buffalo's Delaware Avenue Mansions & Families by Edward T, Dunn.

William Evans & Evans Family

Biographical and Historical Accounts of the Fox, Ellicott and Evans Families and the different
families connected with them by Charles W. Evans.

William Fargo

Through the Mayor's Eyes by Michael F. Rizzo.
buffaloah

Farmer's Brother – Honayawas

History of the city of Buffalo & Erie County by Henry Perry Smith.
An Authentic and Comprehensive History of Buffalo by William Ketchum.
John Stedman: Coward for the Crown, Gallant Frontiersman for Bad Historians. Mike
Hudson. Niagara Falls Reporter. December 19, 2006. niagarafallsreporter.com

MILLARD FILLMORE

Info on East Aurora Home from aurorahistoricalsociety.com
Buffalo: Lake City in Niagara Land by Richard Brown & Bob Watson.
Millard Fillmore's Influence on Buffalo, by Judy Rucki, Forever Young Magazine, February 2019

GEORGE FORMAN

Buffalo Delaware Avenue Mansions & Families by Edward T. Dunn.

HENRY MONTGOMERY GERRANS

Buffaloah
Statler: America's Extraordinary Hotelman by Floyd Miller

CHARLES W. AND FRANK H. GOODYEAR

A History of the City of Buffalo, Its Men & Institutions.
Zoo info from Buffalo Stories by Steve Cichon buffalostories.com
Buffalo's Delaware Avenue Mansions & Families by Edward T Dunn.

ERASTUS GRANGER

Forest Lawn Cemetery: Buffalo History Preserved. Edited by Richard O. Reisem. Published by Forest Lawn Heritage Foundation, Buffalo, NY 2003.
The Story of Erastus Granger, One of Buffalo's Most Prominent Early Residents, forest-lawn.com, January 13, 2019
An Authentic and Comprehensive History of Buffalo by William Ketchum.
When Parkside was the Rugged Frontier. Steve Cichon. Buffalostories.com from The Complete History of Parkside.

WILLIAM GRATWICK

Buffalo Commercial Advertiser. August 15, 1899
North Tonawanda: The Lumber City by Donna Zeller Neal.
Buffalo's Delaware Avenue Mansions & Families by Edward T. Dunn.
Linwood Gardens web page.
Buffaloah.com

ANNA KATHERINE GREEN

The New York Genealogical and Biographical Record. Volume XXXVIII, 1907
Anna Katherine "Kitty" Rohlfs Green, by Patrick Kavanagh. History of Women in Forest Lawn Cemetery.
The Mother of the Modern Detective Story: Anna Katherine Green Rohlfs. Forest Lawn Cemetery.
Anna Katherine Green and Charles Rohlfs: Artistic Collaborators. The Magazine Antiques. 2008

SETH GROSVENOR

Seth Grosvenor and Buffalo. The Grosvenor Library Bulletin. Vol 3, Num 4, Buffalo New York June 1921
Discovering Buffalo, One Street at a Time. Buffalostreets.com. by Angela Keppel
A History of the City of Buffalo: Its Men and Institutions.

CICERO J. HAMLIN

Buffalo's Delaware Avenue Mansions & Families by Edward T. Dunn.
Mambrino King: the horse, the wine bar and the East Aurora legend. By Jane Kwiatkowski Radlich. Buffalo News February 23, 2018.
Second Looks by Scott Eberle and Joseph A. Grande
Buffaloah.com
History of Hamlin Park Part IV: Hamlin's Driving Park and the Home Builders. Mike Puma. Buffalo Rising. August 21, 2013
Buffalo's Historic Neighborhoods: Hamlin Park. Mark Goldman, Buffalo Spree July/August 2000.
Buffalo Beer: The History of Brewing in the Nickel City by Michael F. Rizzo and Ethan Cox.

WILLIAM HENGERER

Picture Book of Earlier Buffalo by Frank H. Severance.
A Descriptive work on Erie County, New York by Truman C. White.
Fierce Fire in Buffalo: Barnes, Hengerer & Company's Great Establishment Burned. Daily News. February 1, 1888

SARA HINSON

Sara Hinson – Founder of Flag Day. Forest Lawn Cemetery. June 10, 2018
Wisconsin Wins This One, Chris Carosa. Chriscarosa.com June 14,2015
History of Flag Day includes connection to Erie County. Observer Today. Dunkirk, NY. observertoday.com. June 14, 2015

WILLIAM HODGE

Hodge Papers. Publications of the Buffalo Historical Society, Volume 26.
Genealogical and Family History of WNY. Volume 2 by William Richard Cutter.

BIRDSILL HOLLY

Birdsill Holly Jr: The American Society of Mechanical Engineers, by Marion Hart, asme.org, May 7, 2012
Birdsill Holly, Lockport Cave & Underground Boat Ride, lockportcave.com
Documentary History of American Water-works. Birdsill Holly and the Holly Manufacturing Company. Waterworkshistory.us
Attempts to Hide Scandalous Private Life May Have Caused Inventor's National Obscurity, by Heather R. Hare, The Buffalo News, October 4, 1998.

LUCIEN HOWE

Buffalo's Delaware Avenue Mansions and Families by Edward T. Dunn.
Pioneer Ophthalmologist: Lucien Howe, M.D., by Susan Eck, Western New York Heritage, November 18, 2015.

WILLIAM BALLARD HOYT

1150/1180 Amherst Street, Buffalo: The Mansion that Moved. Susan J. Eck, wnyhistory.com 2016
Torn Down Tuesday: The Glenny/Hoyt House on Amherst Street. Steve Cichon
buffalostories.com

Our County and its people. A descriptive work on Erie County, New York. by Truman C. White.

Memorial and Family History of Erie County Volume 2.

History of the Hoyt Mansion. Buffalo Rising

Discovering Buffalo One street at a Time. William Ballard Hoyt

William Ballard Hoyt, online biographies

ELAM JEWETT

History at Main & Jewett by Steve Cichon buffalostories.com

Parkside after the War of 1812 by Steve Cichon buffalostories.com

The Complete History of Parkside. Steve Cichon. Staffannouncer.com. Buffalo, NY 10/31/2009

Beltline info – The Belt Line Railroad: Its Influence on the Development of Buffalo's Neighborhoods. By Daniel Zornick, Buffalo 2002.

Parksidebuffalo.org

SHERMAN S. JEWETT & FAMILY

Olmsted in Buffalo: Buffalo's Parks and Parkways System. Sherman S. Jewett.

Olmstedinbuffalo.com

Memorial and Family History of Erie County, unknown author, The Genealogical Publishing Company, New York – Buffalo, 1906-1908.

Buffaloah.com

EBENEZER JOHNSON

Affordable Delaware Avenue Mansions & Families by Edward T. Dunn

An Authentic and Comprehensive History of Buffalo by William Ketchum

WILLIAM JOHNSTON

An Authentic and Comprehensive History of Buffalo by William Ketchum

JONCAIRE

The Buffalo History Gazette. Establishing Buffalo in 1758, Joncaire or Indian, or Both? 4/16/2011

Niagara Falls Reporter. Fur Trapper, Frontiersman Joncaire Made Early Niagara History Here. By Bob Kostoff 3/20/2012.

Daniel Joncaire's Memoire by John Fagant reprinted in buffaloah.com

Oldforniagara.org

Niagarafallsinfo.com

Niagara Discoveries: The lost islands of the Niagara River. Ann Marie Linnabery, Lockport Union Sun & Journal. 1/28/2017.

JESSE KETCHUM

An Authentic and Comprehensive History of Buffalo by William Ketchum

Jesse Ketchum: Philanthropist dedicated to education in the U.S. and Canada. Forest Lawn Cemetery 9/8/2018

Jesse Ketchum and his Times by E.J. Hathaway.

Grace Celia Taylor and the Jesse Ketchum Metal: A triumphant Scholar in the Gilded Age, by William R. Greco, Western New York Heritage Winter 2019.

GERHARD LANG

Looking Back at Buffalo's Brewing History. Resurgence Brewing Company News. Resurgencebrewing.com. June 19, 2017.
Gerhard Lang Brewery. By Stephen R. Powell
A History of the City of Buffalo, Its Men & Institutions.
History of the City of Buffalo and Erie County by Henry Perry Smith.
Discovering Buffalo One Street at a Time by Angela Keppel

JOHN D. LARKIN

John D. Larkin, by Daniel I. Larkin.
The Larkin Company by Shane E. Stephenson.
Conversations with Shane E Stephenson and Sharon Osgood.

LASALLE

Niagarafallsinfo.com The French Settlement in Niagara
Historiclewiston.org History of Lewiston
A History of Buffalo and Niagara Falls: Including a concise account of the aboriginal inhabitants of this region; The first white explorer and missionaries; the pioneers and their successors by John Devoy.
Buffalo: Good Neighbors, Great Architecture by Nancy Blumenstalk Mingus.

WILLIAM PRIOR LETCHWORTH

Famous Residents of Forest Lawn. Forest-lawn.com
William Pryor Letchworth. Glimpses of the Past: People, Places and Things in Letchworth Park History. by Tom Cook and Tom Breslin. letchworthparkhistory.com
A History of the City of Buffalo: Its Men and Institutions.

JENNY LIND

Encyclopedia.com
History of Buffalo Music & Entertainment by Rick Falkowski.
America's Crossroads: Buffalo Canal Street/Dante Place by Michael N. Vogel, Edward J. Patton and Paul F. Redding.

MARIA LOVE

Buffalo's Delaware Avenue Mansions and Families by Edward T. Dunn.
Buffaloah.com
Marialovefund.org

STEELE MACKAYE

Steele MacKaye: Inventor-Innovator, thesis of Richard A. Mangrum.
Epoch: The Life of Steele MacKaye by Percy MacKaye.
Buffalo's Steele MacKaye, the "Father of Modern Acting." by Jerry M. Malloy, Buffalo History Gazette June 16, 2011
The Columbian Exposition and Spectatorium, Illinois Historical Art Project, illinoisart.org

OTHNIEL CHARLES MARSH

Lockport's Bone Warrior. By Richard G. Waite. WNY Heritage Winter 2019.
Niagara Discoveries: Othniel C. Marsh. By Ann Marie Linnabery. Lockport Journal October 24, 2015.

JOSEPH GRIFFITHS MASTEN

Patriot's War on the Niagara Frontier and the Buffalo Barracks on National Parks Service Theodore Roosevelt Inaugural National Historic Site. nps.gov

Mayors of Buffalo by Sister Mary Jane S.S.M.N. and Sister Mercedes O.S.F. May 1961 on buffaloah.com

Through the Mayors' Eyes, Michael F. Rizzo. Lulu Enterprises Inc, Morrisville NC. July 2005.

How the Wilcox Mansion came to be – and how it was almost lost. Steve Cichon. Buffalostories.com

The Ansley Wilcox House, Historic Structure Report, by Lance Kasparian, U.S. Department of the Interior, Lowell, Massachusetts, October 2006.

JOHN G. MILBURN

Buffalo's Delaware Avenue Mansions and Families by Edward T. Dunn.

Western New York Heritage - The Milburns and their Famous Home: 1168 Delaware Avenue. September 16, 2018

High Hopes: The Rise and Decline of Buffalo, NY. Mark Goldman. Published by SUNY Buffalo. 1983.

MAJOR LUDOWICK MORGAN

Lodowick at the Bridge/The Battle of Scajaquada Creek – August 3, 1814, buffalorising.com 9/10/2014 by Mason Winfield

CHARLOTTE MULLIGAN

Forest Lawn: The Remarkable Life of Charlotte Mulligan, forest-lawn.com

New Phoenix Theatre website newphoenixtheatre.org

The Twentieth Century Club of Buffalo website history written by Philip Nyhuis of Buffalo Spree Magazine

SAINT JOHN NEUMANN

St. John the Baptist Church. Parish History from their website stjohnskenmore.org

25th Anniversary of St. John Neumann's Canonization by Eileen Buckley wbfo.org. June 2002

Sisters of St. Francis of the Neumann Communities website sosf.org

St. John Neumann at the catholic.org website

MORDECAI MANUEL NOAH

Mordecai Manuel Noah by Michael Feldberg in My Jewish Learning. myjewishlearning.com

Two Hundred year later, Grand Island proclaims Mordecai Noah Day by Michael Canfield, Buffalo News April 6, 2016

Noah's Grand Island, A Refuge for His People. The Buffalo History Gazette, May 23, 2011

Navy Island as the Capital of the World: The Niagara Proposal for the United Nations Headquarters, by Don Glynn, Western New York Heritage, Spring 2019

FREDERICK LAW OLMSTED

Buffalo Olmsted Parks Conservancy, bfloparks.org

Buffalo's Parks and Parkways System, olmstedinbuffalo.com

Municipal Parks and City Planning: Frederick Law Olmsted's Buffalo Park and Parkway System, by Francis R. Kowsky, Journal of the Society of Architectural Historians, March 1987.

Niagara Falls State Park Information, niagarafallsstatepark.com

ROSWELL PARK

Most Info from *Who was Dr. Roswell Park?* Roswell Park Comprehensive Cancer Center, January 19, 2016 and other info from Roswell Park Cancer Institute Main Lobby Display. roswellpark.org

ELY PARKER

History of the city of Buffalo & Erie County by Henry Percy Smith.
An Authentic and Comprehensive History of Buffalo by William Ketchum.
The Life of Ely Parker, by Terry Belke, wgrz.com November 23, 2017
Historical Society of the New York Courts: Ely S. Parker, nycourts.gov

WILLIAM PEACOCK

Biological and Historical Accounts of the Fox, Ellicott and Evans Families by Charles W. Evans

COMMODORE OLIVER HAZARD PERRY

Doreen DeBooth artspherestudio.com and Black Rock Historical Society
Black Rock Historic Resource Survey. Clinton Brown Company. November 2010

DOCTOR RAY VAUGHN PIERCE

Buffalo's Delaware Avenue Mansions and Families by Edward T. Dunn
Second Looks by Scott Eberle and Joseph A. Grande
Buffalo, Good Neighbors, Great Architecture by Nancy Bluenstalk

JOHN PITASS

Second Looks by Scott Eberle and Joseph A. Grande
Poloniamusic.com The History of St. Stanislaus Parish in Buffalo, NY
Sitting with the forgotten Pitass, by Gregory Witul, Ampoleagle.com

PETER BUELL PORTER

Memorial and Family History of Erie County Volume 1
Peter B. Porter and the Buffalo Black Rock Rivalry by Joseph A. Grande in Adventures in WNY History – Buffalo & Erie County Historical Society Vol. XXVII
Second Looks by Scott Eberle and Joseph A. Grande
Buffalo Lake City in Niagara Land by Richard C. Brown and Bob Watson
War of 1812: Part V – Heroes and Villains, by Rich Kellman, news.wbfo.org, December 7,2012

CAPTAIN SAMUEL PRATT AND FAMILY

Historicbuffalo.com – info on Hiram Pratt
Wnyhistory.com by Susan J. Eck
Tifft Nature Preserve – Historical Timeline. Buffalo History Museum literature
Through the Mayor's Eyes by Michael F. Rizzo
The Picture Book of Earlier Buffalo by Frank Severance – house info
Revolutionary War Veterans at Forest Lawn. July 6, 2017. forest-lawn.com
Memorial and Family History of Erie County, New York, Volume 1.
Discovering Buffalo One Street at a Time, Buffalostreets.com by Angela Keppel
Genealogical and Family History of WNY, Volume 1 by William Richard Cutter
TDA-WNY.com – Buffalo Theatre District Association web page
Second Looks by Scott Eberle and Joseph A. Grande

ASA RANSOM

Centennial History of Erie County by Crisfield Johnson
An Authentic and Comprehensive History of Buffalo by William Ketchum
A Tavern Within the Trees, by Joe McGreevy, Western New York Heritage Magazine, Winter 2019.
Village of Williamsville, Erie County New York, Intensive Level Historic Resources Survey. Copyright by Clinton Brown Company Architecture Buffalo, NY, 2013.
Ransom property info from History of the Town of Clarence by Oneta M. Baker.
Glancing Back: A Pictorial History of Amherst New York by Joseph A. Grande.
Discovering Buffalo: One Street at a Time. Angela Keppel. Buffalostreets.com

BENJAMIN RATHBUN

Buffalo: Lake City in Niagara Land. Richard C. Brown & Bob Watson.
The Rise and Fall of a Frontier Entrepreneur: Benjamin Rathbun, "Master Builder and Architect." by Roger Whitman, edited by Scott Eberle and David A. Gerber.

RED JACKET – SAGOYEWATHA

Centennial History of Erie County, New York by Crisfield Johnson
Burial information from WNY Heritage Magazine 2004 based on information from Buffalo Historical Society publication in 1885
History of the city of Buffalo & Erie County by Henry Perry Smith
An Authentic and Comprehensive History of Buffalo by William Ketchum
Seneca Nation of Indians webpage, sni.org

GENERAL BENNETT RILEY

Delaware Avenue Mansions and Families by Edward T. Dunn.
Discovering Buffalo, One Street at a Time, Bennet Riley by Angela Keppel

AARON RUMSEY & FAMILY

Buffalo's Delaware Avenue Mansions and Families by Edward T. Dunn.
Picture Book of Earlier Buffalo by Frank H. Severance
Conversations with David Rumsey.

JOHN NEWTON SCATCHERD

Buffalo's Delaware Avenue Mansions & Families by Edward T. Dunn.
A History of the City of Buffalo, Its Men and Institutions.
Discovering Buffalo One Street at a time. Scatcherd Place. By Angela Keppel
Hardwood Record, Builders of Lumber History. Vol. XXV No. 1. Chicago, October 25, 1907

JACOB SCHOELLKOPF

Buffalo: Lake City in Niagara Land by Richard C. Brown and Bob Watson
Delaware Avenue Mansion and Families by Edward T. Dunn
Genealogical and Family History of WNY Vol 1 by William Richard Cutter
Back to the memorial monuments at city hall. Niagara Gazette by Norma Higgs, November 19, 2018.

JOHN C. AND WILLIAM F. SHEEHAN

Against the Grain: The history of Buffalo's First Ward. by Timothy Bohen
The Last Hurrah of Buffalo's Sheehan Brothers. Max McCarthy. Buffalo News January 12, 1991.
The National Cyclopedia of American Biography. Volume IX. James T. White & Company, New York 1899

WILLIAM SHELTON

History of St. Paul's Church, Buffalo, NY 1817 to 1888, by Charles W. Evans.
Forest Lawn Cemetery, Forest Lawn Facts.
Houses of Worship: A Guide to the Religious Architecture of Buffalo, NY by James Napora.
Discovering Buffalo, One Street at a Time, Build a Church (or 3) and Rename a Street

JAMES D. SHEPPARD

Family Life in Early Buffalo. Olga Lindberg. Buffalo & Erie County Historical Society. Vol 23
History of Buffalo Music & Entertainment by Rick Falkowski

FRANKLIN SIDWAY

Historic Plymouth Avenue in the Kleinhans Neighborhood by Christopher N. Brown.
Buffaloah – The Sidway Family of Buffalo, NY
Memorial and Family History of Erie County.

ELBRIDGE GERRY SPAULDING

Research paper on the Live and Accomplishments of Elbridge Gerry Spaulding by Author Unknown, reprinted by permission from Buffalo Arts Commission Executive Director David Granville in buffaloah.com
Second Looks by Scott Eberle and Joseph A. Grande
Through the Mayor's Eyes by Michael F. Rizzo
History of the City of Buffalo and Erie County by Henry Perry Smith. Bio page 677

EBEN CARLTON SPRAGUE

Buffaloah.com Carlton Sprague Summer House
Buffalo's Delaware Avenue Families and Mansions by Edward. T. Dunn
Memorial and Family History of Erie County.
A History of the City of Buffalo, Its Men & Institutions
Buffalopitts.com. Company History.

MARGARET ST. JOHN

Recollections of the Burning of Buffalo and Events in the History of the Family of Gamaliel and Margaret St. John. By Mrs. Jonathan Sidway, published in the Buffalo Historical Society Publications, Vol. 16.
Historic Plymouth Avenue in the Kleinhans Neighborhood by Christopher N. Brown.

JOHN STEDMAN

A History of Buffalo and Niagara Falls: Including a concise account of the aboriginal inhabitants of this region; The first white explorer and missionaries; the pioneers and their successors. by John Devoy
Historiclewiston.org History of Lewiston

John Stedman: Coward for the Crown, Gallant Frontiersman for Bad Historians. By Mike Hudson. Niagara Falls Reporter. December 19, 2006. niagarafallsreporter.com

OLIVER GREY STEELE

Second Looks by Scott Eberle and Joseph A. Grande
City on the Lake by Mark Goldman.
Through the Mayor's Eyes by Michael F. Rizzo.
The Buffalo Common Schools. Read before the Buffalo Historical Society on January 23, 1863 by Oliver G. Steele
History of Schools in Buffalo New York 1837-1901. From National Register of Historic Places application form for Buffalo Public school #24.
Centennial History of Erie County by Chrisfield Johnson.

CHARLES F. STERNBERG

Delaware Avenue Mansions & Families by Edward T. Dunn.
Buffaloah.com

NIKOLA TESLA

120 years ago, city celebrated 'weird electric genius' Tesla, by Maki Becker, Buffalo News January 12, 2017
Niagara Falls Power Project 1888 – Inventions & Experiments of Nikola Tesla. https://teslaresearch.jimdo.com
History of electricity preserved in North Tonawanda by Nancy A. Fischer. Buffalo News June 22, 2014.
Discussions with Dr. Francis Lestingi

SHELDON THOMPSON

The Mansion on Prospect Hill 1835-1921. Western New York History by Susan J. Eck. wnyhistory.org
Through the Mayors' Eyes by Michael F. Rizzo
A History of the City of Buffalo, Its Men & Institutions.

GEORGE WASHINGTON TIFFT

A Genealogy of the Tifft Family by Maria E. Maxon Tifft.
The Beginning of Buffalo Industry. By Robert Holder. Online 2013. In Buffaloah.com
Vintage Machinery. George W Tifft Sons & Company. Vintagemachinery.org
Tifft Nature Preserve – Historic Timeline
Discovering Buffalo One Street at a Time by Angele Keppel.

BISHOP JOHN TIMON

Bishop John Timon, the father of our diocese. By Paul Lubienecki. WNY Catholic Newspaper. June 15, 2017
High Hopes by Mark Goldman
Discovering Buffalo One Street at a Time, Bishop John Timon, Angela Keppel
Second Looks by Scott Eberle and Joseph A. Grande.

MARK TWAIN

Buffalo's Delaware Avenue Mansions & Families by Edward T. Dunn.
Just Buffalo Literary Center. justbuffalo.org

GEORGE URBAN

Memorial and Family History of Erie County.
A History of the City of Buffalo, Its Men & Institutions
The George Urban Milling Company. Western New York History. Susan J. Eck.
wnyhistory.org 2016

EBENEZER WALDEN

Through the Mayors' Eyes by Michael F. Rizzo
Discovering Buffalo, One Street at a Time – Ebenezer Walden. Angela Keppel.
Signal Corps Association. Albert James Myer by Mark C. Hageman, civilwarsignals.org
The Ansley Wilcox House, Historic Structure Report, by Lance Kasparian, U.S. Department
of the Interior, Lowell, Massachusetts, October 2006.

STEPHEN V.R. WATSON

Our Country and Its People: A Descriptive Work on Erie County, New York. Volume 1
edited by Truman C. White.
Buffalo's Delaware Avenue Mansions & Families by Edward T. Dunn.
Courier Express, March 23, 1952. Information on the Christmas play.
Camp Onota – Buffaloah.com

PARKHURST AND SOLON WHITNEY

Thousands Mourned Whitney, by Bob Kostoff, Niagara Falls Reporter, September 24, 2002
Niagara Discoveries: Cataract House, by Ann Marie Linnabery, Lockport Journal, June 27,
2015
Niagara Discoveries: Parkhurst Whitney, pioneer and hotelier, by Ann Marie Linnabery,
Lockport Journal, July 4, 2015
The Whitney Mansion, Niagara Falls Historic Preservation Society.
Worst Niagara Falls promotion ever: Sending helpless animals in cages over the waterfall in a
"Pirate" boat, by Terri Likens, The Vintage News, April 3, 2018.

JAMES PLATT WHITE

Second Looks by Scott Eberle and Joseph A. Grande
The Legacy of James Platt White. Buffalo Gynecological and Obstetric Society.
Buffalogynobsociety.org.
Memorial and Family History of Erie County New York

ANSLEY WILCOX

How the Wilcox Mansion came to be – and how it was almost lost. Steve Cichon. Buffalo
News, February 27, 2017.
Buffalo's Delaware Avenue Mansions and Families by Edward T. Dunn
TR Inaugural Site webpage trsite.org

SAMUEL WILKESON

Erie Canal Info Buffalo, Good Neighbors, Great Architecture by Nancy Blumerstalk
Tonawanda info from Our County and Its People, A descriptive Work on Erie County, New
York. Edited by Truman C. White.
Civil War info from Imperfect Union by Charles Raasch.
Buffalo's Delaware Avenue: Mansions and Families by Edward T. Dunn

BIBLIOGRAPHY LIST

Profiles Volume I: Historic & Influential People from Buffalo & WNY – the 1800s

Residents of Western New York that contributed to local, regional and national history, commerce and culture

A History of the City of Buffalo, Its Men & Institutions. Buffalo: Buffalo Evening News, 1908.

Baker, Oneta M. *History of the Town of Clarence*. Clarence Center: Diane C. Baker, 1983.

Blumenstalk, Nancy. *Buffalo, Good Neighbors, Great Architecture*. Charleston: Arcadia Publishing, 2003.

Bohen, Timothy. *Against the Grain: The History of Buffalo's First Ward*. Buffalo: Bohane Books, 2012.

Brown, Christopher N. *Historic Plymouth Avenue in the Kleinhans Neighborhood*. Buffalo: Kleinhans Community Association, 2006.

Brown, Richard C. & Watson, Bob. *Buffalo: Lake City in Niagara Land*. Sponsored by Buffalo & Erie County Historical Society: Windsor Publications, 1981.

Cutter, William Richard. *Genealogical and Family History of Western New York – Volume 1*. New York:

Lewis Historical Publishing Company, 1912.

Devoy, John. *A History of Buffalo and Niagara Falls: Including a concise account of the aboriginal inhabitants of this region; The first white explorer and missionaries; the pioneers and their successors*. Buffalo: The Buffalo Times, 1896.

Dunn, Edward T. *Buffalo's Delaware Avenue: Mansions and Families*. Buffalo: Canisius College Press, 2003.

Dunn, Walter Jr. (Ed,). *History of Erie County 1870 – 1970*. Buffalo: Buffalo & Erie County Historical Society 1971

Eberle, Scott and Grande, Joseph A. *Second Looks:* A Pictorial History of Buffalo & Erie County. Virginia Beach VA: Donning Company, 1987.

Evans, Charles E. *Biographical and Historical Accounts of the Fox, Ellicott and Evans Families and the different families connected with them*. Buffalo: Press of Baker, Jones & Company, 1882.

Evans, Charles W. *History of St. Paul's Church, Buffalo, NY 1817 to 1888*. Buffalo: Matthews-Northrup Works, 1903.

Falkowski, Rick. *History of Buffalo Music & Entertainment*. Williamsville: 2017.

Goldman, Mark. *City on the Lake*. Amherst: Prometheus Books, 1990.

Goldman, Mark. *High Hopes: The Rise and Decline of Buffalo New York*. Albany: State University of New York Press, 1983.

Grande, Joseph A. *Glancing Back: A pictorial History of Amherst New York*. Virginia Beach: The Donning Company Publishers, 2000.

Hathaway, E.J. *Jesse Ketchum and his Times*. Toronto: McClelland & Stewart Limited Publishers, 1929.

Johnson, Chrisfield. *Centennial History of Erie County, New York*. Buffalo: Printing House of Matthews & Warner, Office of the Buffalo Commercial Advertiser, 1876.

Ketchum, William. *An Authentic & Comprehensive History of Buffalo Vol 1*. Buffalo: Rockwell, Baker & Hill Printers, 1864.

Ketchum, William. *An Authentic & Comprehensive History of Buffalo Vol 2*. Buffalo: Rockwell, Baker & Hill Printers, 1865.

Kowsky, Francis R. et al. *Buffalo Architecture: A Guide*. Cambridge: MIT Press, 1981.

Larkin, Daniel I. *John D Larkin*. Buffalo: 1998.

Learned, Josephus Nelson. *A history of Buffalo: Delineating the Evolution of the City Vol 1 & 2*. New York:

Progress of the Empire State Company, 1911.

MacKaye, Percy. *Epoch: The Like of Steele MacKaye*. New York: Boni & Liveright, 1927.

Mangrum, Richard A. *Steele MacKaye: Inventor-Innovator*. Denton: North Texas State University, 1970.

Memorial and Family History of Erie County, New York Volume 1 & 2. Buffalo: The Genealogical Publishing Company 1906-8.

Miller, Floyd. *Statler: America's Extraordinary Hotelman*. Buffalo: Statler Foundation, 1968.

Napora, James. *Houses of Worship: A Guide to the Religious Architecture of Buffalo, NY*. Buffalo: SUNY at Buffalo, 1995.

Neal, Donna Zeller (ed.). *North Tonawanda: The Lumber City*. North Tonawanda: North Tonawanda History Museum, 2007.

Raasch, Charles. *Imperfect Union: A Father's Search for His Son in the Aftermath of the Battle of Gettysburg*. Lanham Maryland: Stackpole Books, 2016.

Reisen, Richard O. (ed.). *Forest Lawn Cemetery: Buffalo History Preserved*. Buffalo: Forest Lawn Heritage Foundation, 2003.

Rizzo, Michael F. *Through the Mayor's Eyes*. Buffalo: Lala.com, 2009.

Rizzo, Michael F. and Cox, Ethan. *Buffalo Beer: The History of Brewing in the Nickel City*. Buffalo: The History Press, 2015.

Severance, Frank H. (ed.). *Picture Book of Earlier Buffalo*. Buffalo: Buffalo Historical Society, 1912.

Smith, Henry Perry. *History of the City of Buffalo & Erie County Vol 1 & 2*. Syracuse: D Mason & Company Printers 1884

Stephenson, Shane E. *The Larkin Company*. Charleston: Arcadia Publishing, 2018.

Taylor, Betsy. *The Ivy Grows Again: A History of the Albright Estate from 1890 to Present*. Buffalo: Nardin Academy, 1998.

Tifft, Maria E. Mason. *A Genealogy of the Tifft Family*. Buffalo: The Peter Paul Book Company, 1896.

Turner, O. *Pioneer History of the Holland Purchase of Western New York*. Buffalo: Jewett Thomas & Co, Geo. H. Derby & Company 1850.

Vogel, Michael N., Patton, Edward J., and Redding, Paul F. *America's Crossroads: Buffalo Canal Street/Dante Place*. Buffalo: Heritage Press, Canisius College, 1993.

White, Truman C. (ed.). *Our County and Its People: Descriptive Work on Erie County New York Vol 1 & 2*

Boston: The Boston History Company publishers, 1898.

Whitman, Roger. *The Rise and Fall of a Frontier Entrepreneur: Benjamin Rathbun, Master Builder and Architect*. Buffalo and Erie County Historical Society: Syracuse University Press, 1996.

ARTICLES

Information from following publications was consulted in the preparation of this book. The specific authors and articles are listed in the source notes of the referenced profile.

Am-Pol Eagle

Buffalo Commercial Advertiser

Buffalo (Evening) News

Buffalo History Gazette

buffalorising.com

Buffalo Spree

Courier Express

Daily News

Forest Lawn Cemetery

Forever Young

Lockport Sun & Journal

Niagara Gazette

Observer (Dunkirk)

U.S. Department of the Interior

Vintage News

Washington Post

Western New York Heritage Magazine

WNY Catholic Magazine

LECTURES

Barton, James. "Early Reminiscences of Buffalo & Vicinity." Read before The Buffalo Historical Society of Buffalo, NY on March 19, 1866.

Hodge, William. "Buffalo Cemeteries." Presented to the Buffalo Historical Society on February 4, 1879.

Steele, Oliver G. "The Buffalo Common Schools." Read before the Buffalo Historical Society on January 23, 1863.

INTERNET SOURCES

Information from the following internet sites was consulted in the preparation of this book. Specific information is listed where applicable in the source notes of the referenced profile.

African American History of Western New York. Math.buffalo.edu

Albright-Knox Art Gallery. Albrightknox.org

American Society of Mechanical Engineers. asme.org

Artspherestudio.com

Buffalo Architecture and History. Buffaloah.com by Chuck LaChiusa

Buffalogynobsociety.org

Buffalo History Museum. buffalohistory.org

Buffalo Olmsted Parks Conservancy. bfloparks.org

Buffalo's Parks and Parkway System. olmstedinbuffalo.com

Buffalo Pitts Company. Buffalopitts.com

Buffalo Stories. Buffalostories.com by Steve Cichon

Buffalo Theatre District Association. tda-wny.com

Catholic.org

Civilwarsignals.org

Discovering Buffalo, One Street at a Time. Buffalostreets.com by Angela Keppel

Encyclopedia.com

Forest-lawn.com

Historiclewiston.org

Historical Marker Project. historicalmarkerproject.com

Illinoisart.org

Just Buffalo Literary Center. justbuffalo.org

Letchworthparkhistory.com

Lockportcave.com

Marialovefund.org

Myjewishlearning.com

New York Heritage. nyheritage.org

National Parks Service. nps.gov

New Phoenix Theatre. newphoenixtheatre.org

Niagarafallsinfo.com

Niagarafallsstatepark.com

Niagara Falls Reporter. niagarafallsreporter.com

NYcourts.gov

Oldfortniagara.org

Parksidebuffalo.org

Poloniamusic.com

Resurgencebrewing.com

Roswellpark.org

Seneca Nation of Indians. sni.org

Sisters of St. Francis. sosf.org

Smithonian.com

St. John the Baptist Church. stjohnskenmore.org

Staffannouncer.com by Steve Cichon

Teslaresearch.jimdo.com

TR Inaugural site. trsite.org

Vintagemachinery.org

Waterworkhistory.us

Wbfo.org

Wgrz.com

Western New York History. WNYhistory.org by Susan J. Eck

Wikipedia.org

TABLE OF FIGURES

Due to the time period covered in this book, most of the images are in the public domain. However, many photos were acquired from organizations and they are credited accordingly. Current time frame photos that do not have a photo credit were taken by the author.

The author apologizes if any copyright photo was considered public domain or a photo was not properly credited. Any unintentional errors or omissions, upon notice, will be corrected in future printings or editions of this book.

INDEX

Made in the
USA
Middletown, DE